The Church in God's Program

Robert L. Saucy

The Church in God's Program

ROBERT L. SAUCY

MOODY PRESS • CHICAGO

To
Nancy, Mark, Brenda, and Rebecca,
companion disciples of
the Way

Library of Congress Catalog Card Number: 70-175496

29 30

ISBN: 0-8024-1544-0

Printed in the United States of America

Contents

Preface

THROUGHOUT THE COURSE OF HISTORY God has worked in the world in a variety of ways through individuals, nations, and peoples. The focus of His present work is the church. That which was begun in the Scriptures, as men and women were called to acknowledge the Lordship of Christ, continues today in fulfillment of Christ's promise to build His church. Not only is Christ building His church, but it is the primary instrument through which He ministers in the world. As Christ was sent by the Father, so the church bears the ambassadorial role for its Lord as sent ones with a message of reconciliation to the world (Jn 20:21).

The reality of the church as the instrument of God and as His primary concern today is met with skepticism and incredulity, not entirely without reason. Amid the blustering crosscurrents of our time, which have shaken all of man's institutions down to the foundations—and in some cases are periling even these, if they have not already been destroyed—the church has not stood unscathed. That which bears the name of God has suffered confusion with the rest. The resultant widespread weakness and uncertainty have caused many to turn aside, rejecting with castigation the church as the locus of God's activity. While it is true that certain forms of church life, accretions of time more than biblical patterns, may be rejected, the follower of Jesus Christ cannot profess allegiance to Him *and* deny His church. What is needed far more than denunciations is constructive criticism and renewed effort to seek God's ways in which one may be a part of the building process. For His purpose still remains: His church will endure.

The chaos over the church today stems primarily from the disengagement of its leaders from the Lord of the church and His patterns of church life. Perplexing questions as to the nature

7

of the church, the role of the ministry, and the very purpose of
the existence of the church can be answered only by a return to
the origins of the church in the Word of its Lord. Progress in
the church comes not from advancing beyond the biblical patterns but from building squarely upon them.

This work is written with the belief that there are basic guidelines for answers to the problems facing the church today, and
even to those of the future until God is finished with His program of the church. These guidelines do not spell out an exact
pattern for the church in all ages, as particular circumstances and
historical settings call for specific adaptations; but the fundamental principles are outlined. The Architect of the church
would not omit a blueprint for its structure. His revelation
presents patterns of church structure and life which are for our
instruction.

This is not a plea to reproduce in detail the New Testament
churches. From the picture we get of some of them, it would be
preferable to be different. Times have changed and so have the
circumstances; nevertheless, to hold to the revealed Word of God
as the norm for the principles of the church and to observe the
course on which the church was set in its foundational period is
the only hope of building on a firm base.

This work was written to explore these basic principles revealed
in the Scriptures. The first five chapters are primarily concerned
with the church universal in its nature as a living organism
vitalized by God's own life, its Pentecostal inauguration, and its
purpose and place in the program of history. The four remaining
chapters look at the pattern of the organized church, including
its ministry and worship. An exhaustive treatment of every
aspect of the biblical teaching on the church is beyond the scope
of this work. It is hoped, however, that sufficient scripture data
is included to make possible a glimpse of the magnitude of God's
church.

Although this is not a critique of church life designed specifically to call for the transformation of particular areas of our
contemporary church scene, it is hoped that the reader will take
the time to relate the biblical data to his own particular church
existence. That all will agree with every detail which is presented
is not expected. Any such unanimity could only reflect a tragic

absence of vital interest in this subject. This book is sent forth only with the hope that it may stimulate and encourage the reader to examine God's biblical patterns for His church, in order that his own church life may be as full of meaning, as rich in fellowship, and as effective in witness as purposed by God and, at least to a certain extent, as portrayed in the church of the New Testament.

1

The Meaning and Uses of the Word *Church*

THE ENGLISH TERM CHURCH

THE ENGLISH TERM *church*, along with the Scottish word *kirk* and German *Kirche*, is derived from the Greek *kuriakon*, which is the neuter adjective of *kurios*, "Lord," and means, "belonging to the Lord." *Kuriakon* occurs only twice in the New Testament, neither time with reference to the church as commonly used today. In 1 Corinthians 11:20 it refers to the Lord's Supper and in Revelation 1:10 to the Lord's Day.

Its application to the church stems from its use by early Christians for the place where they met together, denoting it as a place belonging to God, or God's house. With the realization that the place had significance only because of the people of God who met in it, the term was applied to the assembly itself. From this its meaning has extended to various contemporary uses: (1) a place of meeting, (2) a local organization of believers, (3) the universal body of believers, (4) a particular denomination, for example, the Lutheran Church, and (5) an organization of believers related to a particular area or nation, for example, the Church of England.

THE GREEK WORD

THE ETYMOLOGICAL MEANING

The Greek word in the New Testament for the English word *church* is *ekklesia*. It is derived from the verb *ekkaleo*, a compound of *ek*, "out," and *kaleo*, "to call or summon," which together mean "to call out." While often this etymological meaning is used to support the biblical doctrine of the church as a people called out, separated from the world by God, the usage of this term both in secular Greek and the Greek Old Testament, which provides the background for the New Testament language, does not lend support to this doctrine from the word *ekklesia* itself.[1]

IN SECULAR GREEK

Ekklesia was used by the early Greek-speaking people with its full meaning of those called forth. It was a term for the "assembly of citizens summoned by the crier, the legislative assembly." The idea of summoning, however, soon passed away in usage.[2] In Athens, *ekklesia* signified the constitutional assembly which met on previously fixed dates and did not need to be specifically summoned, much like our modern legislature,[3] while special assemblies summoned to deal with urgent matters were called *sunklētoi*, in distinction from the ordinary *ekklesiai*.[4] The word came to stand for any assembly, regardless of its constituents or manner of convening. This broad use is evident even in the New Testament where a confused mob which had rushed into the theater at Ephesus is twice called an *ekklesia* (Ac 19:32, 41), and in the same context the term is used for "a lawful assembly" (v. 39).

In addition, in secular Greek *ekklesia* refers only to the assembly or meeting and never to the people which compose that assembly. When the people are not assembled, they are not considered as composing an *ekklesia*. A new *ekklesia* existed each time people assembled.[5]

It is questionable whether *ekklesia* was ever used in the Greek society for a religious group. The secular use, therefore, provides little for an appreciation of the rich meaning of the New

1. The fact that neither the verb *ekkaleo*, "to call out," nor the adjective *ekkletos*, "called out" is used in the New Testament lends weight to this conclusion. Also the Hebrew word *qahal*, which is always behind the Greek *ekklesia* in the Septuagint, does not carry with it the linguistic expression "out of." Cf. Karl Ludwig Schmidt, *"ekklesia"* in *Theological Dictionary of the New Testament* (hereafter cited as *TDNT*), ed. Gerhard Kittel, 3:530; James Barr, *The Semantics of Biblical Language*, pp. 119-29; F. J. A. Hort, *The Christian Ecclesia*, p. 5.
2. A. T. Robertson, *A Grammar of the Greek New Testament in the Light of Historical Research*, p. 174.
3. J. Y. Campbell, *Three New Testament Studies*, p. 43.
4. Ibid.
5. Ibid.

Testament term outside of the formal analogy of an assembly of people meeting for a particular purpose.[6]

IN THE SEPTUAGINT

The primary background for the New Testament use of the term *ekklesia*, as with most New Testament word thought, is the Old Testament, specifically the Greek translation of the Hebrew Scriptures in the third century B.C. The word *ekklesia* occurred almost a hundred times in the Septuagint and always translated the Hebrew *qahal* or a word of the same root.[7] Although *qahal* is also rendered by seven other Greek words, including *sunagoge*, which indicates its breadth of meaning, *ekklesia* is the preeminent translation. *Qahal* means simply an assembly, convocation or congregation and can be used for almost any type of gathering of people. It refers to assemblies gathered for evil counsel (Gen 49:6; Ps 26:5) ; for civic affairs (1 Ki 12:3; Pr 5:14) ; for war or invasion (Num 22:4; Judg 20:2) ; for a company of returning exiles (Jer 31:8) ; or for a religious assembly to hear God's Word (Deu 9:10) or worship Him in some way (2 Ch 20:5; Neh 5:13) . The word is used for the congregation of Israel (Mic 2:5; Num 16:3) , but it is also used for angels (Ps 89:5, ASV) and simply for an assembled multitude (Gen 28:3; 35:11) .[8]

This varied use indicates that no technical meaning was attached to *qahal* in the Old Testament or to its Septuagint Greek translation, *ekklesia*. Apparently in the interest of demonstrating continuity between Israel and the New Testament church, it is often argued that *qahal* became a sort of technical term for Israel in the Old Testament, meaning the people of God. This meaning is then said to provide the real background for the New Testament use of *ekklesia* as the early disciples saw themselves as the new Israel of God, the continuation of the Old Testament Israel.[9] There is no evidence, however, that such is the case.[10] *Qahal* and its Greek translation simply mean an

6. Schmidt, p. 514.
7. Campbell, p. 44.
8. Francis Brown, S. R. Driver, and Charles A. Briggs, *A Hebrew and English Lexicon of the Old Testament*, p. 874.
9. George Johnston, *The Doctrine of the Church in the New Testament*, pp. 36, 43-45; Bruce M. Metzger, "The New Testament View of the Church," *Theology Today* 19 (Oct. 1962):369-70.
10. P. S. Minear, "Church, Idea of" in *The Interpreter's Dictionary of the Bible*, ed. G. A. Buttrick, 1:608; Schmidt, p. 527; Barr, pp. 119-29.

assembly. Who assembles and the significance of the assembly
must be added explicitly or implicitly in the context. It is only
the addition of "Lord" which makes it plain that an assembly
is the congregation of God. Campbell examines the seven passages in the Old Testament where the terminology *"qahal* of the
Lord" is used. This terminology is suggested as that which gives
the technical meaning of "people of God" to the term *ekklesia*.
He concludes that these passages afford no adequate basis for the
assertion that the *"qahal* of the Lord" is the usual term for
Israel as the people of God, nor for the supposition that a
Christian reader of the Septuagint would be led to think that
"ekklesia of the Lord," which is found in only five of the seven
passages, had that meaning. He notes that if this is true even
with the addition of the qualifying phrase "of the Lord," it is
surely clear that *qahal* alone cannot have had such a technical
meaning. Corroboration of this conclusion appears in the fact
that in the book of Romans, which concerns itself with the relationship of the New Testament church with God's Old Testament people, and also in 1 Peter, where perhaps the most notable
of Old Testament references describing Israel is applied to the
church (1 Pe 2:4-10), the term *ekklesia* is entirely absent.[11]

Moreover, the Old Testament *qahal* with its Septuagint translation, *ekklesia*, like the secular Greek use, never seems to refer
to other than an actual meeting. However, a synonymous term,
edah, did come to have the broader meaning referring to the
congregation, whether actually assembled or not. In this sense
it is nearer to the New Testament use of *ekklesia* than *qahal*;
yet, it is never translated *ekklesia* in the Septuagint but, rather,
predominantly by *synagoge*, which is also a common translation
of *qahal*.[12]

Although the Septuagint use of *ekklesia* based upon the meaning of *qahal* does not reveal any of the technical sense or the full
meaning of the New Testament *ekklesia*, its use for a worshiping
assembly, especially in the Psalms, makes it the most suitable
biblical word for the early meetings of the New Testament

11. Campbell, pp. 45-48, 53; Hort, p. 12, agrees, noting that neither *qahal*
    nor *edah* is used in any important passages describing Israel as a
    peculiar people, nor do they have a place in the great prophecies of
    Messianic times.
12. Campbell, pp. 44-45; Hort, pp. 4-5; Barr, pp. 125-26.

believers. As we shall see, it is with this primary meaning that the word enters New Testament usage. *Synagoge* meant essentially the same thing to the Jewish people and could be used for an early Christian meeting (Ja 2:2). But its distinct Jewish reference, along with the fact that *synagoge* came to have particular reference to the *place* of meeting, hindered its general acceptance by the Christian community.[13]

An interesting development of the term *ekklesia* appears in the apocryphal book of Ecclesiasticus where, in addition to using the term *ekklesia* in its Old Testament and secular sense of assembly, the writer appears to go beyond this sense to the people who make up the group even when not actually together. Very probably such usage provides the transition from the limited meaning of the Old Testament to the broader concept of the New.[14]

IN THE NEW TESTAMENT

The New Testament meaning of ekklesia. The New Testament reveals a development of the term *ekklesia* from the simple nontechnical meaning of assembly to the full-blown technical designation for the Christian people of God. That *ekklesia* does not immediately mean something entirely different from the secular and Septuagint usage is evident by these uses retained in the New Testament. In Acts 19 the purely secular meaning is used twice for an unruly mob (vv. 32, 41) and again for a lawful assembly (v. 39). The Septuagint usage occurs in Acts 7:38, where it describes the assembly of Israel in the wilderness, and in Hebrews 2:12, which cites the Septuagint of Psalm 22:22: "In the midst of the *ekklesia* I will sing praises to thee." None of these references alludes to the New Testament church.

The same general nontechnical meaning of assembly occurs in the uses of the term with qualifying phrases. Although the development is probably already taking place where *ekklesia* alone stands for the Christian assembly, there are several uses in the early writings of Paul where modifying words are used, indicating that the term itself had not yet fully developed to its technical meaning. The apostle addresses his first letter "unto

13. Johnston, pp. 40-41.
14. Campbell, pp. 49-50.

the church of the Thessalonians which is in God the Father and in the Lord Jesus Christ" (1 Th 1:1). In the same letter he writes, "The churches of God which in Judea are in Christ Jesus" (2:14), while in the second epistle to the same church, which is still very early, the apostle uses the address: "Unto the church of the Thessalonians in God our Father and the Lord Jesus Christ" (2 Th 1:1). These phrases indicate that *ekklesia* itself still carried a general meaning of "assembly"; the particular kind of assembly had to be indicated by qualifiers similar to the Septuagint usage.[15]

Shortly, however, *ekklesia* developed into its full technical sense. Through use, it became so completely identified with the specific Christian assembly that the term took on that particular meaning itself and could stand for that assembly without being confused with others. The majority of the New Testament references have this technical meaning.

The New Testament use of ekklesia. A Greek concordance reveals that there are 114 occurrences of *ekklesia* in the New Testament.[16] Five of these, as seen above, have no reference to the New Testament church, leaving 109 references that are so related. It is interesting to note in passing that the word does not occur in the gospels except for three references in Matthew 16:18 and 18:17. It is also absent from 2 Timothy, Titus, 1 Peter, 2 Peter, 1 John, 2 John, and Jude.

1. The local church. Predominantly, *ekklesia* applies to a local assembly of all those who profess faith and allegiance to Christ. In this sense the singular *ekklesia* refers to a specific church, as that at Thessalonica (1 Th 1:1) or any nonspecified individual assembly ("every church," 1 Co 4:17). The plural *ekklesiai* also designates a group of churches or assemblies in a particular region ("churches of Judea," Gal 1:22); or a nonspecified number of churches ("other churches," 2 Co 11:8); or for all the churches together ("all churches," 1 Co 7:17).[17]

2. The universal church. *Ekklesia* also designates the universal church. In this usage the concept of a physical assembly gives

---

15. Alfred Plummer, *A Commentary on St. Paul's First Epistle to the Thessalonians*, p. 3.
16. W. F. Moulton and A. S. Geden, *A Concordance to the Greek Testament*, pp. 316-17.
17. Hort, pp. 116-17.

way to the spiritual unity of all believers in Christ. *Ekklesia* in this sense is not the assembly itself but rather those constituting it; they are the church whether actually assembled or not. This is clearly evident in the early persecution of the church at Jerusalem. Even when believers are scattered abroad and in their homes, they are "the church" (Ac 8:1-3). The application of traits of personality, such as edification and fear, to the church also shows that it was a term descriptive not only of the Christian assembly but of Christians themselves (Ac 9:31). The *ekklesia* was therefore all those spiritually united in Christ, the Head of the church. There is no concept of a literal assembly in this sense of *ekklesia*, nor does the New Testament, as will be seen later, have any organizational structure for the church universal. The unity is that of the Spirit in the body of Christ (Eph 4:4).

Although this universal meaning is occasionally found in the earlier records (Ac 8:3; 9:31; 1 Co 12:28; 15:9), and in the foundational promise made by Christ (Mt 16:18), it is primarily used in the later epistles of Ephesians and Colossians, which constitute the epitome of the biblical theology of the church (e.g., Eph 1:22-23; Col 1:18).[18]

The universal church is often termed invisible, yet the New Testament never speaks of the invisible church. Even as members of a local church are concrete people, so are members of the universal church.[19] It is true that the New Testament uses the term *ekklesia* for the spiritual reality of the body of Christ and also for the assembly, in which the genuineness of the spiritual reality of every individual professing member cannot be known. To this extent the exact membership in any individual church and the universal church at large cannot be known and is thereby invisible. But even this invisible membership is very visible in the reality of life. As for membership in an invisible church without fellowship with any local assembly, this concept is never contemplated in the New Testament. The universal church was the universal fellowship of believers who met visibly in local assemblies.

18. Earl D. Radmacher, "The Nature of the Church" (Doctor's diss., Dallas Theological Seminary, 1962), p. 190. Radmacher notes that out of thirteen occurrences of *ekklesia* in the books of Ephesians and Colossians, all but two (Col 4:15-16) have this universal reference to spiritual unity.
19. Hort, p. 169; Schmidt, p. 534, considers the distinction between the invisible and visible church as a form of unrealistic Platonism.

Furthermore, it is important to note that the universal use of *ekklesia* does not denote the one church as the sum of many individual churches, or the many churches together producing the universal church. The one universal church is manifested in a particular locality, yet each individual assembly is the church in that place. Typical of this New Testament concept is Paul's address to the Corinthian believers as "the church of God which is at Corinth" (1 Co 1:1; 2 Co 1:1). The thought of these phrases, as Schmidt explains, is not " 'the Corinthian congregation,' which would stand by the Roman, etc., but 'the congregation, church, assembly as it is in Corinth.' "[20]

It is often difficult and sometimes impossible to separate the local and universal meanings in the early uses of *ekklesia* (e.g., Ac 2:47; 5:11). The assembly at Jerusalem, while definitely a local church, was also a spiritual unity through the baptism of the Spirit. For a time, therefore, the two uses of *ekklesia* coincided in the one assembly of believers. The church of Jesus Christ was manifest in the church at Jerusalem. As new local churches were established and organized in other places, these were still viewed as manifestations of the one "church" as well as individually "the churches."

The use of *ekklesia* in the New Testament is limited to the senses of the local and universal church. Other connotations which have arisen with the English term *church* are not found with the New Testament word. It is never used for a church building, nor are adjectives ever attached to *ekklesia* as titles to denote a particular denomination (e.g., Baptist or Presbyterian Church), or a state or territorial church (e.g., the Eastern Church, Church of England). In the New Testament when the locality of a single church is mentioned, it is described either by the name of its members (e.g., 1 Th 1:1, "The church of the Thessalonians") or as in a certain city (1 Co 1:2, "The church . . . at Corinth"). Churches of a region are described as being "in" or "of" the region (e.g., 1 Th 2:14, "the churches . . . in Judea"; Gal 1:2, "the churches of Galatia"). Titles such as the Church of Ephesus or Galatia are never found. Even such theological concepts as militant or triumphant are never attached to the term *ekklesia* in the New Testament.

20. Schmidt, p. 505; cf. Hort, p. 168.

2

The Nature of the Church–Part One

THE NATURE OF THE CHURCH is far too broad to be exhausted in the meaning of the one word *ekklesia* To describe its manifold meaning the New Testament writers employed numerous descriptive expressions.[1] They explained the concept of the church both in literal terms and in rich metaphorical descriptions. This richness of description precludes a narrow concept of the church and warns against magnification of one aspect to the disregard of others

THE PEOPLE OF GOD

A DIVINE ASSEMBLY

The church is God's assembly; its beginning, its history and its glorious destiny all rest upon the initiative and power of divine grace. It is a people called forth by God, incorporated into Christ, and indwelt by the Spirit.

The elect of God. The church as God's assembly is founded upon the "counsel" and "good pleasure of his will" (Eph 1:5, 11), and "chosen [elected] in him [Christ] before the foundation of the world" (Eph 1:4). As such, the members of the church are "God's elect" (Ro 8:33; Col 3:12) or simply "the elect" (1 Pe 1:2; 2 Ti 2:10), "an elect race" (1 Pe 2:9, ASV; cf. Is 43:20). In a closely related thought, the church consists of those whom God foreknows in sovereign love and predestines to be conformed to the image of Christ (Ro 8:29-30). These are then called in history into fellowship with Him and membership in the assembly. This act of calling becomes a prime identifying mark of the mem-

---

1. Minear estimates the number of New Testament images referring to the church "conservatively" at more than 80 and adds that the number could easily be increased to 100 if the different Greek words were counted separately. Paul S. Minear, *Images of the Church in the New Testament*, p. 28.

bers of the church; they are "the called" of God (Ro 1:6; 8:28; 1 Co 1:24; Rev 17:14).

Being chosen and elected by God, the church belongs to God. It is "the people of God" (1 Pe 2:10), "a people for *God's* own possession" (1 Pe 2:9, ASV; Titus 2:14, ASV), or simply "my people" (Ro 9:25 f.; 2 Co 6:14-16; cf. Ac 15:14; 18:10). These titles which God previously applied to Israel He now applies to the church, showing a historical continuity in His redemptive program, but not a revocation of the original application. The church is God's people in this age, but Israel will yet enjoy this position as a nation (Ro 11:26-29). The accent in this thought for both Israel and the new people of God, the church, does not constitute an egotistical claim to superiority above other peoples, but rather indicates the priority of God. By his loving redemptive grace, He has formed a people for Himself for His own glory (Deu 7:6-8; Titus 2:14).

The divine initiative is further emphasized in the commonly used terms *saint* and *sanctified* as virtually synonymous with the church. Typical of this identity is the address to the church at Corinth: "Unto the church . . . , to them that are sanctified in Christ Jesus, called to be saints" (1 Co 1:2). Over a hundred times in eighteen different writings, the church members are called "saints" or "holy ones," plus numerous uses of the verbal idea involved in "sanctified."[2] The church consists of those sanctified or set apart from the masses by the action of God in Christ. By virtue of His own holiness and the holiness of His work, Christ is able to constitute the church a holy people. He, as "the Holy One of God" (Jn 6:69, NASB) came as the "Holy child [servant]" of God (Ac 4:27, 30; 3:14) to offer himself as a perfect holy sacrifice for his people that He might sanctify them (Heb 10:14, 29; cf. Eph 5:26) and be their "sanctification" (1 Co 1:30; 6:11). The Holy Spirit then completes the divine action of sanctifying the church when He takes up residence within the life of the believer, not only thereby to unite him to Christ but to experientially work the holiness of Christ in his life. Membership in the holy community thus depends upon the call and power of divine grace.

The members of Christ. The eternal purpose of God becomes

2. Ibid., p. 136.

clear in the historical person of Christ. The roots of the new community were planted in His command: "Follow me." From a band of disciples, His followers became the nucleus of the church which acknowledged Him as Lord and Saviour, for it owed its very existence to His person and work. Without His coming there could be no church.

This Christ who historically was the Lord of the disciples on earth, through the sending of the Spirit, became the invisible but real Lord and Head of the church. Members of the church are thus continually characterized as being "in Christ." This formula, which occurs commonly throughout the New Testament, is based on the biblical concept of corporate personality. As fallen mankind is in Adam, so the church, the new creation, is in Christ (Ro 5:14 f.; 1 Co 15:21-22). As Adam was the progenitor of a race and included all its members in himself so that they are dominated by his personality, so Christ is the Progenitor of a new race whose members are in Him, sharing in His salvation act and being dominated by His personality. The believer in the corporate personality of Christ is thus "called unto the fellowship of his Son Jesus Christ our Lord" (1 Co 1:9), sharing in common His death (Ro 6:6; Gal 2:19) and resurrection (Eph 2:5-6; Col 2:12), as well as His present suffering in the church and the glory to follow (Ro 8:17; 2 Ti 2:12). Life in the church is life in common with Christ and His people; it is life in a new sphere which brings new relationship and duties at every point.[3]

The fellowship of the Spirit. Christ lives in His church through the indwelling of the Spirit.[4] In fulfillment of His prophecies to come to His people and always be with them, He sent "another Comforter" to live in them (Jn 14:16-20). The church is therefore the assembly of those united together in the reality of the indwelling Spirit. All in the church have been "made to drink into one Spirit" (1 Co 12:13). They have a common partaking or fellowship of the Spirit (2 Co 13:14; Phil 2:1) and therefore are joined to each other (Eph 4:3-4). His vitality energizes all of their actions. Their ministry in the church is performed

3. Ernest Best, *One Body in Christ* (London: SPCK, 1955), p. 29; Albrecht Oepke, "en" in *TDNT*, 2:541-42.
4. While occasionally Christ is said to dwell in the believer (e.g., Gal 2:20), far more reference is made to the Spirit's indwelling. The believer is "in Christ" and the Spirit is in the believer.

through the gifts of the Spirit (1 Co 12:8 ff.). Witnessing and proclamation are done in the power of the Spirit (Ac 1:8; 4:31; 1 Co 2:4), and missionaries are sent out and directed by the Holy Spirit (Ac 13:2, 4).

The presence of the Holy Spirit gives the church a supernatural dynamic and therefore makes it unique among all human bodies. The real church is manifest only where the holy presence and work of the Spirit are known. Failure of the church as a vital factor in the world is the result of failure to recognize the reality of the person of the Spirit living in the church as its dynamic force.

A RESPONSIBLE ASSEMBLY

Believers, the faithful. If the New Testament portrays the church as a people formed by divine initiative, it also pictures that assembly as one responding to the Convener. People become members of the church by faith in Jesus Christ and are therefore the *pistoi,* the "believers" or the "faithful."[5]

Instead of addressing the epistles of Ephesians and Colossians to the "churches," the apostle writes to "the saints" and "faithful" (Eph 1:1; Col 1:2), the latter term blending together both senses of "belief" and "fidelity."[6] The address itself shows the New Testament explanation of God's work of sanctifying and the related human response.

More frequent than the noun forms is the participial form used to describe the early Jerusalem church as "all those that believe" (Ac 2:44; cf. 4:32). Often this is in the present tense, emphasizing the fact that the church lives in the attitude of faith. Paul could thank God that the Thessalonians received the Word as the Word of God and that it was effectually working in those who were believing (1 Th 2:13). The church in Macedonia and Achaia is described as "all that believe" (1 Th 1:7).

The exclusiveness of the faith of the early disciples is pictured in their unusual name as "those of the way" (Ac 9:2; 19:9, 23; 22:4; 24:14, 22). The uses of this designation center around the

5. The same Greek word, *pistoi,* can have both the passive significance of one who is faithful or trusty, and the active sense of believing or confiding. Cf. Hermann Cremer, *Biblico-Theological Lexicon of New Testament Greek,* pp. 476-77.
6. J. B. Lightfoot, *The Epistle of St. Paul to the Galatians,* p. 157.

story of Paul who saw Christ as the only way of salvation and entrance into the kingdom of God.

Disciples. A prominent name for the early Christians, although found only in the book of Acts, is *disciples.* The word means literally "a learner" and refers to one who is an adherent of a certain leader, by following his teaching. This meaning is evident in the words of Jesus: "If you abide in My word, then you are truly disciples of Mine" (Jn 8:31, NASB). The church as disciples, therefore, gathers around Christ to follow Him and learn from Him (Eph 4:20-21). It is clear from the New Testament that discipleship is not an easy task. Jesus said, "Whosoever . . . forsaketh not all that he hath, he cannot be my disciple" (Lk 14:33; cf. Mk 8:34; Mt 10:37 ff.; Lk 9:57 ff.; 14:26-33). As the "disciples" of Christ, the early church experienced persecution (Ac 9:1); nevertheless, and perhaps as a result of it, the number of disciples multiplied rapidly (Ac 6:1).

Christians. Similar in meaning to *disciple* is the name of *Christian* which has designated disciples of Christ for nineteen centuries. This term was not chosen by the followers of Christ, but was coined by pagans at Antioch (Ac 11:26), probably in derision, in keeping with the Antiochian propensity for nicknames.[7] It is used only two more times in the New Testament, once in Acts about twenty years later when it is again on the lips of an unbeliever, King Agrippa, who refuses to become a Christian through the persuasion of Paul's testimony (Ac 26:28). The other use is that of Peter in relation to suffering as a "Christian" (1 Pe 4:16). Here again it is used as a term by which the world knows the members of the church.

Brethren. The redemptive activity of God calls men not only to a reciprocal love to Him, but also to one another. Developing out of this new reconciliation was one of the favorite names for fellow New Testament believers, *brethren.* All members of the church of Jesus Christ belong to the family of God as sons and are therefore related in a spiritual community of life (Ro 8:29; Eph 6:23; 1 Ti 6:2). The term *brethren* also implies a personal equality before the Lord, as evidenced in the statement of Christ to the disciples: "But do not be called Rabbi; for One is your

7. Bruce Metzger, "The New Testament View of the Church," *Theology Today* 19 (Oct. 1962):375.

Teacher, and you are all brothers" (Mt 23:8, NASB). One may still be a master and the other a servant according to their stations in life, but in the church both master and servant are "brethren" (1 Ti 6:2).

This community of life expresses itself in a community of love. There is no life where there is no love. "He that loveth not his brother abideth in death" (1 Jn 3:14*b*). "He that loveth his brother abideth in the light. . . . But he that hateth his brother is in darkness" (1 Jn 2:10-11). Typically, the slave Onesimus is a "beloved" brother to Paul (Col 4:9), and believing masters are "brethren . . . beloved" to their servants (1 Ti 6:2). The church is the community which experienced the love of God in redemption. This same love has been poured out into the hearts of believers through the presence of the Holy Spirit and is the dynamic of life.

THE BODY OF CHRIST

THE METAPHOR

The apostle Paul's favorite description of the church is the metaphor of the head and the body. Christ is the Head of the body which is His church (Col 1:18; cf. 1:24; 2:19; Eph 1:22-23; 4:4, 12, 16; 5:30; 1 Co 12:12-31; Ro 12:5).

The source. Various sources have been suggested for the origin of this concept as used by Paul, but none are completely analogous to his meaning. Perhaps the nearest is the Stoic use of the body figure for the state in which each member had his part to play.[8] But the biblical figure transcends this use in that the church is more than a unified body. It is the body of a Person. The unity of the members is based not on a mutual relationship within the group but in their vital relationship to the Head of the body, Christ Himself.

The use. The body is composed of all those who are united to Christ through the baptism of the Spirit (1 Co 12:12-13). As

---

8. Other sources which have been suggested include Gnosticism with its "Heavenly Man" and the saved community, the eating of the bread of the Eucharist which is the body of Christ, rabbinic speculation on the body of Adam as including all mankind, the predestined solidarity of the elect with the Messiah, the nuptial idea of the church as the bride, and the concept of "in Christ." For the proponents and a discussion of these, see Best, pp. 83-95.

such, the metaphor refers to the one universal church which is under the headship of Christ (Col 1:18, 24; Eph 1:23; 2:15). While some interpret the apostle as applying the same metaphor to a local assembly, calling the Corinthian church "the body of Christ" (1 Co 12:27; cf. Ro 12:3-5),[9] it is doubtful whether such identity is ever made. However, the single church is never viewed as a member of an inclusive body in such a way that every church can appeal to its special gift as if the one church body were made up of many local churches as its members. The local assembly is the one body of Christ particularized in a certain locality.[10] Members of the body are always individuals, not churches.

It is important to recognize that when Scripture speaks of the church as the body of Christ, it speaks figuratively or metaphorically and not literally or in any realistic sense which makes the church equal to Christ as an extension of His incarnation.[11] Although in some statements the church is directly called the body of Christ without any metaphorical sense expressed, several facts must be borne in mind. Biblical thought often expresses metaphors in realistic language. Israel is called "a scattered sheep" (Jer 50:17), and Christ is called a "door" and a "vine" (Jn 10:7; 15:1). Furthermore, Paul varies in his description of the church as the body of Christ. On the one hand, the head is an ordinary member of the body (1 Co 12:21), while on the other hand, the Head is Christ (Col 1:18; 2:19). Both cannot be reality. Moreover, the church is called a "temple" (1 Co 3:16; cf. 1 Pe 2:5) and a "pure virgin" (2 Co 11:2, NASB; cf. Eph. 5:22-23), which are certainly not to be interpreted literally. These are all simply figures describing certain facets of the church.

9. F. J. A. Hort, *The Christian Ecclesia*, p. 146.
10. Eduard Schweizer, *Church Order in the New Testament*, p. 169; Archibald Robertson and Alfred Plummer, *A Critical and Exegetical Commentary on the First Epistle of St. Paul to the Corinthians*, pp. 277-78.
11. The heart of the Roman Catholic doctrine of a salutary and authoritative church rests upon the literal interpretation which identifies the church as the body of Christ with Christ Himself. "With respect to this question of identity, the very existence of the Roman Catholic church is at stake; it is a matter of 'to be or not to be' for Rome." (G. C. Berkouwer, *The Conflict with Rome*, p. 24). For a full discussion of the Catholic problem see Berkouwer, pp. 15-37, and Per Erik Persson, *Roman and Evangelical*, pp. 59-89. This literal interpretation has also found favor with some Protestants, especially in recent times. Cf. William Robinson, *The Biblical Doctrine of the Church*, pp. 115-24.

THE MEMBERS OF THE BODY

At least three important truths are drawn from the analogy of the relationship of members in the natural body to that of the members of the church.

Unity. As the body is composed of many members and yet is one, so also is the church. This emphasis is particularly applicable in the discussion concerning the ministry of spiritual gifts. The apostle begins his discussion of gifts with the Corinthian church by placing all of the pneumatic gifts under one Lord and Spirit (1 Co 12:3-5). Therefore, there must be no schism in the body (12:25 ff.) caused by a disorderly display of gifts (1 Co 14:33). All of the gifted members are under the same Head and are part of the same body, and such members in a normal body do not oppose each other, thus tearing the body apart. The apostle uses the same figure relative to gifts in his letter to the Romans. However, rather than beginning here with the unity of the body, which is necessary because of the problems in Corinth, he lays emphasis on the multiplicity of members: "For as we have many members in one body, and all members have not the same office; so we, being many, are one body in Christ, and every one members one of another" (Ro 12:4-5).

A similar use of the figure is made in Ephesians 4:7-16 where Paul states that the purpose of gifted members is "for the edifying of the body of Christ" (v. 12), which body he later describes as "fitly joined together and compacted" (v. 16a). The picture is of mutually adapted parts fitted closely together. This compactness is ultimately the work of the Head; however, its immediate efficacy is through "that which every joint supplieth, according to the effectual working in the measure of every part" (v. 16b). Each individual, therefore, by the manifestation of the power of Christ in his particular ministry, contributes not only to the edification but to the unity, the compaction of the body. The same Greek word expressing the compactness of the body is translated "knit together" (Col 2:19). Here the unity of the body comes from holding fast to its Head.[12]

A further application of this figure to emphasize the unity of

12. Both in Eph 4:16 ("compacted") and in Col 2:19 ("knit together") the verb is passive, indicating that the action is performed by the power of the Head.

the church is made relative to the Lord's table. The many believers who partake of the one bread, which symbolizes the body of Christ, are by this partaking bound into a unified body (1 Co 10:17).[13] The body of Christ is one and so also are those who have part in it.

Diversity. Equally significant with the teaching that all members of the body are a unity, is the fact that the body is composed of diverse members. The physical body is not composed of one member, but of many (1 Co 12:14), and these members must be different (1 Co 12:17-20). The members vary in function (v. 17), in strength (v. 22), and in honor (v. 23). So there is similar variation among the members of the body of Christ, and yet all are necessary to the body.

This diversity calls first for a sober evaluation and faithful exercising of one's own gifts to the operation of the body (Ro 12:3-8), along with the recognition of the absolute necessity of the contribution of the other members (1 Co 12:21).

Mutuality. As the operation of the human body demands the cooperation and dependence of its members one upon another, so the body of Christ demands a mutuality. Each member is not only related to Christ the Head, but also to each other. They are "members one of another" (Ro 12:5; Eph 4:25). This implies dependence one upon another and a cooperative functioning of the body (1 Co 12:21-25). It also demands a loving concern through which each member enters into the very life of the others, experiencing their life with them. Members are to "have care" for one another, which expression implies anxious care or thoughtful trouble.[14] Although the believer is taught to cast his own cares upon the Lord (1 Pe 5:7; Phil 4:6), this does not relieve him of the responsibility of sharing the cares of other believers. As one member of a human body cannot help but be affected by the condition of another, so the members of the body of Christ are to share with each other their suffering and rejoicing (1 Co 12:25-27). There are no separated individuals in the church which is His body.

13. Some would also use the reference to "the body" in 1 Co 11:29 (NASB) as meaning the church. Cf. Best, pp. 107-10.
14. Robertson and Plummer, p. 276.

THE HEAD AND THE BODY

Just as significant as the teaching concerning the members and their mutual relationship in the body are the truths drawn from the relationship of the head to the body.

Sovereign leadership. Prominent among the meanings the head has for the body is its sovereign leadership. This is the thrust of the apostle in the epistles of Ephesians and Colossians. The church at Colosse was plagued by heresy which combined Judaism with an incipient Gnosticism described by Moule as "a kind of 'theosophy'—in this instance, a 'gnostic' type of Judaism or a Jewish type of 'gnosticism.'" This false system included strains of legalism (Col 2:16-18, 21 f.) and speculation on the unseen world with the tendency to interpose many mediary spirit beings between God and man, some of which had to be worshiped (2:10, 15, 18).[15]

Against this heretical background, the apostle asserts the absolute preeminence of Christ and His unique mediatorship. He is not one of many mediating emanations from God to man, but rather, He is God directly come to man. He is in Himself the image, the representation and manifestation of the invisible God (Col 1:15) in whom the fullness of the Godhead dwells bodily (Col 2:9). By virtue of His divine creative activity, Christ is the absolute Sovereign over all creatures (Col 1:15b-17).[16] And, by virtue of an equally great re-creative power, He has a parallel sovereignty as Head over the new spiritual creation which is His body, the church (1:18).[17]

15. For a full description see C. F. D. Moule, *The Epistle of Paul the Apostle to the Colossians and to Philemon*, p. 33.
16. The term "firstborn of every creature" does not mean that Christ is the first creature. The context definitely excludes this sense. "Firstborn" can also refer to the priority of position enjoyed by the firstborn without any temporal connotation. Both meanings may be involved here, designating Christ as the begotten of God (eternal generation) prior to the creation, and, as such, having an absolute priority of position over it. The latter sense seems to be prominent in the context (cf. especially v. 18). Cf. Lightfoot, *Saint Paul's Epistles to the Colossians and to Philemon*, pp. 146-50.
17. It is argued by many interpreters from this close connection between Christ's supremacy over all creation and His headship over the church, along with the statements that He is the Head of "all principality and power" (Col 2:10) and "head over all" (Eph 1:23, ASV), that the body ultimately embraces the universal cosmos. Minear states, "Christ's headship over all heavenly rulers implies that he is head over all the men who live in subjection to those rulers. He is the head of every man, whether that man believes in Christ or not. If we allow this

As Head of the church, Christ exercises His lordship over the church. This aspect of headship is especially noted in the figure of husband and wife who are conceived as one flesh (Eph 5:28-31). Christ is the Head of the church as the husband is the head of the wife. Therefore, "the church is subject unto Christ" (Eph 5:24). The false theology and practice of the Colossian church were the result of following "fleshly mind, and not holding the Head" (Col 2:18-19). Only as members of the body are in subjection to the Head and respond to His commands can the body function healthily and properly.

In the single Lordship of the Head, the various members find their unity. The multiplicity of gifts and personalities in the church are "knit together" or "compacted" as they individually respond to the command of the Head (Col 2:19; Eph 4:15-16). These terms, along with the anatomical illustrations of joints and ligaments in the physical body, suggest an almost frictionless relationship between the members under the lordship of the Head.

The source of life. Christ as Head of the church is also the source of its vitality. "He is the head of the church . . . who is the beginning, the firstborn from the dead" (Col 1:18). As the "firstborn from the dead" Christ by His resurrection is the originator of a new realm of life in which He is the first and over which He is preeminent. This new resurrection life is communicated to His body, the church, through spiritual union with Him in His death and resurrection (Col 2:11-13; Ro 6:4). The life of the body is nothing less than the very resurrection life of its Head. Christ is "our life (Col 3:4); He is "a life-giving spirit" (1 Co 15:45).

conception to condition our picture of the church, we will be forced to agree with Markus Barth that the church 'includes virtually all who are still unbelievers' " (Minear, p. 206; cf. W. L. Knox, *St. Paul and the Church of the Gentiles,* p. 160).

While Christ is clearly said to have a universal headship, it is evident that this headship does not include the reconciliation of all things in the sense of their salvation and inclusion in the church. By His work at Calvary, Christ has "spoiled" these powers, "triumphing over them" (Col 2:15). This sense of subjection of all powers is also found in other scriptures (Eph 1:22; Phil 2:9-11; 1 Pe 3:22; 1 Co 15:24; Heb 2:5-9). It is better, therefore, to see the reconciliation of all things (Col 1:20) as including a kind of "pacification" which restores universal harmony. Christ's headship over the universe is thus not that vital relationship which He sustains with His body the church, but a headship of absolute sovereignty. Cf. Best, pp. 115-26; F. F. Bruce, *Commentary on the Epistle to the Colossians,* p. 210.

As a source of life, the Head is the channel through which the divine fullness goes to the body. There are no other mediators between God and man, for it is in Christ alone that the "totality of the Divine power and attributes" dwell (Col 2:9; 1:19).[18] In Him are hid all the treasures of divine wisdom and knowledge (Col 2:3) and the fullness of grace and truth (Jn 1:14).

Because of the fullness in Christ, the body need seek no other, for it is "complete [Greek, 'made full'] in him" (Col 2:10). The believer is to "be filled with all the fulness of God" (Eph 3:19), and it is unto this goal that all edification of the body is directed, namely, to the attaining of "the measure of the stature of the fulness of Christ" (Eph 4:13). This communication of Christ's fullness to His body is probably also the thought of Paul when he calls the church "the fulness" of Christ (Eph 1:23). "All the Divine graces which reside in Him are imparted to her; His 'fulness' is communicated to her; and thus she may be said to be Pleroma [fulness]. . . ."[19]

As the life in the natural body is in a sense concentrated in the head and from it flows to the members of the body, so in relation to the divine life of the body of the church, it is concentrated in the Head, who Himself is filled with life and communicates this life to the members of His body.

The sustenance of life. The life of the church is not only given in the past act of regeneration, but it is also continually sus-

---

18. Lightfoot, *Colossians and Philemon,* p. 181. It is probable that Eph 1:23 is to be explained in this sense. The Greek participle by form is either middle or passive. Many commentators understand it as middle, giving it the active sense of the AV, "that filleth all in all." However, Best notes, "There appears to be no sufficient grammatical reason for giving it an active sense. 'The active sense . . . finds no support in the use of the word in the N.T.' (Wescott ad loc.). When an active sense is required, as in Eph 4:10, we find that the active voice is used. The passive sense is supported also by the early versions (see A. Robinson, ad loc)" (Best, p. 143, n. 2). Taking the passive, the thought would then be that as Christ fills the church, so also He is perpetually filled with "all things" or "completely filled."

19. Lightfoot, *Colossians and Philemon,* p. 263. The idea of Armitage Robinson and F. F. Bruce, which views the body as the complement of the head in the sense that Christ is not complete without His church, is very improbable, for as Robinson notes, "Nowhere else does Paul speak of Christ being filled by Christians . . . whereas he frequently talks of the fulness which is in Christ being communicated to and filling the life of His members" (J. A. T. Robinson, *The Body,* p. 69). For the view which sees the "fulness" as referring back to Christ instead of the church, see Moule, pp. 168-69.

tained by the Head. Particularly pertinent to this thought is Paul's statement that "the body by joints and bands having nourishment ministered, and knit together, increaseth with the increase of God" (Col 2:19). The Greek word translated "having nourishment ministered" suggests a generous supply motivated by love.

> The root of this word is the Greek word *choregia*. In the ancient days in Greece at the great festivals the great dramatists like Euripides and Sophocles presented their plays; Greek plays all have a chorus; to equip and train a chorus was expensive, and public-spirited Greeks generously offered to defray the entire expenses of the chorus; later, in war time patriotic citizens gave free contributions to the state. That is described by the word *choregia*. In still later Greek, in the papyri the word is common in marriage contracts and describes the support that a husband, out of love, undertakes to give his wife. The word underlines the generosity of God, a generosity which is born of love, of which the love of the citizen for his city and of a man for his wife are dim suggestions.[20]

The word was also used for equipping an army with all possible necessities for the approaching battle.

The body of Christ is thus lavishly supplied with all necessities for health and growth and this takes place as it holds fast to its Head. The sustenance is ministered to the body by means of the joints and bands or ligaments, the contacts and attachments within the body.[21] The individual members of the body are channels of nutrition in relation to one another that the body might grow "with a growth which is from God" (Col 2:19, NASB).

A similar thought is elaborated in the Ephesian letter. To everyone in the church there "is given grace according to the measure of the gift of Christ" (4:7). The purpose of this grace in each member is that we "may grow up into him in all things, which is the head, even Christ: from whom the whole body fitly joined together and compacted by that which every joint supplieth, according to the effectual working in the measure of every part, maketh increase of the body unto the edifying of itself in

20. William Barclay, *Letters to the Galatians and Ephesians*, pp. 26-27.
21. Lightfoot, *Colossians and Philemon*, p. 200.

love" (4:15-16). The body grows through the supply of energy distributed to each part through the Head. As each member, receiving his gift of grace, contributes to the whole, the body grows. The same Greek term as used in Colossians 2:19, suggesting a liberal generous nourishment, is here translated "supplieth." There is absolutely no necessity for the growth and edification of the body which is not graciously and lovingly supplied by its Head.

It should be noted in conclusion that the metaphor of the body and its head is not used to teach truths concerning the activity of the church in relation to the world, but rather the mutual relations of member to member and, above all, the members to their Head. It "looks inward and not outward." Christ fills His body, giving it life and direction, not that it might move in the world as a body. The church acts in the world as individuals—individuals, however, who are never apart from the body.[22]

22. Best, p. 157.

3

The Nature of the Church—Part Two

THE TEMPLE OF GOD

THE FIGURE OF THE BUILDING or temple of God bears similarities to that of the body. For example, the spiritual gifts are given to edify or *build* up the body (1 Co 14:12; Eph 4:12, 16) and the building *grows* (Eph 2:21). This combination is not unnatural, for the ancients often conceived of the body as a building or a house.[1] Paul himself speaks of the temporal body as the "earthly house" or "tabernacle" and calls the resurrection body "a building of God, an house not made with hands" (2 Co 5:1).[2] Peter also refers to his mortal body in the figure of a building, calling it "my tabernacle" (2 Pe 1:14) and Christ spoke of His body as a temple (Jn 2:19-21). While there are similarities in these metaphors, primarily in the concept of growth, the building or the temple of God adds several new facets to the understanding of the church.

THE COMPOSITION OF THE BUILDING

The foundation. The building of the church is founded upon the historical person and work of Jesus Christ. After referring to the Corinthian church as "God's building," the apostle states, "According to the grace of God which is given unto me, as a wise masterbuilder, I have laid the foundation, and another buildeth thereon. But let every man take heed how he buildeth thereupon. For other foundation can no man lay than that is laid, which is Jesus Christ" (1 Co 3:10-11). The apostle has laid the foundation

---

1. Otto Michel, "oikos, oikia," in *TDNT*, ed. Gerhard Friedrich, p. 132.
2. Philip E. Hughes, *Commentary to the Second Epistle to the Corinthians*, pp. 160 ff. The view of J. A. T. Robinson (*The Body*, pp. 76-78) and E. Ellis ("II Corinthians v. 1-10 in Pauline Eschatology" in *New Testament Studies* 6 [Apr. 1960]:211 f.) that Paul is here speaking not of individual bodies but of the corporate bodies of Adam and Christ, is shown by Hughes to be inadequate for the language of the text.

by teaching the doctrines of Christ and bringing men into a relationship with Him who is the only foundation that is laid. The church is not built upon a man or a creed but upon the person of the living Christ. Without Him as a foundation, a church is only a human construction and not a building of God. "Other builders there are besides the architect, but no other *ground* for them to build upon."[3]

While Christ is the only foundation, the apostles and prophets are also in a certain respect foundational. The building is built "upon the foundation of the apostles and prophets" (Eph 2:20). Although some interpret this as the foundation laid by the apostles and prophets, the appositional sense is preferred. The foundation is the apostles and prophets, both of whom are seen as chief gifts to the first-century church (Eph 4:11).[4] Their position is due to the fact that they were recipients of foundational revelation of God. The New Testament prophets were instrumental in God's immediate instruction to the primitive churches before the canonical revelation was complete. Although foundational, the prophets were subordinate to the apostles (1 Co 14:37), who received the permanent revelation preserved in the Scriptures. While the foundation of the church is Christ, He is truly revealed only in the inspired apostles' doctrine, which is in reality the teaching of the exalted Christ through them (Jn 16:12-15; Gal 1:12; Rev 1:1). The church, therefore, is only built upon the true foundation of Christ as it stands upon inspired Scriptures.

The cornerstone. Closely associated with the foundation of the building is the cornerstone, which is also identified as Christ (Eph 2:20; 1 Pe 2:6; cf. v. 7, "head of the corner"). The cornerstone, unlike a foundation stone, was visible and controlled the

3. G. G. Findlay, "St. Paul's First Epistle to the Corinthians," *The Expositor's Greek Testament*, 2:790.
4. That the reference is to New Testament prophets rather than Old is seen by the following: (1) The obvious reference to New Testament prophets in the near context (Eph 3:5); (2) The close relationship of prophets with apostles as gifts to the church (Eph 4:11; 1 Co 12:28); (3) New Testament prophets are more appropriate as foundational for the new work of God than those of Israel, and also more evident to Gentile believers; (4) The order of "apostles and prophets" would more aptly be reversed if Old Testament prophets were in view; and finally, (5) The closeness of the relationship of "the apostles and prophets" is emphasized by the use of one article with both.

design of the building.[5] It was the stone that brought unity, harmony and symmetry to the edifice. It is thus in Christ, as the cornerstone, that "all the building fitly framed together groweth unto an holy temple unto the Lord" (Eph 2:21). As the stone of cohesion, it is the primary stone of the building. Therefore Peter calls Christ the "elect, precious" cornerstone (1 Pe 2:6, citing Is 28:16), the one uniquely chosen and honored or prized. This one "was made the head," that is, "chief of the corner" (1 Pe 2:6, citing Ps 118:22). Without this cornerstone there is no building.

The stones. The stones of the building are described by the apostle Peter as "living stones" (1 Pe 2:5). They have received life from *the* "living stone" who has life in Himself (Jn 5:26) and communicates His life to those who come to Him. The "coming" denotes a "coming to stay" for a continual personal relationship.[6] Only through this relationship with the "living stone" is one constituted a "living stone" and therefore a part of the edifice of God's house.

Harmonious with the concept of building is the word *lithos* which is used for the stones. In distinction from *petros,* a loose stone lying on a field or roadside, and *petra,* a rock, or simply rock in contrast to other material, *lithos* is the usual word for a worked stone.[7] The stones of the building of the church are hewed and shaped by the Lord for proper fitting and functioning in His edifice.

THE CONSTRUCTION OF THE BUILDING

The process of building the edifice is detailed by the apostle in Ephesians 2:20-22. Three steps are involved in the construction: placing the stones upon the foundation, their being fit together, and the addition of more stones.

Joining the foundation. Each stone in the building is "built upon the foundation." The Greek *epi,* "upon," suggests "a real resting upon,"[8] denoting here the fact that the members of the building are in close contact with the foundation, resting solidly

5. Edward G. Selwyn, *The First Epistle of St. Peter,* p. 163.
6. Ibid., p. 158.
7. Ibid.
8. A. T. Robertson, *A Grammar of the Greek New Testament in the Light of Historical Research,* p. 600.

upon the apostles and prophets as instruments of the revelation of Christ.

Fitting the stones. As the stones are brought into a relationship with Christ, they are continually being "fitly framed together" (Eph 2:21). This term, derived from *harmos,* "joint," represents the whole elaborate process in which stones are fitted together.[9] The building stones are not piled loosely one on top of another, nor are they held together by some cumbrous external device. Each stone is shaped and formed for a perfect fit in relation to the others in the building. Each has a niche to fill and is adequately fitted for it by the "measure of the gift of Christ" (Eph 4:7, 16) that they might be "built together" (Eph 2:22, NASB). The building is framed together "in the Lord" as the mortar by which each stone is held in position and in proper relationship to the others.

Increasing the structure. The building of the church is conceived by the apostle as yet in the process of its completion (Eph 2:21).[10] Paradoxical, even as the "living stones" out of which it is built, the edifice is said to be "growing." As new members are constantly added, it is "being built up," as Peter says, into "a spiritual house" (1 Pe 2:5).

THE NATURE OF THE BUILDING

A temple. The metaphor of the building reaches its climax in the revelation of its nature. The church is no ordinary building, no matter how great; it is "a holy temple in the Lord" (Eph 2:21). It is because of this tremendous importance of the building of the church that Paul earlier had warned the Corinthians concerning doing harm to the church: "Know ye not that ye are the

9. J. Armitage Robinson, *St. Paul's Epistle to the Ephesians,* p. 262. Robinson describes the process involved in this word as it was used in reference to the construction of large buildings in ancient Greece. It denotes "the preparation of the surfaces, including the cutting, rubbing and testing; the preparation of the dowels and dowel-holes, and finally the fixing of the dowels with molten lead."

10. Because of the omission of the article in the better Greek manuscripts, "all the building" is translated by some as "every building" (cf. ASV). The context, however, definitely favors the popular rendering. There are not several buildings of God which would necessitate several "temples," but the one church founded upon the one foundation and cornerstone (cf. ibid., p. 70). It has been suggested that "building" be considered as a proper name in the sense that there is only one such building.

temple of God, and that the Spirit of God dwelleth in you? If any man defile the temple of God, him shall God destroy; for the temple of God is holy, which temple ye are" (1 Co 3:16-17). The English word *temple* translates two Greek words, *naos* and *hieron*. *Naos*, which is used here, although not always distinguishable from *hieron*, which denotes the entire temple precinct, usually refers to the temple building proper or the sanctuary. The distinction is seen, for example, when the Pharisee and publican pray in the *hieron* (Lk 18:10). Jesus drives the traders out of the same place (Mk 11:15), but it was in the *naos* that the angel appeared to Zecharias (Lk 1:9), and it was the veil of the *naos* that was rent at the crucifixion (Mk 15:38). Deriving from the verb *naiō*, "to dwell, to inhabit," *naos* meant to the Greek "the abode of the god"[11] and particularly the shrine in which the image of the god was placed.[12] In the Jewish temple, which provides the background for New Testament thought, the *naos* consisted of the holy place and the holy of holies. But the church no longer worshiped in that literal temple. The time predicted by Jesus to the woman of Samaria had come, "when ye shall neither in this mountain, nor yet at Jerusalem, worship the Father" (Jn 4:21). The old order with its temple sacrifice had passed away, being fulfilled at Calvary. The new order had come with a new temple composed of "living stones," the church.

The habitation of God. The significance of the temple seen in the meaning of *naos* was the fact that God dwelt there. So the apostle specifies the church as "an habitation of God." It was the great privilege of Israel to have the Lord who dwelt in heaven, also dwell among His people in the sanctuary of the temple (1 Ki 8:29-30; cf. Ex 25:8). In an even more intimate way, this privilege is granted to His New Testament people: "For ye are the temple of the living God: as God hath said, I will dwell in them, and walk in them; and I will be their God, and they shall be my people" (2 Co 6:16).

God dwelt in the temple of Israel, as in the earlier tabernacle, for the purpose of having communion with His people. Speaking of the tabernacle, God told Moses, "I will meet you, to speak

11. Otto Michel, "Naos" in *TDNT*, 4:880.
12. James H. Moulton and George Milligan, *The Vocabulary of the Greek Testament*, p. 422.

there unto thee. And there I will meet with the children of
Israel" (Ex 29:42b-43). For this reason the tabernacle was called
the tent of meeting, the place where God met His people. It was
also termed the tent or dwelling of the testimony, signifying the
place of revelation where God made known His will. It was there
that Moses brought the causes of the people "before the LORD."
Furthermore, the temple was the appointed place where God received the services of His people through the priests—the tithes,
offerings and sacrifices. Above all, the temple was the dwelling
place of the glory of God. From its position between the cherubim
above the ark of the covenant, the Shekinah glory went out in
acts of power. At the beginning of the sacrificial ministry this
glory appeared to all the people and fire came out "from before
the LORD" to consume the offering (Lev 9:24). This same fire
went out to kill the sons of Aaron who offered strange fire to the
Lord (Lev 10:2). God now dwells in His New Testament temple,
the church, to perform these same functions. Rather than a temple made with hands, He has created a temple in the hearts of
men through faith in Christ. The body of each member of the
church, as well as the church collectively, is a temple (1 Co 6:19;
1 Co 3:16-17; Eph 2:21-22). The glory of God indwells this New
Testament temple, and therefore Paul can say, "But we all, with
unveiled face beholding as in a mirror the glory of the Lord, are
being transformed into the same image from glory to glory, just
as from the Lord, the Spirit" (2 Co 3:18, NASB).

THE PRIESTHOOD

A temple is not complete without a priesthood to minister in
it. As the temple of the Old Testament had a priest, so does the
church. Thus Peter declares that New Testament believers, "as
living stones, are being built up as a spiritual house for a holy
priesthood, to offer up spiritual sacrifices acceptable to God
through Jesus Christ" (1 Pe 2:5, NASB). The nature of the
church is a "spiritual house" and its vocation is a "holy priesthood." Using language which was applied to Israel in the Old
Testament (Ex 19:5-6), the apostle in the same context calls the
members of the church "a chosen race, a royal priesthood, a holy
nation, a people for God's own possession" (1 Pe 2:9, NASB).
As Israel was formed by God to be a priestly nation, so now, fol-

lowing her setting aside during this age, the church functions as God's mediatorial people.[13]

THE OFFICE OF PRIEST

The basic term for priest in the Old Testament, *cohen,* comes from a root meaning "to stand," and therefore signifies one who stands before God and therefore serves Him.[14] The concept also carries the thought of standing to represent another, bringing out the primary mediatorial function of the priesthood.[15] The entire nation of Israel was called a "kingdom of priests" at Sinai (Ex 19:6) and is yet destined to function as a priestly body (Is 61:6). But during Old Testament times it was necessary that a special priesthood be chosen by God to represent even that nation before Him. In contrast to Israel, the entire church stands as a "royal priesthood," a priestly fellowship belonging to the King and sharing His glory.[16]

In further contrast to Old Testament practice, whereby only the high priest could enter the holy of holies into the presence of God once a year, the church as a priesthood has permanent access open to it through its High Priest. In the Old Testament the presence of God was cut off from the people by the thick veil. But that veil was rent through the rending of the body of Christ, making it possible now for the believer to enter with confidence into the "holy place" through Christ (Heb 10:19-21). Nor is it into an earthly tabernacle that the church enters, but rather the High Priest of the church entered into the holy of holies, there to present His finished work once and for all (Heb 9:24-28). The believer is therefore encouraged to "draw near" into the very presence of God. This term was the cultic term used for the priest's approach to God. How different is the church from all which preceded it. Whereas all nations had priests to perform the functions, the church has none. It is a priesthood. While all others brought sacrifices that they might approach God, the

13. Some, on the basis of this similarity of language, make Israel typical of the church, and therefore the church is considered to be real Israel. While there is much that is typical in the Old Testament economy of Israel, the nation itself is not strictly typical.
14. Franz Delitzsch, *Biblical Commentary on the Psalms,* 3:192.
15. Gustave Oehler, *Theology of the Old Testament,* p. 209.
16. Gottlob Schrenk, "hierateuma" in *TDNT,* 3:250.

church brings none, but approaches boldly through the finished sacrifices of Christ, its great High Priest.

THE QUALIFICATIONS OF THE PRIESTHOOD

Requisites for the priestly office are succinctly summed up in conditions laid down at the confirmation of Aaron's house to the priesthood. The issue of the identity of the priests was to be settled by God, as Moses declared, "The LORD will shew who are his, and who is holy; and will cause him to come near unto him: even him whom he hath chosen will he cause to come near unto him" (Num 16:5). The priesthood is thus composed of those chosen by God from among men and set apart as holy. Only such can approach God. These same qualifications are met by the priesthood of the church.

Chosen by God. Peter makes it abundantly clear that members of the New Testament priesthood do not choose this honor for themselves, but rather, are set apart by God. They are the "elect according to the foreknowledge of God the Father," an "elect race." This election is only in Christ, who is the appointed High Priest (Heb 5:1, 4). As He is Himself installed High Priest (Heb 7:28), so He installs the members of the church as priests (Heb 10:10, 14).[17] Therefore Peter says it is through coming to Him that believers are built up "an holy priesthood" (1 Pe 2:4-5).

Sanctified by God. As the Old Testament priest was set apart as holy unto God, so the New Testament priest is also a "holy priesthood" (1 Pe 2:5). The emphasis on holiness of the Old Testament priests, seen in the elaborate rites of consecration,[18] is also evident in the sanctification of the priesthood of the church. These rites began by the washing of the whole body, symbolic of spiritual cleansing (Ex 29:4). The New Testament believers likewise have their "bodies washed with pure water" (Heb 10:22), an obvious reference to cleansing through the "washing of regeneration" (Titus 3:5).

This negative preparation of cleansing was followed by a cere-

17. The Greek verb *teleioō* as used in Heb 7:28, "consecrated" and 10:14, "perfected," is employed in the Septuagint to describe the installation of the priests to their work (Ex 29:1, 33, 35; Lev 4:5; 8:33; 16:32; 21:10; Num 3:3). Cf. Ernest Best, "Spiritual Sacrifice," *Interpretation* 14 (July 1960):285; B. F. Westcott, *The Epistle to the Hebrews*, p. 63.
18. Oehler, pp. 210-11.

mony of robing (Ex 29:5-6) with robes made of fine, shining white linen symbolic of purity (Ex 28:40-41). The fulfillment of this aspect in the New Testament is the robe of purity which the believer wears. Having "put on Christ," he is clothed in His righteousness.

Next the priest was anointed with oil made with four sweet-smelling substances. This act, symbolic of the communication of the Holy Spirit, finds its part in the New Testament priesthood anointing of the Holy Spirit received by each member of the church (1 Jn 2:20, 27).

These preparations of the priest were followed by a threefold sacrifice: a sin offering, a burnt offering, and a modified thank offering—signifying their placing "into all the functions and rights of the priesthood."[19] In the last offering the blood of the ram was sprinkled upon the altar, but also upon the priests, significantly upon their ear, thumb and toe, denoting their duty to hear the Word, to execute it, and walk in it (Ex 29:20). Similarly, Peter speaks of the New Testament priesthood as "elect . . . unto obedience and sprinkling of the blood of Jesus Christ" (1 Pe 1:2; cf. Heb 12:24).

All of these consecration rites bespeak the purity demanded of the priest and his devotion of life to God. With similar thrust Peter calls the priesthood of the church to a holiness of life (1 Pe 1:16) and walk which glorifies God among all men (1 Pe 2:11-12).

THE FUNCTIONS OF THE PRIESTHOOD

The great privilege of the priesthood in access into the presence of God carries with it a responsibility of service. Again viewing the priests of the old covenant, their functions may be broadly divided into the service of the altar (or sacrifices) the service of witness (proclamation of the law), and the service of intercession for the people. The New Testament reveals the same functions for the church as a priesthood.

The service of sacrifice. In sharp contrast to the priest of the old covenant, the priesthood of the church has no sacrifice for sin to offer. Christ has "offered one sacrifice for sins for ever" (Heb 10:12). Once for all He "appeared to put away sin by the

19. Ibid., p. 210.

sacrifice of himself" (Heb 9:26), and so "there is no more offering for sin" (Heb 10:18). Nevertheless, there are sacrifices to be
performed by the New Testament priesthood. According to Peter,
the church is "built up a spiritual house, an holy priesthood, to
offer up spiritual sacrifices, acceptable to God by Jesus Christ"
(1 Pe 2:5). The word that Peter uses for "offer up" is that which
is regularly used for sacrifices (cf. Heb 7:27), denoting "the notion of an offering made unto God and placed upon his altar."[20]
Thus the writer to the Hebrews can speak of an altar which belongs to the believer (Heb 13:10) upon which Christ has already
made the primary offering but upon which the believer also has
sacrifices to make (vv. 15-16).

The primary sacrifice is the believer himself. In the language
of sacrificial ministry,[21] the members of the New Testament
priesthood are called upon to present their own bodies, that is,
their total persons, as "a living sacrifice, holy, acceptable unto
God" (Ro 12:1). This act is described as "reasonable service,"
denoting an action involving the active mind of the offerer and
not something mechanically ritualistic. The effect of this sacrifice is the gradual transformation of the entire person (Ro 12:2).
This self-sacrificing priestly ministry is also seen in Paul's statement to the Philippians: "But even if I am being poured out
as a drink-offering upon the sacrifice and service of your faith,
I rejoice and share my joy with you all" (2:17, NASB). Here,
as in 2 Timothy 4:6, the reference is to the apostle's martyrdom;
nevertheless, even in this he is voluntarily offering his life in
sacrifice to God.

Along with this primary sacrifice, there are other sacrifices
imperative upon the New Testament priesthood. The writer to
the Hebrews exhorts his readers, "By him therefore let us offer
the sacrifice of praise to God continually, that is, the fruit of our
lips giving thanks to his name" (Heb 13:15). This sacrifice, the
highest form of peace offering for a graciously bestowed favor
which was an exceptional service in the Old Testament, is now
the continual, normal service of the believer in the church. But
one cannot truthfully offer the sacrifice of praise to God without
also serving his fellowman. Therefore the writer to the Hebrews

20. Westcott, p. 197.
21. H. Strathmann, "latreuo, latreia" in *TDNT*, 4:65.

adds immediately, "But to do good and to communicate forget not: for with such sacrifices God is well pleased" (Heb 13:16). "To do good" signifies general kindly service, while "to communicate" indicates that the service includes the free sharing of our possessions with those in need. The apostle similarly describes the gifts of the Philippians toward his own need as "an odour of a sweet smell, a sacrifice acceptable, wellpleasing to God" (Phil 4:18). Thus, the kind deeds of believers not only glorify God before men (Mt 5:16; 1 Pe 2:12), but they are indeed priestly acts toward God.

One other sacrifice of the New Testament believer-priests is the offering up of new converts to God. The apostle Paul saw himself by the grace of God as a minister to the Gentiles "that the offering up of the Gentiles might be acceptable, being sanctified by the Holy Ghost" (Ro 15:16; cf. Is 66:20). Although the apostle Paul was uniquely a minister to the Gentiles, every New Testament believer has the privilege of making this sacrifice of the fruits of evangelism.

The service of witness. In the mediatorial capacity between God and man, the priest also bears the responsibility of witness. The Old Testament priest was called "the messenger of the Lord" because the people were to "seek the law at his mouth" (Mal 2:7; cf. Lev 10:11; Deu 33:10). The church likewise has the responsibility of being God's witness to the world. Peter says that the purpose of New Testament priests is to "shew forth the praises of him who hath called you out of darkness into his marvellous light" (1 Pe 2:9). Rendered more literally, the believer is to advertise the excellencies or noble acts of God, "especially the redemption brought about by Christ's death and resurrection, and the divine wisdom, love, power, and mercy which lay behind it and in it."[22] The church performs this priestly ministry by proclaiming the message of the gospel as ambassadors of Christ (2 Co 5:20) and by a holy manner of life before the world (1 Pe 2:12), which includes suffering for righteousness' sake after the pattern of Christ, the great High Priest (1 Pe 2:20-25). The believer is thus to consider his body a temple in which to perform priestly acts which display positively the

22. Selwyn, p. 167.

glory and especially the holiness of God who resides in it (1 Co 6:19).

The service of intercession. While the priestly office itself under the old order was intercessory in character, there appears to have been a special ministry of intercession as well. In Joel 2:17 the priests are exhorted to "weep between the porch and the altar, and . . . say, Spare thy people, O LORD." Malachi also appeals to them for intercession (1:9). This intercessory service was symbolized by the engraving of the names of the twelve tribes upon the shoulder pieces worn by the high priest (Ex 28:12). As their mediator, he carried the people before God.

The New Testament reveals a similar intercessory activity performed by the members of the church. Although all members are priests and therefore have equal access through Christ, the High Priest, intercessory prayer for one another was natural for the early church. Prayer was made for physical needs (Ac 12:5, 12; Ja 5:14-18), missionary activity (Ac 13:3), and, above all, for the spiritual needs of the church (Ac 14:23; cf. the numerous prayers of Paul in his epistles, e.g., Eph 1:16-23; 3:14-21).

The intercessory activity of the New Testament priest included those outside of the faith. Stephen's last recorded words were words of intercession for his murderers. The plight of Israel outside of Christ moved Paul to prayer (Ro 10:1), and his concern for the ministry of the gospel urged him to command that prayer be made for all men everywhere (1 Ti 2:1-2). Thus the church stands as God's priesthood in the ministry of intercession to invoke His blessing on herself and the world.

In the ministries of believer priests it must be remembered that they do not act as individuals alone, but are members of a priesthood which has its position and authority only in its High Priest, the Lord Jesus. All the ministries of the New Testament priesthood become valid and effectual through Him.

THE BRIDE

One of the most beautiful images of the church is that of the bride of Christ. This same figure of marriage was used in the Old Testament for the bond between God and Israel. Looking forward prophetically to the restoration of the nation, Isaiah declares, "Thy Maker is thy husband; Jehovah of hosts is his name. . . . For Jehovah hath called thee as a wife forsaken and grieved in spirit, even a wife of youth" (Is 54:5-6, ASV). Again he writes, "As the bridegroom rejoiceth over the bride, so shall thy God rejoice over thee" (62:5; cf. Ho 2:7). Although not used extensively in the New Testament, this concept carries significant meaning for the relationship of the church to Christ.

THE LOVE OF THE BRIDEGROOM

In a discourse on the practical expression of the grace of salvation in marriage, the apostle uses the union of Christ and His church to illustrate the relation of husband and wife (Eph 5:22-23). As human marriage involves the intimacy of oneness, so members of the church are united to Christ as "members of his body, of his flesh, and of his bones" (v. 30). But the dominant theme in the relationship is love between husband and wife. The man is to love his wife, "even as Christ . . . loved the church, and gave himself for it" (v. 25).

The extent of love. The love of Christ for His bride far surpasses anything known in the human level, even though it is set forth as the ideal of married love. Never has a husband loved as Christ loved the church. For Christ did not love those worthy of love, but sinners and enemies (Ro 5:8-10). Westcott aptly remarks, "Christ loved the church not because it was perfectly lovable but in order to make it such."[23] The extent of this love is seen in the price paid to acquire the bride. Among the ancients there was the practice of the groom giving a price to the father or brother of the bride.[24] Christ did not give of the wealth of creation for the church, which He could have given without end, but He gave Himself. Such love is beyond comprehension, surpassing all human knowledge, and yet it is the object of ultimate knowledge and the subject of all true experience of the bride (Eph 3:19).

The expression of love. The evidence of the love of a husband to his wife is his concern for her welfare. A loving husband nourishes and cherishes his wife as he does his own body. Literally, the two words suggest the supply of nutrition and warmth

23. Westcott, *St. Paul's Epistle to the Ephesians*, p. 84.
24. W. P. Paterson, "Marriage" in *A Dictionary of the Bible*, ed. James Hastings, 3:270.

to the body. But the idea goes beyond these to the tender care of the total well-being.

So Christ as the Bridegroom nourishes and cherishes His bride, supplying her with every necessity for her health and welfare (Eph 5:29; cf. 4:7 ff.). This is certainly included in Paul's description of Christ as the Head and Saviour of the body (5:23). The head is responsible to plan for the safety and protection of the body and to provide for its welfare. So Christ as Head and Saviour has not only redeemed His bride, but His love continues to be shown making daily provisions in every area for her.

THE RESPONSE OF THE BRIDE

Although there was no initial love on the part of the bride, there is a response to His love. John frequently speaks of this response on the part of the church as "love." "We love him, because he first loved us" (1 Jn 4:19). In contrast, Paul seldom refers to the attitude of the believer toward Christ as that of love, but rather prefers to speak of faith and obedience.[25] Undoubtedly these too are to be understood as the expression of responsive love, which needs to be spelled out because of the failure of believers to properly interpret it.

The church as the bride is therefore "subject unto Christ" (Eph 5:24), even as the wife to the husband in the marriage relationship. The word translated "subject" means literally to "arrange under." The life of the church in each member is to be arranged under the headship of Christ. Their authority and leadership are found in Him. His thoughts and attitudes must be theirs. As the apostle calls the woman the glory of the man (1 Co 11:7), so the church as the bride is the glory of her Bridegroom, reflecting His majesty as a queen does a king's.

Following the scriptural emphasis to fidelity in marriage, the apostle Paul applies this aspect of responsibility to the church in Corinth in relation to Christ. He is jealous to present them to Christ "as a pure virgin" (2 Co 11:2, NASB), fearing that Satan might lead them "astray from the simplicity and purity of devotion to Christ" (v. 3, NASB). As the love of God for His people in the Old Testament was a jealous love, demanding a

25. Ernest Best, *One Body in Christ* (London: SPCK, 1955), p. 175.

single-hearted devotion in response, so the love of Christ for His Bride calls for a response of absolute faithfulness. Simplicity, coming from the verb meaning "that which is *spread out*, and thus without folds or wrinkles,"[26] suggests a heart totally and wholeheartedly devoted to Christ with no duplicity or secret loves. The Corinthians were in danger of being seduced through the subtlety of impostor teachers of another gospel. Until the bride is finally united to her Bridegroom, she must be on guard against the alluring and yet lying attractions which Satan uses to draw her away from Christ. Marriage love is an exclusive love.

THE FUTURE UNION

A problem is presented in the use of this figure which demonstrates the truth that the images of the church must not be pressed into every detail. In 2 Corinthians 11 the church is represented as betrothed, with the consummation of the marriage yet future. This has caused some to refer to the union of Christ and His bride as being only future and therefore the Bride as the idealized church of the end. However, the same apostle in the Ephesian letter uses the present union of Christ and the church as illustrative of the consummated married state (Eph 5:28-33). That the marriage can be viewed as having already taken place and yet still in the future is in harmony with the biblical tension between the present possession of salvation in Christ and its being an inheritance which will be fully realized in the future. The church is united to Christ as His bride and yet the complete entering into the state of this blessed position awaits the future when Christ will take His bride to be *with* Him forever (1 Th 4:17).

Therefore, this figure speaks of a future day when the church, which is now the bride, will enter into the fullness of that position. Now her position is hidden before the eyes of the world, even as the power and life of her Bridegroom are hidden. When He is manifest in glory then His bride will also be revealed for what she is and exalted to share in the glory of her spouse.

It is possible to see this progression of relationship in the Oriental practice of marriage which consisted of three stages. First came the betrothal, which was more than the promise of

26. Richard C. Trench, *Synonyms of the New Testament*, p. 204.

marriage. It was the very initiation of marriage, for the bride
was legally considered a married woman from the time of betrothal. She could become a widow, receive a bill of divorce-
ment, or be punished for unfaithfulness.[27] The church is presently the betrothed bride of Christ (2 Co 11:2), having been purchased by the Bridegroom (Eph 5:25; Ac 20:28). She is therefore bound to faithfulness and purity because the marriage has
been initiated.

After an indefinite interval, the actual marriage took place.
On that day the bridegroom and his friends went to the home
of the bride and then, in company with the bride and her
friends, the festal company proceeded to their future home.[28]
Following the analogy of the Oriental practice, the church as
the bride now awaits the coming of Christ to take her to Himself. The apostle Paul speaks of this day when he says, "For the
Lord himself shall descend from heaven with a shout, with the
voice of the archangel, and with the trump of God: and the
dead in Christ shall rise first: then we which are alive and remain
shall be caught up together with them in the clouds, to meet the
Lord in the air: and so shall we ever be with the Lord" (1 Th
4:16-17).

When the bride and groom arrived at their future home, the
actual marriage ceremony took place, with the bride being presented to the groom. Although in the Oriental weddings it was
a friend of the bridegroom who made the presentation, Christ
Himself presents His own bride to Himself. "He and none other
presents the bride, and He and none other receives her to Himself. No inferior agency is permitted; a proof in itself, as well
as His death, of His love to the church."[29]

After the presentation, the marriage supper or feast began.
It could last for several days until finally consummated with the
bridal pair being led to the bridal chamber. The apostle John
refers to this event for the church in Revelation 19:7-9:

> Let us be glad and rejoice, and give honour to him: for the
> marriage of the Lamb is come, and his wife hath made herself
> ready. And to her was granted that she should be arrayed in fine

27. Joachim Jeremias, "numphē, numphios" in *TDNT*, 4:1099.
28. Jeremias, *The Parables of Jesus*, rev. ed., p. 173.
29. John Eadie, *Commentary on the Epistle to the Ephesians*, p. 421.

linen, clean and white: for the fine linen is the righteousness of saints. And he saith unto me, Write, Blessed are they which are called unto the marriage supper of the Lamb.

Whether the supper takes place in heaven following the rapture[30] or in connection with the Lord's return to earth itself,[31] it is associated with the revelation of the glory of Christ and His bride at the second advent. At this time the church will partake of the great eschatological banquet expressive of the joy of perfect fellowship with Christ in the kingdom.[32]

OTHER IMAGES

At least two other images add significantly to an understanding of the nature of the church. Jesus directed both toward His disciples and their relationship to Him, which was to continue even after His physical departure and the inauguration of the church at Pentecost.

THE FLOCK

The metaphor of the shepherd and his flock is frequently used in the Old Testament. God is the Shepherd who loves and tenderly cares for His sheep. "The LORD is my shepherd," the psalmist says (Ps 23:1). "Give ear, O Shepherd of Israel, thou that leadest Joseph like a flock" (Ps 80:1). The gentle care of the shepherd is viewed in this prophecy of Isaiah: "He shall feed his flock like a shepherd: he shall gather the lambs with his arm, and carry them in his bosom, and shall gently lead those that are with young" (Is 40:11). God's flock is composed of Israel which He has made His own possession through redemption and covenant (cf. Ex 19:3-8). "So," the psalmist says, "we thy people and sheep of thy pasture will give thee thanks for ever" (Ps 79:13). "We are his people, and the sheep of his pasture" (Ps 100:3*b*; cf. 95:7).

The flock of the New Testament church is composed of sheep from both Israel and the Gentiles. Speaking to His disciples before going to the cross, Jesus looks forward to the breaking

30. William R. Newell, *The Book of the Revelation*, p. 260.
31. John F. Walvoord, *The Revelation of Jesus Christ*, p. 270.
32. Already in the gospels Jesus associates the marriage feast with the Messianic times or the kingdom of heaven (Lk 14:16 ff.; Mt 22:1 ff). Cf. Ethelbert Stauffer, "gameo, gamos" in *TDNT*, 1:653-55.

down of the wall of partition between Jew and Gentile in the
church when both will become one flock: "And I have other
sheep, which are not of this fold; I must bring them also, and
they shall hear My voice; and they shall become one flock with
one Shepherd" (Jn 10:16, NASB).[33] The sheep of the New
Testament church from every nation are one flock because of
common relationship to the one Shepherd.

The prominent concepts involved in the metaphor of the
shepherd and the sheep are the ownership and tending of the
flock on the part of the shepherd and the subjection of the
sheep to the rule of the shepherd.

The ownership of the flock. The church as God's people in
the New as in the Old Testament is the "flock of God" (1 Pe
5:2). But something new is added; it is also Christ's flock. Jesus
declared, "My sheep hear my voice" (Jn 10:27); "Feed my sheep"
(Jn 21:16). In this the unity of the Son and the Father is
revealed. "My Father, which gave them me, is greater than all;
and no man is able to pluck them out of my Father's hand.
I and my Father are one" (Jn 10:29-30). The ultimate Shepherd-
Owner is God, who has sent His Son as "the great shepherd of
the sheep."

In addition, the method of procurement is made known. For
God to acquire ownership of the flock it was necessary for Him
to redeem it from the bondage of sin. This He did at the highest possible cost. He purchased it "with his own blood" (Ac
20:28).[34] The threat of the enemy against the life of the sheep
was conquered by the good Shepherd who gave His own life for
the sheep (Jn 10:11). All of this serves to show the value which
God has placed upon the flock that He might have absolute right
of ownership over it.

The shepherding of the flock. Christ the Shepherd has not

---

33. It is important to note the distinction between "fold" and "flock" which
    is blurred in the Authorized Version. "Fold" denotes an outward or-
    ganization and refers to Israel, some of whom were Christ's sheep but
    some who were not because they did not believe. "Flock" speaks of the
    inner unity of the sheep "created in and by Jesus" (C. K. Barrett, *The
    Gospel According to St. John*, pp. 312-13).
34. It is probably best with Bruce to translate the Greek possessive *idios* as
    "His own one" which sense is well attested in the papyri. The church
    would then be purchased by God "by means of the blood of His own
    one" (F. F. Bruce, *The Book of the Acts*, p. 416, n.59).

only purchased the church, but He also provides for its every need. The shepherd's task is that of care in the widest sense. He guards the sheep from danger, tends the sick, searches for the lost and, above all, leads them to good pasture. In the East the relationship of the shepherd to his sheep was one of considerable intimacy. Often the same sheep would be in the flock for as long as eight or nine years so that the shepherd came to know each one, calling them by name, and the sheep in turn knew the voice of their shepherd. Such is the relationship between Christ and His people. He knows those who are His and provides every need for them.

While in the ultimate sense Christ Himself tends His sheep, going before them (Jn 10:4), the work of shepherding has also been committed to undershepherds as His ministers in the church. Thus he says to Peter in John 21:16, "Shepherd My sheep" (NASB). Peter, in turn, charges the elders to "shepherd the flock of God among you" (1 Pe 5:2, NASB). Paul gives the same charge to the elders of Ephesus in Acts 20:28: "Be on guard for yourselves and for all the flock, among which the Holy Spirit has made you overseers, to shepherd the church of God which He purchased with His own blood" (NASB). The ascended Christ has given "pastors" to the church (Eph 4:11), which term is simply the Latin word for *shepherd*. There is therefore no better description of the work of the leaders of the church than "undershepherds" of the "chief Shepherd" whose ministry is to care for each member as a shepherd cares for his sheep.

Primary among the shepherd's tasks was the provision of nourishment for his sheep. Christ, the chief Shepherd, also makes provision for the spiritual nourishment of His sheep. This feeding is done through the ministry of the Word. Thus Paul's charge to the young minister, Timothy, was "preach the word" (2 Ti 4:2). It is the Scripture which is profitable and makes the man of God "perfect, throughly furnished unto all good works" (2 Ti 3:16-17). Paul could take satisfaction in the fact that he had fed the flock at Ephesus: "For I have not shunned to declare unto you all the counsel of God" (Ac 20:27). There is no greater responsibility for the undershepherd than to provide that spiritual food which makes for a healthy flock.

The shepherd also rules the flock, leading it in the way it

should go and disciplining those that stray. In like manner the Scriptures connect the shepherding of the flock with the task of "overseer" of the church. Christ is the "Shepherd and Bishop" of His sheep (1 Pe 2:25). "Bishop" is the translation of *episcopos*, which means literally "to look or watch over." It was the title used by Athenians for the officers sent to manage the affairs of subject states. As Shepherd, Christ is the Overseer of the flock, but He has also committed this task to His undershepherds. Paul says that the Holy Spirit had made the Ephesian elders overseers of the flock (Ac 20:28). According to Peter, the elders are to shepherd the flock, "taking the oversight" (1 Pe 5:2). Thus the term *bishop* or *overseer* became the name of a church office (1 Ti 3:1).

One further task of the shepherd, with great importance for the sheep, was that of protection. The shepherd's equipment included his rod and his staff (Ps 23:4). The staff was a long, crooked stick used for pulling back straying sheep, while the rod was a stout piece of wood about three feet long with a lump on one end; it was used as a weapon against wild beasts and robbers. It was also the practice of some shepherds to lay down across the opening of the fold during the night so that their bodies became literally the protecting door. Christ the great Shepherd and His undershepherds similarly bear the responsibility of protecting the flock of God. "Grievous wolves" threatened the flock in New Testament times (Ac 20:29-30), and warning is given of increasing dangers throughout the church age (2 Ti 3:1-13; 2 Pe 2:1-3).

As the shepherd went before his sheep through every place of danger, assuring safe passage for the sheep, so Christ has passed along the way of His sheep, suffering every threat that besets them. He even went into the very lair of the enemy to conquer death itself so that no harm may ultimately befall His sheep. As the shepherd lay down to form the door, so Christ is the door to His fold (Jn 10:9). While the flock may have to suffer and is, in fact, promised tribulation, yet protection and, ultimately, victory are assured.

The undershepherds serve in this same protective ministry, watching over the souls committed to them, for they must give an account to the chief Shepherd for the sheep (Heb 13:17).

Their protection comes by way of the faithful ministry of the Word through which Christ guards His sheep.

The subjection of the sheep. This metaphor of sheep not only carries meaning in relation to the position of the Shepherd, but also that of the sheep. It says first of all that the church is totally dependent upon Christ, for there is perhaps no animal born as helpless as a sheep. As Bigg notes, the figure "brings out the general ignorance and helplessness of man, who, without aid from above, can only go astray like sheep without a shepherd."[35] Essentially, the sheep can provide nothing for itself and can only prosper as it follows the direction of the shepherd. Its only obligation is to submit to his leading and authority. Thus the church is directed as the flock of God to submit to His authority and that of the chief Shepherd. Because this direction is communicated through the Word and the ministry of the under-shepherds which God has placed in the church, the members are exhorted to "obey them that have the rule over [literally, lead] you, and submit yourselves" (Heb 13:17). As even the leaders of the church are sheep, they also are obligated to submit ultimately to the chief Shepherd.

THE VINE AND THE BRANCHES

The Old Testament again provides the background for the figure of the vine and the branches used by Christ in John 15. Repeatedly Israel is symbolized by a vine which God has planted, but it has failed to bear the desired fruit (Eze 15:1-5; 19:10-14; Is 5:1-7; Jer 2:21). Against this failure of the Old Testament vine, Jesus comes as the "true vine" (Jn 15:1) who does bring forth fruit through the branches abiding in Him, namely, His disciples of the New Testament church.

The organic union of the vine. The branch not only is attached to the vine and so may be said to be in it, but the vine by its very life is also in the branch. Thus Jesus exhorts His disciples to "abide in me, and I in you" (Jn 15:4). "He that abideth in me, and I in him, the same bringeth forth much fruit" (v. 5).

Although fruit-bearing depends upon this mutual relationship, the power for production flows only one way, from the vine

35. Charles Bigg, *A Critical and Exegetical Commentary on the Epistles of St. Peter and St. Jude,* p. 149.

to the branches. As the branch bears fruit from what it receives from the vine, so the believer is fruitful only as Christ lives in him. Only that done in the spiritual supply of Christ is considered to be fruit in the sight of the husbandman. Christ puts it pointedly, "Without me ye can do nothing" (Jn 15:5*b*). Nevertheless, it should also be noted that the vine does not bear the fruit by itself, but rather through the branches living in it. So Christ does not directly bear the fruit, but produces it through His life in the believer.

The abiding of the vine. The production of fruit has but one requirement for the branch. It must remain in the vine, in order that the vitality of that vine might bring forth fruit through it. Jesus makes only this demand upon His disciples that they may be productive. The husbandman "purges" or prunes the branches, making them clean to bear more fruit; the branch simply remains in the vine (Jn 15:4-7). The word abide (*menō*) which Christ uses denotes "an inward, enduring personal communion."[36] This does not have primary references to a second stage of intimacy between the vine and branches beyond the fact of union, but rather emphasizes the necessity on the part of the branch to persevere in its relationship to the vine. The same "abiding" relationship is in accord with other biblical references and is implied in the varying productions of fruit (Jn 15:2, 8). Christ, however, in this metaphor is pointing to the imperative incumbent upon every branch to abide or remain in personal relationship with Him as the vine. There is no life in the branch of itself and consequently no prospect of fruit outside of abiding in the vine.

The fruit of the union. While other wood is of some value in itself, the branch of the vine is notoriously useless severed from its source. The sole purpose of a branch is to produce fruit; this it can do only as it lives in the vine. So the believer is without purpose apart from bearing fruit in Christ. The husbandman

36. W. F. Arndt and F. W. Gingrich, *A Greek-English Lexicon of the New Testament and Other Early Christian Literature,* p. 505. Speaking of the phrase "to abide in," Hauck states, "In the Johannine writings such phrases are developed into distinctive personal statements concerning the lasting immanence between God and Christ or Christians and Christ" (F. Hauck, "menō" in *TDNT*, 4:576).

tends the vineyard for fruit and is "glorified" when the branches "bear much fruit" (v. 8).

The nature of this fruit is not defined, although two characteristics listed as fruit of the Spirit (Gal 5:22-23) are prominent in the context: joy (Jn 15:11) and love (vv. 9, 10, 12, 13). All of the manifestations of the Spirit are undoubtedly included in this fruit, as it is by the Spirit that Christ lives in the branches (Eph 3:16-17). Perhaps it is best to say with Godet, "By *fruit* Jesus designates the production and development of the *spiritual* life, with all its normal manifestations, either in ourselves or in others, through the strength of Christ living in us."[37]

For the furtherance of production, the husbandman "purges" the branches (Jn 15:2).[38] The word means to purify or make clean and in the figure refers to the pruning away of superfluous wood by the vinedresser. Manifestations of self which clog the production of genuine fruit are cut away through the convicting ministry of the Word (cf. vv. 3, 7), and the disciplinary action of God comes upon His children, not for the purpose of destruction or stunting the growth, but that more fruit might be borne. Again the pertinency of this particular metaphor is seen in the fact that no tree requires such extensive pruning as that of the vine, and yet it is the characteristic of the vine, that even though it is severely cut back, it does not die but grows again.

The figure of the vine thus demonstrates the vital relationship

37. F. Godet, *Commentary on the Gospel of John*, 2:294. Barrett, p. 395, similarly remarks, "The bearing of fruit is simply living the life of a Christian disciple—(see vv. 5, 8); perhaps especially the practice of mutual love (v. 12)."
38. Some see v. 2a also as the work of the husbandman to encourage production of fruit by translating *airō*, "taketh away" (AV), as "lifted up" in the sense of exposing it to the benefit of sunlight and the atmosphere. However, nothing is said of this act promoting fruit as in 2b. While the basic meaning of the verb is "to lift up," it frequently carries with it the idea of removal and is probably best so understood here (cf. Arndt and Gingrich, p. 24). The reference is then to those who have an outward relationship to Christ through profession but are not organically joined to His life and consequently do not "abide" or "remain" in Him. Jesus spoke of some in the parable of the sower who received the word but had no root in them (Mk 4:16-17). John also referred to those who "went out from us, but they were not of us; for if they had been of us, they would no doubt have continued [*menō*] with us" (1 Jn 2:19). An example of such a person near at hand to Jesus, bearing an unreal relationship to Him, was Judas (cf. Jn 10:10-11).

between the members of the church and Christ. Abiding in Him
means life and fruitfulness; apart from Him there is worthless-
ness and death.

4

The Inauguration of the Church

MUCH DISAGREEMENT exists over when the church began. Some
who interpret the church essentially as God's covenant people
of all ages go back to the call of Abraham and the covenant made
with him for the beginning of the church.[1] Others go back
even earlier to include all those who exercised faith in the promise of God beginning with Adam (Gen 3:15)[2] Even among those
who understand the church as a distinct New Testament work
of God there is considerable variation. Some suggest that Jesus
Himself began the church while here on earth.[3] Others, while
recognizing the fact that the disciples of Jesus did constitute the
nucleus of the church, believe that the church did not become a
reality until the coming of the Spirit at Pentecost. Ultradispen-
sationalism, however, delays the inauguration of the church
which exists today until the time of the apostle Paul.[4] A different
church is said to have existed in the earlier portion of the book
of Acts.

New Testament evidence seems to point clearly to the Pentecostal origin of the church. It is not found as such in the Old
Testament, and is yet future in the teaching of Christ. Moreover, the church, by its very nature as the body of Christ, is
dependent upon the finished work of Christ (Ac 20:28) and
the coming of the Spirit (1 Co 12:13). The Old Testament
saints were quickened by the Spirit, but they were not united
with a risen Lord.

1. D. Douglas Bannerman, *The Scripture Doctrine of the Church*, p. 43;
Charles Hodge, *Systematic Theology*, 3:549.
2. R. B. Kuiper, *The Glorious Body of Christ*, pp. 21-22.
3. Johnston notes four alternatives which are proposed for the beginning
of the church in relation to the historical Jesus: "(1) The call of the
first disciples; (2) the confession of Peter as representative of the
twelve; (3) the Last Supper, which established a New Covenant, to be
sealed by Christ's death; (4) the union of the disciples in the Resurrection faith" (George Johnston, *The Doctrine of the Church in the
New Testament*, pp. 46-47).
4. Ethelbert Bullinger, *The Mystery*, p. 40; J. C. O'Hair, *A Dispensational
Study of the Bible*, p. 32.

THE NEW WORK OF GOD

The church is a new work of God begun in the New Testament era. Jesus Himself predicted its establishment during His earthly life, and the apostle Paul taught its character as a mystery not revealed in previous times as it is now, identifying it as a "new man" (Eph 2:15).

A SUBJECT OF CHRIST'S TEACHING

The prophecy of Matthew 16:18. The gospel of Matthew presents Christ as the King of Israel, tracing the presentation of the kingdom in the person of the Messiah. The kingdom is at hand (Mt 4:17) and, in fact, is already present in the power of Christ (Mt 12:28). But the people of Israel reject their King and His kingdom, refusing the demand for repentance which is requisite for its establishment (Mt 11-12). In the midst of His ministry, Christ reveals the mysteries of the kingdom to His disciples (Mt 13:11). In light of the rejection, a new phase of the kingdom is going to take place. The opposition continues from those outside (13:54—16:12), and Christ begins to instruct His disciples in preparation for the ensuing events. They must be assured of His person and know of His purpose following these days. Thus Christ reveals Himself as the Christ, the Son of the living God who purposes to build His church (Mt 16:13-19).

Although He does not lay down rules for a specific organization, the words "I will build my church" clearly express Christ's intent to establish a new community. The future tense here expresses not only futurity but probably also volition. The church will be established "and the gates of hell [Hades, NASB; death, RSV] shall not prevail against it" (Mt 16:18). Not until the power of sin and death was broken by the death and resurrection of Christ, and He held the keys of death and Hades (Rev 1:18), could such a church be founded. Therefore, He immediately predicts these coming events at Jerusalem (Mt 16:21).

Other teachings on the church. Along with the explicit prophecy of Matthew 16:18, there are many other implications of the church in Christ's teachings. Frequently the idea of establishing a new fellowship occurs in the words and works of Jesus. The metaphor of the good shepherd implies a flock and, in fact, Jesus calls those who believe in Him a "flock" (Lk 12:32; cf. Mk 14:27; Jn 10:16), "my lambs" and "my sheep" (Jn 21:15-16). The teaching of the vine and the branches (Jn 15) likewise implies a coherent group with a life of its own. A similar conclusion may be drawn from Christ's calling Himself the Bridegroom (Mk 2: 19). In the institution of baptism and the Lord's Supper, Christ also made reference to the future church as both were commanded for His disciples near the end of His time with them, and specifically for that period during His absence. The initiatory rite and the table of communion have no meaning without a definite fellowship.

Another explicit reference to the "church" is in the instructions for discipline in Matthew 18:15-20. While some feel that this is "hardly intelligible" unless it refers to a contemporary Jewish community,[5] it is best to view the use of the term church as anticipating the congregation to which these addressed would belong. Even then the group of disciples was the preparatory company of the church and churches to come after Pentecost.[6] The presence of the prophecy of the church in the near context (Mt 16:18) supports this position, along with the fact that had the Jewish community been in view, *synagogue* would have been the more probable term used. Moreover, the promise of the presence of Christ whenever two or three are gathered together in His name (v. 20) can only refer to His presence through the Holy Spirit following Pentecost.

A MYSTERIOUS CHARACTER

The new aspect of the church is further revealed in the mysterious character of its composition. Mystery in the New Testament sense signifies something which previously has been hidden but now is revealed (Ro 16:25; 1 Co 2:7, 10). A special mystery prominent to the apostle Paul is the incorporation of the Gentiles on equal terms with the Jews to form the church, the body of Christ. Writing to the church at Colosse, he explains that this mystery "hath been hid from ages and from generations,

5. F. J. A. Hort, *The Christian Ecclesia*, p. 10; Alfred Plummer, *An Exegetical Commentary on the Gospel According to St. Matthew*, p. 253.
6. John A. Broadus, *Commentary on the Gospel of Matthew*, pp. 388-89.

but now is made manifest to his saints: to whom God would make known what is the riches of the glory of this mystery among the Gentiles; which is Christ in you, the hope of glory" (Col 1:26-27). This mystery is amplified in the Ephesian letter where it is revealed "that the Gentiles are fellow-heirs and fellow-members of the body, and fellow-partakers of the promise in Christ Jesus through the gospel" (Eph 3:6, NASB). This is a new truth not previously made known to the sons of men (Eph 3:5). To be sure, God's blessing of Gentiles was a recurrent theme of Old Testament prophecy, beginning with the promise to Abraham (Gen 12:3) and onward. The Gentiles would be blessed during the glorious reign of the Messiah (Is 60:1-3; 62:1-2). Hint was even given of their blessing before the kingdom age during a time of Israel's disobedience (Deu 32:21; cf. Ro 10:19; 11:11). But the fact of the body of Christ in which there is neither Jew nor Gentile, bond or free, male or female (Gal 3:28) was not foreseen in Old Testament times. It is the mystery of the church age.

A NEW MAN

Corresponding with its mystery character, God's creation in the church is termed a "new man" (Eph 2:15). The law with its elaborate system of observances separating Jew and Gentile was abolished in Christ breaking down the wall of partition that both might be reconciled in one body (Eph. 2:14-16). The result is the "new creation" (Gal 6:15, NASB), "one new man" (Eph 2:15). The Greek word *kainos* ("new") used in both passages suggests something new in nature or kind. The church belongs to the new age of salvation that dawned with the coming of Christ. While it yet lives its life out in this world, it already partakes of the "age to come" (Heb 6:5, NASB), being the beginning of the new creation in which God will finally "make all things new" (Rev 21:5).

THE FOUNDATION OF THE CHURCH

The church as the new creation of God rests upon the person and work of Jesus Christ. It came into actual historical reality when Christ baptized His disciples with the promised Holy Spirit on Pentecost. From this small beginning at Jerusalem the church spread rapidly throughout Asia, Africa and Europe as new members were added daily by God through the regeneration of the Spirit.

THE FOUNDATION OF CHRIST

The church rests upon the foundation of Jesus Christ, as the apostle writes, "Other foundation can no man lay than that is laid, which is Jesus Christ" (1 Co 3:11). Although the apostles and prophets are also foundational (Eph 2:20), Christ is the cornerstone upon which the whole foundation depends. During His earthly ministry Jesus chose twelve apostles so that they might be with Him to learn of Him and go forth to preach (Mk 3:14). At first their message, as that of Christ Himself, was the proclamation of the near kingdom and the imperative of repentance for its coming. Later, however, with His rejection, Christ began to instruct them concerning the new age which would be inaugurated before the kingdom comes, the time of the mysteries of the kingdom (Mt 13), and His impending suffering, death and resurrection (Mt 16:21). He announced the church (Mt 16:18), and gave command for the two ordinances of baptism (Mt 28:18-20) and the Lord's Supper (Mt 26:26-29). He also commissioned the church with its worldwide mission, defining its power and authority (Mt 28:18-20; Lk 24:46-49), promising to be with it "to the end of the age" (Mt 28:20, NASB). Thus in the twelve and in His instructions to them Christ laid the groundwork for His church.

The choosing of the disciples and His words to them would have been empty, however, without His work at Calvary. Having united Himself to the old creation, He brought it to an end in His judgment of death. In His resurrection He inaugurated the new creation. He purchased the church with His own blood (Ac 20:28; Eph 5:25-27), and through the resurrection became its Head and source of life (Col 3:1-4). Without the death and resurrection of Christ there could be no church.

But the church also awaited the ascension, for it was "when He ascended on high" that "He gave gifts to men" (Eph 4:8, NASB). These spiritual gifts on which the function of the church depends were bestowed through the Spirit, who was sent only after Christ ascended to the Father (Jn 16:7). Thus the church is built upon the entire work of Christ's first coming and is sustained through His present headship.

THE FOUNDATION OF THE APOSTLES AND PROPHETS

The Scriptures also refer to the apostles and prophets as foundational elements in the structure of the church. The "household of God" is "built upon the foundation of the apostles and prophets, Jesus Christ himself being the chief corner stone" (Eph 2:20). Some suggest the foundation to be that which was laid by the apostles and prophets, namely, Christ.[7] But here His relation to the building is pictured as the "chief corner stone" and it is best to see the foundation as the apostles and prophets of the New Testament church.[8]

These are foundational through their unique ministry as channels of the revelation, the prophets for the immediate edification of the church (1 Co 14:30), and the apostles for the permanent teaching upon which the church is founded. This foundational ministry of the apostles is in reality that of the risen Christ. Those who were formerly known as disciples, except when sent on a preaching mission (Mt 10:2; Mk 6:30), are following the resurrection apostles. Sent forth by Christ, they were to bear witness of Him even as He witnessed to the Father through the Spirit (Jn 15:26-27), who would lead them into the truth concerning the person and work of Christ. Their teaching is not from man, but from Christ Himself (Gal 1:1-12), and therefore foundational. It was the norm of the early church (Ac 2:42) and was to be passed on to all succeeding generations of believers (2 Ti 1:13; 2:2). Because of this unique relationship to Christ, the apostles are foundational and they are pillars (Gal 2:9) of the church of Christ.

Salmon aptly summarizes this apostolic ministry when he states,

> . . . in the same manner as any human institution is said to be founded by those men to whom it owes its origin, so we may call those men the foundation of the Church whom God honored by using them as His instruments in the establishment of it; who

7. John Eadie, *Commentary on the Epistle to the Ephesians*, p. 197. This is also Calvin's interpretation.
8. See pp. 34-35.

were themselves laid as the first living stones in that holy temple, and on whom the other stones of that temple were laid; for it was on their testimony that others received the truth so that our faith rests on theirs; and (humanly speaking) it is because they believed that we believe.[9]

It is also probable that the "rock" upon which Christ predicted that He would build His church was a reference to the apostle Peter as the leader and representative of the apostles. Throughout the history of the church the "rock" has been variously interpreted as a reference to Peter, Peter's confession, Christ, or all of the apostles.[10] The most natural interpretation, however, would appear to be the best. Using a play on words, Christ calls His disciple Peter (*Petros*) which means "a rock" and then adds, "upon this rock [*petra*] I will build my church" (Mt 16:18), which would most naturally mean "upon you."[11] The change of Greek words from *petros* to *petra* is best explained by reference to the meaning of the words. *Petra* denotes a massive rock which would be suitable for a foundation, while *petros* means a stone. *Petra*, however, being feminine, was not suitable as a name for Simon, so he is called by the masculine *petros*. While in other places Scripture calls Christ a rock (1 Co 10:4; Ro 9:33; 1 Pe 2:8), this does not preclude this term being attached to the apostle, even as the concept of foundation can apply to both.

In support of His reference to Peter, Christ gives to him the keys of the kingdom of heaven (Mt 16:19), signifying that he will have authority as the human instrument over the doors of Christ's house, even as the key of the house of David was laid on the shoulders of his servant Eliakim "so he shall open, and none shall shut; and he shall shut, and none shall open" (Is 22:22). In fulfillment of this prediction it is Peter who opens the door to the Jews on Pentecost (Ac 2:14 ff.), to the Samaritans (Ac 8:14 ff.), and finally to the Gentiles (Ac 10:34 ff.).

This interpretation is not entirely exclusive of the other sug-

9. George Salmon, *The Infallibility of the Church*, p. 338.
10. For a brief history of the leading interpretations, see Oscar Cullmann, *Peter, Disciple, Apostle, Martyr*, pp. 164-76.
11. In all probability Christ spoke in Aramaic, which has only the one word for rock, *kepha*, and therefore makes the word play even more obvious: "You are *kepha* and upon this *kepha* I will build my church." Cf. Cullmann, pp. 192-93; Broadus, pp. 355-56.

gestions. Certainly Peter is so named because of his faith in Christ, the Son of the living God, but this faith cannot be abstracted from his person. This is consistent with the testimony of the New Testament "in which not doctrines or confessions, but men, are uniformly called pillars or foundations of the spiritual building."[12] He is therefore foundational as a confessor of Christ. The keys also are operative not by personal power but through the proclamation of the saving efficacy of the death and resurrection of Christ. Finally, Peter stands only as the first among equals,[13] who shares, as has been shown previously, foundational activity with the other apostles. The same authority of binding and loosing is common to all the apostles (Jn 20:23) and ultimately to the entire church (Mt 18:18).[14]

The Origin of the Church

The actual historical formation of the church occurred in Jerusalem on the day of Pentecost. On that day the Spirit was poured out upon the disciples to form the body of Christ, the church.

THE CHURCH FORMED BY THE SPIRIT

Writing to the Corinthians, Paul states, "For by one Spirit are

12. Milton S. Terry, *Biblical Hermeneutics*, p. 127.
13. It is interesting to note the primacy of Peter among the disciples in the gospel accounts. Along with Andrew he is the first called (Mk 1:16). He with James and John constitute an inner circle, but even in this circle, he stands in the forefront (Lk 5:1-12; Mt 14:28). He acts as chief spokesman (Mk 8:29; 9:2-5; etc.). In every list of disciples, Peter's name occurs first (cf. Mt 10:2), with "Peter and those with him" being a characteristic expression. He is also the first to see the risen Christ. Cullmann, p. 31, concludes, "*Among the disciples of Jesus Peter, according to the united witness of the gospel tradition, occupies a peculiarly representative position.*"
14. Further support for the view expressed is seen in the grammatical structure of the verse. The two words for "rock" (*petros* and *petra*) are connected by the conjunction "and" (*kai*) indicating a close relationship which would not be true if the latter "rock" were a reference to Christ or the confession of the previous verse. Also, following the general rule that the demonstrative pronoun "this" refers to the near antecedent, the antecedent of "this rock" would most naturally be Peter. The change to the feminine gender is explained in the distinct meanings of the words. Along with taking exception to the above usual rules of Greek grammar, viewing the "rock" as Christ Himself or Peter's confession loses the force of the obvious play on words involving Peter (*petros*) and rock (*petra*). It would seem difficult to understand the significance of calling Simon a rock if the further reference to "this rock" had nothing essentially to do with it.

we all baptized into one body . . . and have been all made to drink . . . [of][15] one Spirit" (1 Co 12:13). "By one Spirit," which may also be translated "in one Spirit,"[16] signifies the means by which the body is formed. As believers are placed in the sphere of the Spirit, they are fused into the spiritual body which is identified as the church (Eph 1:22-23; 5:30; Col 1:18). Christ, who promised to send the Spirit, is the Baptizer who baptizes His people with the Spirit. The Spirit, however, being a personal Being, actively indwells the members of the church, uniting them together in Himself.

The same dependence upon the Spirit's work for the existence of the church is seen in the metaphor of the building. As "an holy temple in the Lord," the members of the church "are builded together for an habitation of God through the Spirit" (Eph 2:21-22). Only when the Spirit came to dwell within the believers was the church formed as the temple of God.

THE CHURCH FORMED AT PENTECOST

The outpouring of the Spirit which initiated the church occurred at Pentecost. Before His ascension into heaven, Christ commanded His disciples to wait at Jerusalem to receive the promise of the Father, saying, "Ye shall be baptized with the Holy Ghost not many days hence" (Ac 1:5b). While the term *baptized* is not used in the account of the Spirit's coming on Pentecost (Ac 2), it can easily be shown that this was the fulfillment of Christ's prediction. Reporting on the outpouring of the Holy Spirit upon the Gentiles in the case of Cornelius (Ac 10:45), Peter said, "And as I began to speak, the Holy Ghost fell on them, as on us at the beginning. Then remembered I the word of the Lord, how that he said, John indeed baptized with water; but ye shall be baptized with the Holy Ghost" (Ac 11:15-16). The "beginning" can only refer to Pentecost, thus identifying it as the time of the "baptism with the Holy Ghost."

Pentecost marks not only the beginning of the church as the spiritual reality of the body of Christ, but also the visible church.

15. The best texts omit "into." Cf. RSV, NASB.
16. The construction is the same as Mt 3:11 where John the Baptist says, "I indeed baptize you with [en] water . . . but he . . . shall baptize you with [en] the Holy Ghost." Cf. also Ac 1:5.

Luke describes this first group of believers at Jerusalem meeting together for instruction and fellowship, and sharing their goods with one another, as an expression of the new life in the Spirit (Ac 2:41-47). Although meetings were held in various homes in Jerusalem, it was apparently one church under the authority of the apostles.

THE SPREAD OF THE CHURCH

From its beginning at Jerusalem, the church spread to other regions and finally throughout the then-known world. The early believers witnessed to their risen Lord "both in Jerusalem, and in all Judea, and in Samaria, and unto the uttermost part of the earth" (Ac 1:8b).

The beginning. The point from which the church spread out was the city of Jerusalem. Every Christian mission began there. Even Paul, the apostle to the Gentiles, counted his starting point not at Damascus or Antioch, but at Jerusalem (Ro 15:19). It was at Jerusalem that the foundation of the church had been laid in the death and resurrection of Christ. There He "presented Himself alive, after His suffering" and taught the apostles "concerning the kingdom of God" (Ac 1:3, NASB). Finally, it was from Jerusalem that He was "received . . . out of their sight" (Ac 1:9) to ascend to the presence of the Father from where He poured out the Spirit on the day of Pentecost. Thus Jerusalem, the holy city, becomes the focal point of the new work of God in this age. The same Lord of Israel was the one now forming the church.

The news of the amazing happenings in Jerusalem soon spread so that the people of the neighboring cities began to bring in their sick and demon-possessed to be healed (Ac 5:16). Although threatened by the Jewish leaders, the apostles continued to preach Jesus Christ (Ac 5:42), and thousands were added to the company of believers (Ac 2:41; 4:4; 6:7).

The transition. The gospel had undoubtedly already begun to spread into other areas via those who had witnessed the events of Pentecost and the travelers who came to Jerusalem—as seen in the later incident of the Ethiopian eunuch who returned to his country rejoicing in his newfound faith (Ac 8). But it was the pressure of persecution which provided the occasion for the first great outreach of the church. Luke records that immediately following the violent martyrdom of Stephen, "there was a great persecution against the church which was at Jerusalem; and they were all scattered abroad throughout the regions of Judea and Samaria, except the apostles" (Ac 8:1). Everywhere they went, they preached the word (v. 4). Particular attention is given to the spread of the church to Samaria (Ac 8). The preaching here was a surprising action, for the Jews normally avoided the Samaritans because of their mixture of Gentile blood. But Philip believed that his message was for these also, and the response was amazing as "the people with one accord gave heed unto those things which Philip spake" (8:6). The apostles, who had so far remained in Jerusalem, hearing of these things, delegated Peter and John to go up to Samaria to see what had transpired and to minister the Holy Spirit to these new converts. It might be noted that the introduction of the Holy Spirit to each new class of people, the Samaritans (Ac 8:17), the Gentiles (Ac 10:44-46), and the disciples of John the Baptist at Ephesus (Ac 19:6), came through the apostles. Thus the unity of the church, including all peoples, was assured under the apostles' authority and doctrine. During the period of transition the church spread throughout most of the eastern end of the Mediterranean as the preaching of the gospel was heard in remote parts of Judea, Samaria, Damascus, Phoenicia, Cypress and Antioch. The expansion was also in the constituency of the church which now included Samaritans and Gentiles.

The universalization. The final expansion of the church occurred primarily through God's "chosen instrument" (Ac 9:15, NASB), the apostle Paul, who was ordained to be "his witness unto all men" (Ac 22:15; cf. 26:16). Through his missionary activities, the church spread through Asia Minor and into Europe, reaching the very capital of the Mediterranean world, Rome.

Although the book of Acts relates only Paul's missionary journeys during this time, it is clear that many others were involved in the work. This is implied by Paul himself when he refers to the apostles and the brethren of the Lord taking their wives with them as they traveled about (1 Co 9:5). Furthermore, the apostle's desire to preach the gospel in Spain rather than build upon another man's foundation (Ro 15:20-24) suggests that the gospel had been preached by others in the closer regions of North Africa, Italy and perhaps even southern France.

Undoubtedly this rapid extension was aided by the easy flow of travel and trade within the unity of the Roman Empire. The primary strategy of the apostle was preaching in the cities and towns. Here traveling merchants, tourists and soldiers came in contact with the gospel and they in turn took it to the remote regions of the empire. So much had the gospel been spread abroad during this early period of the church that the apostle could speak of it going into "all the world" (Col 1:6). Justin Martyr, writing in about the middle of the second century, corroborates this rapid expansion:

> There is no people, Greek or barbarian, or of any other race, by whatever appellation or manners they may be distinguished, however ignorant of arts or agriculture, whether they dwell in tents or wander about in covered wagons, among whom prayers and thanksgivings are not offered in the name of the crucified Jesus to the Father and Creator of all things.[17]

17. William Hendriksen, *Colossians and Philemon*, p. 51.

5

The Church in God's Program

THE INAUGURATION OF THE CHURCH at Pentecost marked a new phase in the outworking of God's historical plan whereby He purposes to establish His will on earth as it is in heaven (Mt 6:10) and ultimately dwell with His people (Rev 21:3).[1] Although the Old Testament contains hints of a time when Israel would be scattered among all nations (Deu 28:37; 30:1 ff.; Amos 9:9), and God would visit the Gentiles with salvation, provoking Israel to jealousy and causing her return to God (Deu 32:21; cf. Ro 10:19), the church was not a theme of prophecy. Rather, it belongs to that period of the mysteries by which Christ revealed to His disciples a new operation of the kingdom which was not previously known (Mt 13).

As the present work of God, the church is vitally related to the ongoing program of God and its other phases.

THE CHURCH AND ISRAEL

Much discussion has centered around the relationship of the church and Israel. Some biblical interpreters, emphasizing their similarity, view them essentially as one people of God.[2] The term *Israel* represents not a national people but the spiritual

1. God's historical plan is best described as the establishment of His kingdom on earth. This kingdom theme is prominent in the Old Testament prophecies, in the gospels and epistles, and in the Revelation where "the kingdoms of this world are become the kingdoms of our Lord, and of his Christ; and he shall reign for ever and ever" (Rev 11:15). Bright notes that "the concept of the Kingdom of God involves, in a real sense, the total message of the Bible. Not only does it loom large in the teachings of Jesus; it is to be found, in one form or another, through the length and breadth of the Bible" (John Bright, *The Kingdom of God*, p. 7). Sauer concurs, stating, "The 'kingdom' is the real basic theme of the Bible" (Eric Sauer, *From Eternity to Eternity*, p. 75); cf. George N. H. Peters, *The Theocratic Kingdom*, 1:31.
2. Louis Berkhof, *Systematic Theology*, p. 571; cf. also the Roman Catholic position stated in the *Dogmatic Constitution on the Church of Vatican II*, Walter M. Abbott, ed., *The Documents of Vatican II*, pp. 24-37.

people of God. Therefore, the members of the church are considered to be New Israel. Spiritual Israel was related to national
Israel in the Old Testament but it has now been enlarged to become a universal spiritual work in the church. The Israel of the
Old Testament is thus superseded by the church, and the prophecies concerning the nation of Israel are, for the most part, no
longer literally applied to the nation but rather to the church
now and in the future.

A preferable position sees Israel and the church as distinct
phases of God's program; not so distinct as to preclude relationship in the historical plan and purpose of God, but having a distinction which recognizes the calling and election of Israel as a
nation among nations (cf. Deu 7:6-8; 10:15-17; Num 23:9) to be
"without repentance" (cf. Ro 11:27-29). This does not deny the
spiritual qualifications necessary for Israel to enter into the fulfillment of her promises. Physical descent alone is not sufficient to
reap God's blessings. This was already true of Israel in the Old
Testament. There has always been a true Israel within national
Israel, but this true Israel is a part of the nation.[3] This interpretation allows for the natural understanding of the Old Testament
prophecies portraying a future for Israel as a nation. It is also
consistent with the New Testament teaching of the church as
distinct from Israel and yet sharing in God's salvation program.

THE CHURCH DISTINCT FROM ISRAEL

The New Testament never confuses Israel and the church.
As opposed to the church, which is a religious body composed of
individuals from all nations, the term *Israel* retains its reference
to that people which came physically from the loins of Abraham.
After the beginning of the church, Israel is still addressed as a
national entity. When on the day of Pentecost Peter addresses his
audience as "ye men of Israel" (Ac 2:22), he is obviously referring to those of the physical nation and not the church. Similar
uses of the term *Israel* are found throughout Acts, demonstrating
the fact that the church had not taken this term for itself (Ac
3:12; 4:10; 5:21, 31, 35; 21:28). Paul's prayer for "Israel" (Ro

3. Compare the concept of the Servant of the Lord in Isaiah, where in
   many places the Servant is identified merely with Israel (e.g., 41:8;
   43:10; 44:21), but in other instances it is clear that only the true Israel
   is involved (51:1, 7).

10:1; cf. 11:1) and his references to Israel throughout the discussion of God's program in Romans 9—11 concern his "kinsmen according to the flesh" (9:3). If "Israel" were a reference to the church, the reference to Israel's "blindness in part . . . until the fulness of the Gentiles be come in" (11:25) would be meaningless.

Two references are often used against this consistent use of *Israel* for the nation in an attempt to substantiate that the church is New Israel. One is Paul's statement: "For they are not all Israel, which are of Israel" (Ro 9:6).[4] An examination of the context reveals, however, that Paul is speaking only of a division within Israel. He has introduced the subject concerning his "brethren, my kinsmen according to the flesh" who are identified as "Israelites" (vv. 3-4). The subsequent discussion concerns God's elective purpose within the physical seed of Israel as illustrated in the choice of Isaac over Ishmael and the other children of Abraham and Jacob over Esau (vv. 7-13). Verse 6 then also has reference to Israel. "Those 'of Israel' are the physical seed, the natural descendants of the patriarchs" while "in the other expression 'they are not all Israel,' obviously the denotation is much more limited and the thought is that there is an 'Israel' within ethnic Israel."[5] Gutbrod, linking this passage with Romans 2:28-29, where a similar Jewish context is often overlooked, states forthrightly, "We are not told here that Gentile Christians are the true Israel. The distinction at Rom. 9:6, does not go beyond what is presupposed at Jn. 1:47, and it corresponds to the distinction between *Ioudaios en tō kruptō* [a Jew inwardly] and *Ioudaios en tō phanerō* [a Jew outwardly] at Rom. 2:28f., which does not imply that Paul is calling Gentiles true Jews."[6]

Perhaps the words most often cited for the identity of the church as Israel are those of the apostle to the Galatians: "And as many as walk according to this rule, peace be on them, and mercy, and upon the Israel of God" (Gal 6:16). The meaning of "Israel of God" in this verse rests upon its relationship to the

---

4. Louis Berkhof, *The Kingdom of God*, p. 161; Arndt and Gingrich also define Israel in this passage as "a fig. sense of the Christians as the true nation of Israel" (W. F. Arndt and F. W. Gingrich, *A Greek-English Lexicon of the New Testament and Other Early Christian Literature*, p. 382).
5. John Murray, *The Epistle to the Romans*, 2:9.
6. Walter Gutbrod, "Israel" in *TDNT*, 3:387.

previous expression, "as many as walk according to this rule,"
and this relationship depends upon one's understanding of the
"and" (Greek, *kai*) which connects them. Three different interpretations have been suggested. Lenski, expressing the view
which sees the church as the Israel of God, understands *kai* in the
explicative sense of "even." " 'As many as will keep in line with
the rule,' constitute 'the Israel of God.' "[7] A second view clearly
separating the two phrases as distinct groups is that of Walvoord,
who states, "God's blessing is declared on those who walk according to this rule (among the Galatians who were Gentiles), and
also 'upon the Israel of God.' "[8] According to this interpretation
the *kai* ("and") is used as a simple copula joining two separate
entities.

The third interpretation, which seems preferable, understands
the use of the *kai* ("and") as adding a specially important part
of the whole in the sense of "and especially."[9] Ellicott interprets
the passage according to this use as well as refuting the position
of identity when he says,

> Still, as it is doubtful whether *kai* is ever used by St. Paul in
> so marked an explicative force as must be assigned . . . and as it
> seems still more doubtful whether Christians generally could be
> called "the *Israel* of God" . . . the simple copulative meaning
> seems most probable. . . . St. Paul includes all in his blessing,
> of whatever stock and kindred; and then with his thought turn-
> ing (as it ever did) to his own brethren after the flesh (Rom.
> ix. 3), he pauses to specify those who were once Israelites accord-
> ing to the flesh (1 Cor. x. 18), but now are the Israel of God . . .
> true spiritual children of Abraham.[10]

The truth of Burton's statement that "there is, in fact, no instance of his [Paul's] using *Israel* except of the Jewish nation or

7. R. C. H. Lenski, *The Interpretation of St. Paul's Epistles to the Galatians, to the Ephesians and to the Philippians*, p. 321; cf. J. B. Lightfoot, *The Epistle of St. Paul to the Galatians*, pp. 224-25.
8. John F. Walvoord, *The Millennial Kingdom*, p. 170.
9. For this use of *kai*, see Arndt and Gingrich, p. 392.
10. Charles J. Ellicott, *St. Paul's Epistle to the Galatians*, p. 139; Eadie
    comments, "The simple copulative meaning is not to be departed from,
    save on very strong grounds; and there is not ground for such a
    departure here, so that the Israel of God are a party included in, and
    yet distinct from the *hosoi* [as many as]" (John Eadie, *Commentary on
    the Epistle of Paul to the Galatians*, p. 470).

a part thereof,"[11] renders the possibility of that use in this verse highly doubtful.[12] The context of Galatians supports the inclusion of the Israel of God among those that "walk according to this rule." The apostle wrote to ward off the threat of those Judaizers who insisted upon mingling law with the grace of the gospel, demanding that Christians be circumcised as well as have faith in Christ. It would seem logical to pronounce peace and mercy not only upon Gentiles who recognize that "neither circumcision availeth any thing, nor uncircumcision, but a new creation" (Gal 6:15), but also upon those Jewish Christians who likewise recognize this rule of grace. The special mention of Jewish believers who rejected the error of the Judaizers is logical, as it would be these among the Galatians who would be most likely to succumb.

A further motive might also be suggested for their special mention. Paul's attack upon the Judaizers might incite antagonism on the part of the Gentile believers against all Jews. Perhaps the special mention of the Israel of God was also designed to quell any such animosity. Additional evidence for this interpretation is found in the similarity of this statement with the conclusion of Jewish prayers: "Shew mercy and peace upon us, and on Thy people Israel."[13]

The consistent witness of Scripture is to the distinctiveness of Israel and the church. Israel is an elect nation called to witness to the glory of God as a nation among nations and serve a distinct phase in the kingdom program. The prophecies declare that she will yet fulfill this calling. The church, on the other

11. Ernest DeWitt Burton, *A Critical and Exegetical Commentary on the Epistle to the Galatians,* p. 358.
12. Although the term *Israel* is used 38 times and *Israelite* occurs 8 times in Acts–Revelation, the absence of a clear reference to the church in any of these instances makes one suspect the validity of this popular theological equation. The statement of R. T. Stamm almost incredibly admits to theological deduction unrelated to the evidence: "But although he [Paul] did believe that Christians constituted the true Israel, he never called the church the Israel of God, but used the word 'Israel' to designate the Jewish nation" (*The Interpreter's Bible,* ed. George A. Buttrick [New York: Abingdon, 1953], 10:590-91). If the New Testament writers actually do make the theological equation of the terms *church* and *Israel,* it is difficult to explain their reticence to make such an equation verbally.
13. Gutbrod, p. 388, n. 135; F. F. Bruce suggests that it is "perhaps an echo of Psalm 125:5, 'Peace be upon Israel'" (*The Letters of Paul: An Expanded Paraphrase,* p. 39).

hand, is a people called out from every nation as "a people for his name" (Ac 15:14). She also bears witness to the glory of God and serves His kingdom program along with the nation of Israel.

Having noted this distinction, it is necessary to guard against a dichotomy which fails to see the place of the church as an integral part of God's program along with Israel and thus a coheir of the promises (Gal 3:29). This close relationship of Israel and the church is seen in the concepts of the seed of Abraham and the new covenant.

THE CHURCH AS THE SEED OF ABRAHAM

In the call of Abraham and the covenant promises made to him, God laid the basis for His program of redemption and the ultimate establishment of His rule on earth. It was in fulfillment of the Abrahamic promises that Christ came bringing salvation and will ultimately reign as King over the earth (Lk 1:69-79; Gal 3:14 f.; Ac 3:25-26). The believers in the church as the seed of Abraham share in this promise with Israel.

The biblical use and meaning of "seed of Abraham." The expression "seed of Abraham" has three applications in Scripture. It is used first for the natural descendants of Abraham through Jacob. "But thou, Israel, art my servant, Jacob whom I have chosen, the seed of Abraham my friend" (Is 41:8; cf. 2 Ch 20:7; Ps 105:6; Ro 11:1). Jesus likewise made reference to literal descendants when He said, "I know that ye are Abraham's seed" (Jn 8:37; cf. Lk 13:16; 19:9). He quickly denies, however, that physical lineage is the decisive factor when He says to the same individuals, "If ye were Abraham's children, ye would do the works of Abraham" (Jn 8:39b). As there is a true Israel within ethnic Israel, so there is a genuine seed within the physical seed. The true seed are those "not of the circumcision only, but who also walk in the steps of that faith of . . . father Abraham" (Ro 4:12). However, the fact that the true seed includes spiritual characteristics does not negate the reality of the physical relationship in this use of the concept. It is hardly conceivable that Abraham understood it otherwise when God made reference to "thy seed after thee in their generations" (Gen 17:7) and to his son Isaac "and . . . his seed after him" (v. 19b; cf. 28:13-14).

A second use of this terminology is for Christ Himself. "Now to Abraham and his seed were the promises made. He saith not, And to seeds, as of many; but as of one, And to thy seed, which is Christ" (Gal 3:16). The true posterity of Abraham is ultimately embodied in Christ. He is its summation and Head, for the promise was received through Him. All who inherit the promises inherit them through Christ.

The third application follows logically upon the second. All those in Christ are also Abraham's seed. "And if ye be Christ's, then are ye Abraham's seed, and heirs according to the promise" (Gal 3:29). This includes all, whether Jew and Gentile, who are in Christ, and therefore in His body, the church.

According to its usage, "seed of Abraham" thus has two basic significations in Scripture. It refers to a spiritual seed which is justified through Christ's work by faith after the pattern of Abraham. It also denotes Abraham's physical posterity through Isaac and Jacob which formed the nation of Israel. While all Israelites can be called Abraham's seed, only those of faith are Abraham's true seed who will inherit the promises. The primary significance is thus spiritual, and this spiritual seed is made up of true Israel as well as those outside of Israel.

Both the church and Israel are therefore Abraham's seed and heirs of the promise. But this does not therefore equate the church and Israel. Rather, Abraham is the father of both. Writing to the Romans, Paul states that Abraham is "the father of all them that believe, though they be not circumcised. . . . And the father of circumcision to them who are not of the circumcision only, but who also walk in the steps of that faith of our father Abraham, which he had being yet uncircumcised" (Ro 4:11-12). Thus, as Godet explains, "There was a time in Abraham's life when by his uncircumcision he represented the Gentiles, as later after his circumcision he became the representative of Israel."[14] Children of Abraham may belong to one category or another, but " 'children of Abraham' are not necessarily 'children of Israel', for Israel is not the only seed of Abraham."[15] The members of the church are also Abraham's seed as individuals out of all the

14. F. Godet, *Commentary on the Epistle to the Romans*, p. 295.
15. D. W. B. Robinson, "The Salvation of Israel in Romans 9-11," *The Reformed Theological Review* 26 (Sept.-Dec. 1967):89.

families of the earth, while Israel is his seed as that great nation among nations "through whom the promise would eventually be held out to the rest of the nations."[16]

Church participation in the Abrahamic promises. As seed of Abraham the members of the church participate in the Abraham covenant; they are "heirs according to the promise" (Gal 3:29). The original promise to Abraham included this blessing upon those outside of Israel: "In thee shall all families of the earth be blessed" (Gen 12:3), and the outworking of this promise is the subject of many of the Old Testament prophecies. The vast majority of these relate to that time when converted Israel will be the channel of blessing to all nations during the kingdom reign of Christ on earth (Is 2:2-4; 60:1 ff.; 62:2; Zec 8:22-23). However, with the institution of the mystery phase of the kingdom, the New Testament teaches that this blessing has already come to the Gentiles during the church age. This present blessing does not supersede or cancel the fulfillment of millennial blessings, but is rather part of that program of God which was not clearly revealed in prophecy. There are, in fact, indications of God's turning from Israel to bring salvation to others even during this time before the restoration of Israel. He promises to provoke Israel to jealousy "with those which are not a people" (Deu 32:21*b*). The apostle Paul sees this promise fulfilled in the salvation of the church (Ro 11:11; 10:19).

The participation of the church in the covenant promises made to Abraham rests, as we have seen, on the fact that these promises included blessing for all families of the earth (Gen 12:3). When the apostle speaks of the blessing of Abraham coming on the church, he makes reference specifically to this universal promise and not to the national promises of Israel. "Know ye therefore that they which are of faith, the same are the children of Abraham. And the scripture, foreseeing that God would justify the heathen through faith, preached before the gospel unto Abraham, saying, In thee shall all nations be blessed. So then they which be of faith are blessed with faithful Abraham" (Gal 3:7-9).

The grafting in of the Gentiles onto the root of the olive tree in Paul's figure of Romans 11 represents the fulfillment of this universal promise. The root represents the foundation of God's

16. Ibid.

redemptive program in His covenant promises to Abraham, or perhaps Abraham himself as the father of all those sharing in the promise.[17] The natural branches represent Israel, while the wild branches which are grafted in are the Gentile believers. As branches, both partake of "the root and fatness of the olive tree" (v. 17b). In that Israel is the natural branches, the tree can be said to be "their own olive tree" (v. 24). They had received the promises and covenants and growth from the root as God formed the nation of Israel as His people. But now the Gentiles in the church, as wild branches with whom God had made no covenants, are grafted in to partake of the same root. The Gentiles which were "aliens from the commonwealth of Israel, and strangers from the covenant of promise, having no hope, and without God in the world . . . now . . . are made nigh by the blood of Christ" (Eph 2:12-13). They do not now assume Israel's promises to become a new Israel, but they have become "fellowheirs . . . and partakers of his [God's] promise in Christ by the gospel" (Eph 3:6). "The Gentiles have been made partakers of their [Israel's] spiritual things" (Ro 15:27b).

As seed of Abraham in Christ, the church "participates in all He does to bring the covenant to completion."[18] The present blessings of salvation in Christ, as well as the future glory with Him, are all the realization of the promises made to Abraham. Members of the church are "joint-heirs with Christ" of the promise (Ro 8:17; cf. Gal 3:29). Although this participation is not in the place of Israel in the fulfillment of her national promises, the church nevertheless participates even in these through her relationship to Christ, the fulfillment of all promises.

THE CHURCH AND THE NEW COVENANT

The participation of the church in the promises is seen especially in the blessings of the new covenant which are applied to it. Paul as a minister of the gospel of grace which brings the life-giving Spirit describes himself as one whom God has made adequate as a minister of the new covenant (2 Co 3:6). Similarly,

17. It is possible also to understand the root as Christ, "the seed of Abraham to whom the promise was made" (see Gal 3:16 ff.), and in whom it is fulfilled. Cf. H. L. Ellison, *The Mystery of Israel*, pp. 86-87; cf. Karl Barth, *Church Dogmatics*, 2, 2, 285 ff.
18. J. Dwight Pentecost, *Things to Come*, p. 90.

the writer of Hebrews cites the new covenant (Heb 8:8 ff.; 10:15 ff.) in seeking to persuade his hearers of the superiority of Christ over the old covenant. These applications of the new covenant to the church have been variously interpreted. Some see them as evidence that the church is indeed the New Israel fulfilling the Old Testament prophecies addressed to Israel. "For the gospel age in which we are living is that day foretold by the prophets when the law of God shall be written in the hearts of men (Jer. xxxi. 33) and when the Spirit of God abiding in their hearts will enable them to keep it (Ezek. xi. 19, xxxvi. 26f). The gospel age is the age of the new covenant."[19]

In an attempt to clearly distinguish the prophecies for Israel from those for the church, the position of two new covenants, one for Israel and another for the church, has been espoused. "There remains to be recognized a heavenly covenant for the heavenly people, which is also styled like the preceding one for Israel a 'new covenant'. . . . To suppose that these two covenants—one for Israel and one for the Church—are the same is to assume that there is a latitude of common interest between God's purpose for Israel and His purpose for the Church."[20]

The Scriptures, however, do not reveal a separate new covenant. The blessings for the church of the indwelling Spirit and the inward law (2 Co 3:3-6) are the same as those promised to Israel (Jer 31:33-34). Moreover, as has been indicated, Jeremiah's prophecy is directly applied to believers in the book of Hebrews. The fact of only one new covenant does not, however, necessitate that the church is fulfilling Israel's prophecy in her place. Rather, both Israel and the church share in this covenant, as in the Abrahamic covenant, for the new covenant is the realization of the salvation of the Abrahamic promise.

The promise of the new covenant. Against the background of the impending judgment through Babylon because of the failure to keep the Mosaic covenant, God promised to "make a new covenant with the house of Israel, and with the house of Judah" (Jer 31:31). The essence of this new covenant was in reality nothing but the renewal of the relationship promised in the old covenant: "I will . . . be their God, and they shall be my people"

19. Oswald Allis, *Prophecy and the Church*, p. 42.
20. Lewis Sperry Chafer, *Systematic Theology*, 7:98-99.

(v. 33*b;* cf. Lev 26:12; Ex 29:45). The newness, apart from its futurity, lay in its subjective reality. Whereas the old covenant could only command response, the new covenant contained provisions to effect it. The key provisions were the gracious forgiveness of sins (Jer 31:34) and the writing of the law in the heart through the indwelling power of the Holy Spirit (v. 33). The result of this latter provision would be the universal knowledge of God (v. 34*a*).

Provisions of the new covenant to Ezekiel further elaborate these covenant promises: "Then I will sprinkle clean water upon you, and ye shall be clean: from all your filthiness . . . will I cleanse you. . . . I will put my spirit within you, and cause you to walk in my statutes . . . and ye shall be my people, and I will be your God" (36:25-28; cf. 11:19 ff.; 34:25-29; 37:26 ff.). The new covenant is also the subject of Isaiah's prophecies concerning Messianic salvation (Is 59:20-21). As the result of these spiritual provisions, Israel will also enjoy physical blessing.

In the contexts of the new covenant are promises of restoration to the land, which would continue forever, and multiplied prosperity (Jer 31:36; Ex 36:28-38). As the Abrahamic covenant looked forward to the same conditions, it is evident that the new covenant is in reality the gracious provisions for the fulfillment of the original promises given to Abraham. To him was promised a seed which would be a great nation inheriting the promised land as an everlasting possession (Gen 12:2; 17:6-8). This connection is especially seen in the word of God spoken to Abraham concerning Israel: "I will be their God" (Gen 17:8). As we have seen, this is, in fact, the culmination of the new covenant.

The new covenant is also related to the Davidic promises which are an amplification of the promises to Abraham (cf. Jer 33:14-16; 20-26; Eze 37:21-28). This same relationship is evident in the New Testament as well.[21] Christ came as the fulfillment of God's word "to perform the mercy promised to our fathers, and to remember his holy covenant: the oath which he sware to our father Abraham . . . to give knowledge of salvation unto his people by the remission of their sins" (Lk 1:72-77). The forgiveness of sins through Christ and the coming of the Spirit are likewise connected to the fulfillment of Abraham's covenant in the teaching

21. Leon Morris, *The Apostolic Preaching of the Cross,* pp. 93-94.

of Peter (Ac 3:25-26) and Paul (Gal 3:6 ff.). In summary, the
new covenant contained the provisions for the realization of the
Messianic promises which find their fulfillment in Jesus Christ,
the Seed of Abraham.

Inauguration of the new covenant. The Old Testament prophecy of the new covenant connected the time of the new covenant
with a coming Person. This one whom Isaiah saw as Servant of
the Lord would be given "for a covenant of the people, for a light
of the Gentiles" who would open blind eyes and free those who
were in prisons of darkness (42:6-7; cf. 49:8). The same one is
"the messenger of the covenant" in Malachi 3:1.

Christ clearly revealed Himself as that Person when in the
upper room He linked His death with the new covenant. Taking
the cup, He said, "This cup is the new covenant in my blood,
even that which is poured out for you" (Lk 22:20, ASV; cf. Mt
26:28; Mk 14:24; 1 Co 11:25). In this statement Christ was telling
the disciples that His death would effect the final eschatological
promise of the new covenant for the remission of sins (Mt
26:28).[22] The writer of Hebrews later expressly stated that with
the death of Christ the covenant was in force (Heb 9:15-18). He
is the "mediator of a better covenant, which was established upon
better promises" (8:6).

Thus, from the death and resurrection of Jesus Christ the new
covenant stands open to all who will receive it. The finished
work of Christ at Calvary once and for all provides the basis for
all new covenant blessings. To be sure, Israel as a nation has not
entered into the provisions of Jeremiah 31 and therefore the
specific national fulfillment of the covenant to the "house of
Israel" and the "house of Judah" awaits their future conversion.
But the "messenger of the covenant" has come, and those who receive Him receive the salvation of the new covenant.

Participation of the church in the new covenant. Although the
Old Testament references to the new covenant were for the nation
of Israel, the members of the church also share in its provisions.
Like the Abrahamic covenant which was ratified with Abraham
and his national seed and yet contained blessing for Gentiles, so

---

22. It is historically inconceivable that the Jewish disciples to whom these
    words were spoken could have thought of a new covenant other than
    that of Old Testament prophecy.

the new covenant as an amplification of the salvation of the Abrahamic covenant can also be applied to Gentiles.

Old Testament prophecies looked forward to the salvation of the new covenant extending also to the Gentiles. The Servant of God not only restores Israel, but God says, "I will also give thee for a light to the Gentiles, that thou mayest be my salvation unto the end of the earth" (Is 49:6b; cf. 42:1, 6; 60:3). This prophecy looked forward to the establishment of the Messianic kingdom at the coming of Christ when salvation would flow through converted Israel to all nations. But this salvation has now come to the church during the time of the mysteries of the kingdom between Christ's first and second comings as an earnest or guarantee of the final fulfillment.

The enlargement of the new covenant to those outside of Israel is indicated in the words of Christ Himself when at the inauguration of the Lord's supper He gave His disciples the cup, saying, "This is my blood of the new covenant, which is shed for many" (Mt 26:28; Mk 14:24). In using the word "many" in the Semitic sense of "all," Christ showed that the scope of His death and the new covenant extended beyond Israel to all peoples.[23] The death of Christ for "the many" or "all" was already the subject of Isaiah's prophecy (53:10-12) and was certainly the background for the Lord's words at the inauguration of the memorial feast of the new covenant.[24]

The church thus enjoys the eschatological salvation of the new covenant. Full and final remission of sins is a reality for those in Christ (Eph 1:7). The life-giving Spirit has come to indwell (2 Co 3:3-6) and work out the righteousness of the law in every believer (Ro 8:2-4). No longer is the knowledge of God connected with the mediation of priests and prophets, but all are taught of the Spirit (1 Jn 2:27).

CONCLUSION

This brief study of the church and Israel reveals that the two

---

23. Although in Greek there is a difference in *polloi* ("many") and *pantes* ("all"), the Hebrew and Aramaic have no word for all in the sense of the sum as well as the totality. As a result, the Hebrew *ha-rabbim* ("the many") is also used inclusively for "all." Cf. Joachim Jeremias, "polloi" in *TDNT*, 6:536, 543-45.
24. Ibid., p. 544.

are distinct, and yet both have a part in the outworking of God's program. Prior to the launching of the church, God began His kingdom program through the elect nation of Israel. During this time of the mysteries of that kingdom, when Israel has temporarily been set aside and with her the full blessing of the world, God is calling out a people for His name from all nations, and He is building the church. The church has therefore been grafted into the great promises of blessing which are foundational to God's total salvation program which had prior to this time been covenanted only to Abraham and Israel. This engrafting is not to replace Israel nor to fulfill her specifically national prophecies. In this regard it is interesting to note that none of the physical blessings attendant upon the realizations of the new covenant for Israel are cited in the New Testament with regard to the church (cf. 2 Co 3:6-7; Heb 8:8-13 with Jer 31:31-40; Eze 36:24-38). Rather, both Israel and the church share in their distinctive phases in God's program as the people of God through whom He will be glorified.

THE CHURCH AND THE KINGDOM

The relationship of the church to the kingdom concept in Scripture is of utmost importance for the perspective of the place of the church in God's historical program. History reveals that much harm has come from the misunderstanding of this relationship. Based upon Augustine's *City of God*, the church of the Middle Ages developed the theology which equated the church with the kingdom of God on earth, resulting in the absolute authority of the church in teaching and dispensing salvation grace. In another direction, this equation led to the concept of building the kingdom through the church, forgetting that the fulfillment of the promises of God's reign is yet future.[25] The equation of the church with the kingdom inevitably leads "to an intolerable glorification of the Church" which "is to forget that the power and the glory of the reign of God are still to come . . . that the Church is called to pilgrimage, not to rest. It is to forget that the Church is composed of men, and sinful men at that. . . ."[26] Such exaltation of the church at the expense of the proclamation of

25. Cf. Hans Küng, *The Church*, pp. 90-92.
26. Ibid., pp. 92-93.

Jesus the Lord and the coming kingdom reign has not only often contributed to the failure of the church in its mission of servant in the world, but has also led to dissatisfaction and criticism of the church when it failed to produce a millennial utopia on earth.[27] On the other hand, any radical divorce of the church from the kingdom sunders it unbiblically from participation in the salvation program of divine history.

DISTINCTIONS OF THE CHURCH AND THE KINGDOM

Meaning of the kingdom. The kingdom of God in Scripture is the all-embracing program of God's divine salvation history. All ages, peoples, and saving activities are in some way related to it. It has well been described by Sauer as "the royal saving work of God to the carrying through of His counsels in creation and redemption."[28] Its comprehensive scope is seen in the prayer for the kingdom which the Lord taught His disciples: "Thy kingdom come, thy will be done in earth, as it is in heaven" (Mt 6:9). The coming of the kingdom is nothing less than the coming of the reign of God upon this earth.

Involved in the term *kingdom (basileia)* are both the sovereignty or royal dignity of a king, and the realm or territory in which this kingship is exercised.[29] The kingdom of God thus refers to the sovereign rule of God over His creation. Although there is, in the ultimate sense, one kingdom of God, the Scripture uses this term for two distinct aspects of this kingdom. On the one hand, it signifies God's universal, eternal rule over all creation: "The LORD hath prepared his throne in the heavens; and his kingdom ruleth over all" (Ps 103:19). On the other hand, it refers to the eschatological Messianic kingdom which is to be established in history, which Christ announced as at hand, and for which He taught His disciples to pray. While the first kingdom is ruled directly by God, the second aspect is founded upon covenant promises and ruled through the God-Man, Jesus Christ, the Seed of David. It is the purpose of this mediatorial aspect to establish the reign of God, which is now *over* the earth, directly

27. Ibid., pp. 93-94.
28. Sauer, p. 89.
29. Karl Ludwig Schmidt, "basileia" in *TDNT*, 1:579-80.

upon it, and to make the kingdoms of this world "the kingdoms of our Lord, and of his Christ" (Rev 11:15*b*).

Stages of the kingdom. The kingdom program has been manifest in several forms as it moves toward the ultimate establishment of the kingdom of Christ upon earth. Founded upon the covenant promises with Abraham, it was begun in an initiatory form in the kingdom of Israel. Not only did God rule over Israel with the manifestation of His Shekinah glory in the tabernacle and the temple, but through this nation the way of salvation was prepared for all nations (Jn 4:22; Ro 11:12-15). The next appearance of the kingdom came with Christ. It was present in His person (Lk 17:21) and also in the power of the Spirit demonstrated in His mighty works (Lk 11:20). Again the glory of God was present, this time veiled in human flesh (Jn 1:14; cf. Lk 9:29-32). The kingdom is now present, working in the church according to the mysteries described by Christ in His parabolic teaching (Mt 13:11 ff.; cf. 20:1 ff.; 22:2 ff.) until the end of the age (Mt 13:39, 49). Finally, the mediatorial kingdom will be consummated in the millennial reign of Christ in glory on the earth (Rev 20:4-6). After the final putting of all His enemies under His feet, the kingdom will be delivered up to the Father "that God may be all in all" (1 Co 15:24-28).

The kingdom distinct from the church. From the above outline of God's kingdom program it is evident that, far from equation, several distinctions must be noted between the church and the kingdom:

1. Not only are the terms *church* (*ekklesia*) and *kingdom* (*basileia*) never equated in the New Testament, but each has a distinct etymological and connotational meaning.

2. The introduction of the kingdom and that of the church are entirely different. The kingdom is introduced as something "at hand" from the beginning of Christ's ministry (Mt 4:17), while the church is only the subject of prophecy much later (Mt 16:18).

3. The coming of the kingdom is the breaking in of the perfect heavenly reign of God. It is not the product of growth and organic development as the church of which Christ said, "I will build my church" (Mt 16:18; cf. Eph 2:21-22).

4. Finally, the usage of the terms in the New Testament re-

veals a clear distinction. In the gospels, the term *kingdom* occurs many times, while *church* is used only three times and these in a prophetic sense (Mt 16:18; 18:17). However, in the book of Acts, which forms the historical transition from the time of the gospels to that of the church, the attention of the disciples is turned away from the kingdom by the Lord's statement that it was not for them to know the times and seasons (Ac 1:6-7), and increasing reference is made to the newly established church. This continues in the epistles, which are addressed to the churches or members of the churches but never to the saints of the kingdom. Only in Revelation does the kingdom again become prominent with its establishment at the coming of Christ.

Thus the kingdom appears in Scripture as a distinct concept from the church. Nevertheless, the church shares in the kingdom as a part of God's purpose to reign upon the earth.

THE RELATION OF THE CHURCH AND THE KINGDOM

The two errors of identifying the church with the kingdom or radically separating them are usually associated with a one-sided concept of the nature of the kingdom. Those who would see the kingdom as the church are compelled to stress the abstract aspect of the kingdom, thus viewing it as the present spiritual reign of God in the hearts of men. Likewise, those separating the kingdom from the church stress the futurity and apocalyptic nature of the kingdom. The kingdom (*basileia*) includes both aspects. The church is therefore presently related to the kingdom in its spiritual nature but also looks forward to participation in the glorious culmination in the literal apocalyptic manifestation of the kingdom.

Present relation of the church to the kingdom. The relation of the church to the kingdom at present is based upon the fact of her salvation in Christ. In the gospels, the kingdom of God is so closely associated with Christ that in some passages to speak of the kingdom is to speak of Christ Himself. In Mark 11:10 the people cried, "Blessed be the kingdom of our father David, that cometh in the name of the Lord," but in Matthew 21:9 and Luke 19:38 the same language is used with reference to Christ. A similar close relationship is seen in the phrases "for my sake, and the gospel's" (Mk 10:29), "for my name's sake" (Mt 19:29), and "for the kingdom of God's sake" (Lk 18:29). The coming of the kingdom of God (Mk 9:1; Lk 9:27) is the coming of the Son of man with His kingdom (Mt 16:28). Christ even pointed to His mighty work while on earth as the arrival of the kingdom of God (Mt 12:28).[30] From these passages it is evident that kingdom is, in reality, nothing less than the salvation of God in Christ.

What was announced as imminent in the proclamation of the gospels was begun through the passion and exaltation of Christ. The decisive saving events had taken place, the promised eschatological salvation was present spiritually in the rule of Christ as Lord over the hearts and lives of His people. Temporally they live in this present age, but "spiritually they belong to the heavenly kingdom and enjoy the life of the age to come."[31]

This was the message the apostles proclaimed in Acts. Luke says that Christ for forty days between the resurrection and the ascension spoke to the apostles "of the things pertaining to the kingdom of God" (Ac 1:3). Part of His instruction during this period is related again by Luke when he records that the risen Lord opened the understanding of the disciples that they might understand the Scriptures concerning His suffering and resurrection "and that repentance and remission of sins should be preached in his name among all nations, beginning at Jerusalem" (Lk 24:45-47). Thus the gospel of the gracious remission of sins through Christ is the message of the kingdom. The Samaritans "believed Philip preaching the things concerning the kingdom of God, and the name of Jesus Christ" (Ac 8:12). Likewise, Paul's ministry of "the gospel of the grace of God" was at the same time the "preaching [of] the kingdom of God" (Ac 20:24 ff.). To the end of Acts, both to Jew and Gentile he was "preaching the kingdom of God, and teaching those things which concern the Lord Jesus Christ" (Ac 28:31; cf. v. 23).

The person of Christ and His Lordship became the prominent objects of apostolic preaching, rather than the "kingdom," as in the gospels, because now the reign of God is His. As Küng notes, "The concept of the reign of God becomes of secondary importance; because the glorified Kyrios shows in himself the meaning of the reign of God in which the church lives." The crucified

30. Ibid., pp. 588-89.
31. F. F. Bruce, The Book of the Acts, p. 35.

Jesus has been made "both Lord and Christ" (Ac 2:36) and all authority in heaven and earth are given to Him (Mt 28:18).

The relationship of the church to the kingdom presently involves both her nature and her mission.[32] Concerning her nature, the church is first the fruit of the kingdom. The members of the church are those who have been gathered together, as we have seen, by the preaching of the gospel, which is the word of the kingdom. They therefore have their "citizenship in heaven" as citizens of the kingdom (Phil 3:20, NASB; cf. Col 1:13). So also the "good seed" which is sown during the period of the mysteries of the kingdom "are the sons of the kingdom" (Mt 13:38, NASB).

As citizens, the church is secondly those who acknowledge the regal lordship of Christ (1 Co 12:3; Ro 10:9-10). According to Paul, the gospel carries with it the command to repent (Ac 17:30). Conversion takes place in the act of submission plus the obedience of faith toward Christ the Lord (Ro 16:26; Ac 26:19). It is at the same time the recognition of the kingly rule of God in Christ and entrance into the membership of the church.

Finally, the church, as citizens of the kingdom, enjoys certain blessings of that kingdom even while living in the kingdoms of this world. McClain notes this fact when he says, "From His [Christ's] present throne in the heavens, He is abundantly able to bestow certain of His regal blessings even before the arrival of the Kingdom."[33] These blessings are manifest and operative in the presence and power of the Spirit by whom the risen Lord is present in His church. Through life in the Spirit, the church already experiences "the powers of the age to come" (Heb 6:5, NASB).

The church, as citizens of the kingdom, is called into the service of the kingdom as ambassadors for Christ the King (2 Co 5:20) with the mission of representing "its heavenly government in this world as in a foreign land."[34] Under the full regal authority of Christ, the members of the church are sent forth (Mt 28:18-20) to proclaim the salvation of the kingdom and the command of God to repent and believe (Ac 17:30; Ro 16:26). Through the church the good seed of the kingdom is scattered abroad in order

32. Sauer, pp. 90-93; cf. Herman Ridderbos, *The Coming of the Kingdom*, pp. 354-56.
33. Alva J. McClain, *The Greatness of the Kingdom*, p. 440.
34. Sauer, p. 92.

that sons of the kingdom might be prepared for the arrival of its manifestation in glory (Mt 13:36-43).

In its very nature and mission the church is therefore presently "surrounded and impelled by the revelation, the progress, the future of the kingdom of God without, however, itself being the *basileia,* and without ever being identified with it."[35]

Relation of the church to the future kingdom. Although the church is presently related to the kingdom, the vast majority of references to the kingdom in the New Testament look to the future kingdom. The present mystery phase of the kingdom is not the final act; in fact, the disciples make no mention of it in the gospels but rather look to the future establishment of the kingdom (Mt 19:27-30; 20:21; cf. Ac 1:6). Christ Himself, although referring to the presence of the kingdom in Himself and His ministry, specifically taught in the parable of the nobleman that the kingdom was not going to appear immediately (Lk 19:11). The same forward look characterizes the epistles. The kingdom is an inheritance of the believers in the church from which those of the world will be excluded (1 Co 6:9; Gal 5:21; Eph 5:5; Ja 2:5). It is something for which the church presently suffers that they might be "counted worthy of the kingdom of God" (2 Th 1:5; cf. Ac 14:22) and for which they live fruitful lives that theirs may be an "entrance . . . abundantly into the everlasting kingdom of . . . [their] Lord and Saviour Jesus Christ" (2 Pe 1:11).

Members of the church stand related to the future kingdom first of all as heirs. In its unity with Christ the church as His body is coheir with Christ of the glory of the age to come when the kingdom will be manifest in all creation (Ro 8:17 ff.). Second, as heirs with Christ the church shares in the reign of the coming kingdom. Although believers are often called the servants and slaves of their Lord and are therefore subject to His regal rule, the New Testament avoids referring to them as subjects of the kingdom.[36] For when the kingdom comes, "the saints shall judge the world" (1 Co 6:2) and reign with Christ (2 Ti 2:12; Rev 1:6; 5:10; 20:6). As the bride, they will be one with Him in His kingdom reign.

35. Ridderbos, p. 356.
36. Peters, 1:597.

Thus the church appears in Scripture as vitally related to the kingdom program of God both presently and in the future because of her relation to Christ the Lord, God's mediatorial King.

THE FUNCTION OF THE CHURCH

The ways of God in His workings are beyond our final comprehension (Ro 11:33). Nevertheless, they are founded in wisdom, and each phase has been called into being for a purpose. According to the Scripture, the church as a part of that program has many functions to perform which may be divided into those related to the overall kingdom plan, to the world, to itself as a church, and to God.

TOWARD THE KINGDOM PROGRAM

The provocation of Israel to jealousy. The extension of the blessings of salvation to those outside Israel during the age of the church when Israel is judicially blinded is designed by God to effect the final salvation of Israel and the fulfillment of her covenant promises. This in turn will bring the full Messianic blessing upon all nations (Ro 11:11-15). The apostle explains this intent of God when he says of Israel, "They did not stumble so as to fall, did they? May it never be! But by their transgression salvation has come to the Gentiles, to make them jealous" (v. 11, NASB; cf. 10:10). The apostle magnified his ministry as an apostle to the Gentiles according to his testimony that "somehow I might move to jealousy my fellow-countrymen and save some of them" (11:13-14, NASB).

Through the grafting in of the Gentiles into the root of the Abrahamic blessing which initially belonged to Israel, God purposes by the church to bring a jealousy upon Israel which will cause her to desire to return to the place of blessing through repentance and the acknowledgment of Christ as her true Messiah. Unfortunately, the church has often failed to see itself as the "wild branches" which were grafted into the root which belonged to the natural branches and into which they will again be brought back. History shows, rather, that the church for the most part early turned its back on the Jew, treating him as God's outcast. Failure to demonstrate the true nature of Christianity as the life of the living Christ with His concern for Israel and to

proclaim Christ as the one who came according to the promises
(Ro 1:2) and will yet fulfill them, has resulted in few of Israel
being stirred to jealousy. Nevertheless, in modern times—due
perhaps to an increased interest in Israel on behalf of the church,
and dissatisfaction "prevalent almost everywhere among religious
circles in Jewry"—there is a steadily growing number of Jews who
would be prepared to echo Joseph Jacob's words, " 'If the sons of
Israel slew Jesus, Israel is greater than any of his sons, and the day
will come when he will know thee (Jesus) as his greatest.' "[37]

Display of God's grace and wisdom. God's forbearance in the
face of human sin and His provision of salvation in all ages have
been by the grace of God. The full manifestation of this grace,
however, awaited the church age.[38] For not until God's final and
complete revelation in the person of His Son was rejected could
grace be seen in all of its glory. In the crucifixion, man had done
his worst; he had killed the Lord of glory (1 Co 1:8) in whom
the fulfillment of all promises depended. He deserved nothing
but wrath and death. Instead, because of the cross, God extended
salvation which not only makes the sinner alive, but raises him
to sit with Christ in heavenly places, a son in the family of God
"that in the ages to come he might shew the exceeding riches of
his grace, in his kindness toward us, through Christ Jesus" (Eph
2:7). The church as the assembly of undeserving sinners redeemed in Christ is therefore the crowning display of God's grace
for all eternity.

The church is also the display of God's wisdom in bringing
Jew and Gentile together in one body in Christ. Writing to the
Ephesians, Paul states that the revelation of the mystery "that the
Gentiles should be fellow heirs, and of the same body [with Jews]
and partakers of his promise in Christ by the gospel" is "to the
intent that now unto the principalities and powers in heavenly
places might be known by the church the manifold wisdom of
God" (Eph 3:6, 10). The manifold wisdom is literally the "very-
varied" wisdom displayed in the untraceable ways of the divine
program of redemption. In the church God has worked the reconciliation of Jew and Gentile through the cross, which to the
Jew was a stumbling block, and to the Gentile, foolishness (1 Co

37. Ellison, p. 83.
38. Sir Robert Anderson, *The Gospel and Its Ministry*, pp. 9-23.

1:22-25). Angelic beings had seen the wisdom of God displayed in the creation of the material universe, but God's work in the church is the masterpiece by which He instructs the inhabitants of the heavenlies concerning His incomprehensible wisdom.

Preparation of rulers for the kingdom. The church age is, finally, the time when "sons of the kingdom" are prepared so that when it is established they might "shine forth as the sun in the kingdom of their Father" (Mt 13:43). These, as we have already seen, are to rule in that kingdom with Christ. During this age, through suffering in a hostile world (Ro 8:17; 2 Ti 2:12), and learning the lordship of Christ in this life, the members of the church are fitted to reign with Him in the coming age.

TOWARD THE WORLD

The primary purpose of the church in relation to the world is evangelization. The confusion of the present church concerning her purpose is difficult to understand in light of the unequivocal command of the Lord of the church: "Go therefore and make disciples of all the nations, baptizing them in the name of the Father and the Son and the Holy Spirit, teaching them to observe all that I commanded you" (Mt 28:19-20, NASB). This same exhortation was repeated just prior to the ascension. The church is to witness to her Lord "both in Jerusalem, and in all Judea, and in Samaria, and unto the uttermost part of the earth" (Ac 1:8; cf. Lk 24:46-48). As Christ was sent to the world by the Father, so He sent His disciples (Jn 20:21). If the debatable ending of Mark's gospel is included (Mk 16:15), the Great Commission is repeated five times in Scripture. That it is given to the church at large and not only to the first apostles is seen in the promise of Christ to be with His witnesses "to the end of the age" (Mt 28:20, NASB). According to the instruction of the Scriptures and the example of the early church in Acts, the witness of the church is accomplished through the total life of the members of the church, both in word and act, as a community and as individuals.

The witness of the Word is prominent in the commission itself. Christ instructed His disciples "that repentance and remission of sins should be preached in his name among all nations" (Lk 24:47). In the original Greek the word for preaching stands in the prominent position at the beginning of the verse, indicative of the place of preaching seen in the ministry of the apostles. From Peter's initial proclamation at Pentecost, the record shows that the good news of Christ went verbally into all areas of the then-known world so that they "heard . . . the word of the truth of the gospel" (Col 1:5-6). The spread of the gospel was accomplished not only through special ministers and evangelists but, even with the apostles absent, having remained in Jerusalem in the persecution, the church "went every where preaching the word" (Ac 8:4; cf. v. 1).

The attitude of the early Christians is demonstrated in the words of Peter, who when ordered to stop talking about Christ, replied, "Whether it be right in the sight of God to hearken unto you more than unto God, judge ye. For we cannot but speak the things which we have seen and heard" (Ac 4:19-20). Their witness was characterized by "boldness" (*parrēsia*), a spirit described by Moule as "no timid beating about the bush, but an 'uninhibited' freedom of speech—a literal reckless attitude, which does not stop to reckon what the consequences may be."[39] The early believers made no secret of their loyalty to Christ (Ac 4:13, 29, 31; 9:27, 29; 14:3; 18:26).

The content of the early witness was the great acts of God's grace in Christ. There were no exhortations to be good or any moral homilies but, rather, the proclamation of the facts of the gospel and the evidence for their truthfulness, together with a challenge to act accordingly.[40]

Since the Word cannot be separated from the person speaking, witness is also borne through the lives of those in whom the Word manifests itself in Christian action. The joint impact of word and deed is seen in Peter's counsel to wives of husbands who are disobedient to the Word to be submissive to them that "they may be won without a word by the behavior of their wives, as they observe your chaste and respectful behavior" (1 Pe 3:1-2, NASB). It should be stated, however, that action alone does not fulfill the Great Commission and cannot be used as a substitute for preaching the gospel.

39. C. F. D. Moule, *Christ's Messengers, Part I*, World Christian Books No. 19, p. 26.
40. Bo Reicke, "A Synopsis of Early Christain Preaching" in *The Root of the Vine* by Anton Johnson Fridricksen et al., pp. 134-43.

The witness of Acts is accomplished both within the corporate church life and outward in the world. The church is the place where the new life of Christ in the Spirit is manifest. The gospel reconciles man to God but also reconciles man to man. The evidence of this reality in the church is a witness to the world. Jesus told His disciples that all would know them for what they were if they "have love one to another" (Jn 13:35).[41] This love is expressed not only in kindly words but in beneficent action in meeting the needs of fellow believers (1 Jn 5:16-18).

The sharing of goods in the church at Jerusalem was undoubtedly an expression of this love, as the Scripture says, "The multitude of them that believed were of one heart and of one soul" (Ac 4:32). Not that this act was to be a pattern for all history, for genuine brotherly love will express itself in different ways, depending upon the circumstances. But it will always manifest the reconciliation of men in the tearing down of barriers and concern for others, no matter of what race or status in life. Stott rightly points out that "a truly inter-racial, inter-social Christian fellowship, whose members evidently care for one another and bear one another's burdens, is in itself an eloquent witness to the reconciling power of Jesus Christ."[42] The church has often sought to witness to the world in attempting to heal the breaches of mankind before it has demonstrated a genuine love in its midst. Only as the latter is first manifest will the world be attracted to receive the healing message of the gospel.

The church also witnesses corporately to the world when it meets to worship. The primary end of coming together as a body of believers is Godward in praise and adoration and then toward itself in edification as the various ministries of the Spirit are manifest, especially the preaching and teaching of the Word. Nevertheless, the congregational meeting also serves as a witness to the world. The true manifestation of God's presence in the church cannot be avoided by the unbelievers who are present, with the result that at least some will worship God (1 Co 14:23-25).

The witness of the church toward the world is accomplished

41. The command for love among believers is incessant throughout the New Testament. Cf. Jn 15:12, 17; Ro 12:10; 1 Th 4:9; Heb 13:1; 1 Pe 1:22; 2:17; 1 Jn 2:10; 3:11, 14, 18, 23; 4:7, 8, 11, 12, 20, 21; 5:1, 2.
42. John R. W. Stott, *Our Guilty Silence*, p. 71.

first through the proclamation of the Word. History reveals that the church can fail in its ministry to the world in one of two ways. It may attempt to rule the world through deliberately entering secular forms, or it may withdraw to individual monastic piety. Both result in a faulting of responsibility toward the world. The error of the latter method is obvious, for no witness can be had in isolation. Nevertheless, the church is continually in danger of withdrawing from the world in excessive inward attitudes and so losing contact with the world. Witness can only be effective as the church penetrates the world, not in conformity but in holy worldliness.

The other extreme of leaving the ministry of the Word in an attempt to witness through the more direct secular power has always tempted the church and is again prominent in our time. However, by casting aside its influence through the Word in favor of secular forms such as politics and business, the church loses its function as the servant of God, for only as it proclaims His Word is it His witness to the world. Before the world can experience renewal, the old man which is lord of the world must be judged and put to death by the challenge and judgment of the Word. If the church fails to witness by challenging the world with the Word and instead yields to the world, taking secular forms of power, it loses its holiness and no longer stands separate from the world as God's minister to it.[43]

While the church as church refrains from entering secular forms, its influence is felt in these forms through the influence of individuals who have been transformed by the Word. The member of the church lives not only in the church but in the secular forms of the world. In these structures of human society he is called to a supernatural life, witnessing to the world the reality of the power of the gospel to change the characteristics of this fallen life into those of the life to come. Through every member's attitudes and actions in the world, so different from those of the world that the supernatural is required for their explanation, the church bears witness to her Lord. The effect of this witness is described as being light to the world and salt to the earth (Mt 5:13-16; Phil 2:15). As such, it will most certainly have a beneficial effect upon society. But the transformation of the world is

43. Regin Prenter, *Creation and Redemption*, pp. 538-42.

not the ultimate goal. Neither the Lord in His ministry nor the apostles in theirs set about to reform society as an end in itself. As a matter of fact, if the reformation of the world was envisioned, the injunctions to be separate from it would be pointless. The final end of the church's witness of good works is revealed everywhere in Scripture as that of causing others to acknowledge God and glorify Him (Mt 5:16; 1 Pe 2:12; 3:1). In this function good works are linked to evangelism in the fulfillment of the Great Commission. Thus the total church witness is born when the Word is proclaimed in all its fullness and application to all areas of men's lives, and then lived by each believer in the contacts with the world in which the Lord of the church has stationed him for a witness.

In going to the world, the church is sent forth according to the pattern and with the love of Christ. As He was sent, so we are sent (Jn 20:21). As He loved the world enough to leave heaven's riches and go into the world, so the church cannot fulfill its purpose without the same compassion for a world outside of God's salvation. Jesus, moreover, was willing to live in the world, mixing freely with men and sharing their experiences, even being criticized for fraternizing with publicans and sinners. Finally, He gave His life for a world which, for the most part, did not respond to His love but repaid it with hatred. The church cannot die for the world in the unique atoning sense of Christ, and yet, it can only truly witness with the love of Christ for the world as it dies to self, sharing the sufferings of Christ (Col 1:24) in bearing the sins of the world and the reproaches directed toward God (cf. Ro 15:3).

TOWARD ITSELF

Edification. The edification of the church, while related to outward growth by the addition of new members, is concerned primarily with the building and developing of the community itself in the life of faith (Eph 4:16; Jude 20; 1 Co 14:26). The goal of the edification is that each member might grow to maturity in all things in Christ (Eph 4:13-16; cf. 2 Pe 3:18).

The work of edification is ultimately accomplished by the Lord of the church through the Spirit, first through the special ministries of the leaders (Eph 4:11-12; 1 Co 14:3), but ultimately through every individual (cf. Eph 4:12, 16; 1 Th 5:11). As each member receives edification through the pastoral ministry, he in turn passes it on to his fellow believer. Thus, every member "maketh increase of the body unto the edifying of itself in love" (Eph 4:16*b*).

The ministry of edification is associated in Scripture with the mutual exhortation and comfort of believer to believer. The apostle encouraged the church at Thessalonica to "comfort yourselves together, and edify one another, even as also ye do" (1 Th 5:11; cf. v. 14). The term "comfort" is used both in the sense of exhortation or admonishing, and comfort or consolation. Sometimes it blends the two together, depending upon the circumstance. While there is an urgency and seriousness in exhortation spoken in the power of the Spirit, there can be no thought of a critical polemic spirit. For this, as well as the comfort, is based upon the saving work of God and His mercies.[44] Genuine edification can only be accomplished in love (Eph 4:16) and peace (Ro 14:19).

Purification. Even as edification is possible ultimately by the supply of the Head, so the cleansing of the church is likewise the work of Christ who "gave himself for it; that he might sanctify and cleanse it with the washing of water by the word, that he might present it to himself a glorious church, not having spot, or wrinkle, or any such thing; but that it should be holy and without blemish" (Eph 5:25-27). Although the sanctification of the church is complete and perfect in its positional standing in Christ, it is also a process in the life of the church as the meaning and significance of that complete salvation are continually applied through the operation of the Holy Spirit by means of the Word.[45] So Christ prayed the Father to sanctify His disciples "through thy truth: thy word is truth" (Jn 17:17). This divine cleansing is seen in the work of the husbandman who "purges" (*katharidzō*, "cleanses") the branches in the vine (Jn 15:2) and the heavenly Father who disciplines His sons whom He loves (Heb 12:5-12; 1 Co 11:32).

The responsibility of the church is to allow the divine purifica-

44. Otto Schmitz, "parakaleō, paraklēsis" in *TDNT*, 5:794-99.
45. The fact that the verb, "sanctify" and the participle "cleansing" are both in the aorist tense does not indicate the length of time involved in the action. It simply looks at the total acts.

tion to work in its midst. This demands not only submission to the discipline of the Father (Heb 12:5-7), but self-discipline in obedience to the numerous commands for purity in the Word (cf. 2 Co 7:1; 1 Jn 3:3; 1 Co 11:31). When the health of the body is endangered by the failure of members to discipline themselves, the church as a community is responsible to exercise the needed correction.[46] The importance of purification cannot be overestimated, for only a church which allows the Spirit of God to cleanse it can be used by Him in any service.

TOWARD GOD

The church's final goal in all of its responsibilities, whether to the world or itself, is the ascription of glory to the one who has created it through redemption in Christ. The predestination of believers in the church to adoption as sons through Jesus Christ and the obtaining of an inheritance in Him all redounds "to the praise of the glory of his grace" (Eph 1:5-6, 11-14). So amazing is the display of God's attributes in creating the church and bestowing upon it all blessings in Christ Jesus that the apostle exults in a doxology of praise: "to Him be the glory in the church and in Christ Jesus to all generations forever and ever. Amen" (Eph 3:21).

Glory is first brought to God in the church through a thankful response to His grace: "Whoso offereth the sacrifice of thanksgiving glorifieth me" (Ps 50:23, ASV; cf. Heb 13:15-16). He is further glorified through the lives of believers as they advertise His mighty acts (1 Pe 2:9), yield fruits of righteousness in their lives (Phil 1:10-11), and wholeheartedly devote themselves to the ministry committed to them (1 Pe 4:11). Good works and the presentation of new converts are also sacrifices well pleasing to God and redounding to His glory (Heb 13:16; Phil 4:18).

The church as the habitation of God through the Spirit is the temple in which His glory now resides on earth. As this glory shines forth through the transformation of each member into the glorious image of Christ from glory to glory, the church will fulfill it highest purpose.

46. See pp. 119-26.

6

The Organization of the Church

SINCE THE CHURCH of the New Testament was a new work of God, it was a growing and developing body. For this reason it is difficult to get a unified view of what a mature, fully developed church (if there is such) should be. Rather, we observe the church in various stages of spiritual and organizational maturity. Evidence of variation and development is immediately apparent in the record of Acts where we find leadership first centered in the apostles and later the mention of elders appointed in every city (Ac 14:23) to take the oversight (cf. 20:28). In Acts 6, seven men are appointed to serve directly under the apostles; there is no mention of elders. Later such service is performed by deacons under the elders. Despite the variation due to the transitional nature of inauguration of this new work of God, certain organizational principles appear basic to the church.

THE FACT OF ORGANIZATION

Some have contended against any formal church organization, believing that the church is only a spiritual body whose members are united solely by their mutual relationship to Christ. The New Testament, however, gives clear evidence of a definitely organized church. This does not detract from the vital principle of the church being the spiritual resurrection life of Jesus Christ through the Spirit. Even as the invisible soul of man is manifest through the body, so God has ordained that the spiritual life function through an organized form.

There were already indications of simple organization in the first church at Jerusalem. The believers knew the number of their members (Ac 2:41; 4:4); they united in public worship and prayer meetings (2:42, 47), and practiced the ordinances of baptism and the Lord's Supper (2:41-42, 46). Although they still gathered in the temple for some functions, the "breaking of bread" was "from house to house," apparently following an organized system (2:42) ; they administered the property in common at that time (2:45; 4:32-37) , and exercised discipline (chap. 5) . Soon, however, it was necessary for them to enlist the aid of seven men to care for the poor (chap. 6) . That this early, relatively simple, apostolic-dominated organization developed into a formal church organization is evident from the New Testament.

CHURCH OFFICERS

The New Testament church had offices of elders and deacons. On his first missionary journey Paul "ordained them elders in every church" (Ac 14:23). The salutation to the church at Philippi includes specific mention of the bishops and deacons (Phil 1:1) . The permanent status of these offices is evident by the list of qualifications necessary for the officeholders (1 Ti 3; Titus 1:5-9) .

MEETINGS

The very concept of a group meeting necessitates some organization. Such meetings were commanded of the believer (Heb 10:25) , and evidently the first day of the week was set aside for this purpose. The disciples met immediately after the resurrection on the "first day of the week" (Jn 20:19, 26) . Later Paul instructed the church at Corinth to take a collection on the first day of the week (1 Co 16:2) . He also ministered to the believers at Troas "upon the first day of the week, when the disciples came together to break bread" (Ac 20:7) .

CHURCH DECORUM AND DISCIPLINE

Instructions were given that "all things be done decently and in order" (1 Co 14:40) . The Greek term translated "order" was used as a military term denoting the results of discipline to which an army is subjected. It described the symmetry and arrangement of society and simply signified good order.[1] Orderliness is further commended by the apostle in writing to the Colossian believers (Col 2:5) , while disorderliness is rebuked (2 Th 3:6-7, 11; 1 Th 5:14) . The violation of the ordered decorum was to be

---

1. John Eadie, *Commentary on the Epistle of Paul to the Colossians*, p. 122.

disciplined, implying an organized procedure and an authority
to execute it.

VARIOUS CHURCH PRACTICES

Other practices of the New Testament church also indicate
organization. Letters of commendation were sent from one church
to another, commending the bearer of the letter to the church of
his destination (Ac 18:24-28; 2 Co 3:1). Some ordered decision
had to be made in giving and receiving such letters. Collections
were gathered and sent from one church to another in the name
of the church (Ro 15:26; 1 Co 16:1-2; 2 Co 8:6—9:5). Registers
were kept of the widows under the care of the church (1 Ti 5:9).
Common customs were practiced among the churches, which
evidence a certain uniform organization (1 Co 11:16).

Apart from these various indications and the fact that God
reveals Himself as one who brings order (1 Co 14:33), it is mani-
festly evident that organization is inherent in any human association. "It must be evident," Lightfoot notes, "that no society of
men could hold together without officers, without rules, without
institutions of any kind; and the Church of Christ is not exempt
from this universal law."[2] The ministries of the church to preach
the gospel to all nations, educate the believers, and minister in
material ways to those in need necessitate some organizational
form.

LAWS AND MEMBERSHIP OF THE CHURCH

THE LAWS OF THE CHURCH

The Lord as Lawgiver. The church laws are simply the will
of Christ, the Lord of the church. The beginning of life for the
believer is the confession of Jesus as Lord (Ro 10:9-10; 1 Co
12:3). So also the church exists under His lordship. He is the
one who builds the church and calls it "my church" (Mt 16:18).
The prerogative of legislative authority belongs not to any man
or denomination but to Christ alone.

Christ Himself expressed this right when He commissioned the
disciples: "All authority [power, AV] has been given to me. . . .

2. J. B. Lightfoot, "The Christian Ministry" in *Saint Paul's Epistle to the
Philippians*, p. 181.

Go therefore and make disciples [teach, AV] of all nations, . . . teaching them to observe all that I commanded you" (Mt 28:18-20, NASB). By virtue of His authority, ministers are appointed in the church (Eph 4:7, 11) and gifts distributed (1 Co 12:5-6). Believers as members of the church become disciples, not of the church but "of the Lord" (Ac 9:1).

The Word as law. The will of the Lawgiver is expressed in the inspired Scriptures. Before leaving the disciples, Jesus promised to send the Spirit who would act in His behalf to convey His Word to them: "I have yet many things to say unto you . . . when he, the Spirit of truth, is come, he will guide you into all truth. . . . He shall glorify me: for he shall receive of mine, and shall shew it unto you" (Jn 16:12-14). The inspired word of the apostolic tradition is thus the word of the risen Lord Himself to His church. He is "the direct author of the tradition of the apostles, because he himself is at work in the apostolic transmission of his words, and deeds."[3]

As the Spirit of the Lord, the Holy Spirit not only inspired the writing but illumines the believer to understand the Word that each may be taught of Christ directly. With respect to all believers, John writes, "The anointing which ye have received of him abideth in you, and ye need not that any man teach you: but . . . the same anointing teacheth you of all things" (1 Jn 2:27; cf. 1 Th 4:9). This does not rule out human teachers in the church, for they are explicitly given to the church (Eph 4:11; 1 Co 12:28) and may be viewed as instruments of the Spirit's teaching. But it does declare that the ultimate authority of truth is the Lord of the church through His Spirit. There is no human mediator between any member of the church and the truth of Christ found in His Word illumined by the Spirit. The voice of the Lord of the church is only heard when the believer has abiding in him the apostolic teaching which he has "heard from the beginning" (1 Jn 2:24) and the "anointing" of the Spirit which he has "received" (v. 27; cf. Is 59:21).

The history of God's people in the Old Testament and in the church reveals the constant danger of forgetting the source of authority and listening to the traditions of men. When this

3. Oscar Cullmann, "The Tradition" in *The Early Church*, ed. A. J. B. Higgins, p. 59.

occurs, the church rejects its place as Christ's church as well as the vital ministry by the authority and power of its Lord to which it is commissioned and for which it exists.

THE MEMBERSHIP OF THE CHURCH

Included in the will of Christ for the church are instructions concerning the fellowship of its members. Among these are the necessity of and the qualifications for membership in the church.

The necessity of membership. At the time of salvation, believers are first "called unto the fellowship of his Son Jesus Christ our Lord" (1 Co 1:9; cf. 1 Jn 1:3, 6-7). This fellowship or participation with Christ constitutes the believer a member of the universal church in the sense of the spiritual reality of the unity of the Spirit in the body of Christ.

But the New Testament revelation does not stop with this fellowship. For when one is called into fellowship with God and made a member of the body of Christ, he is at the same time brought into fellowship with fellow members of that body. Stibbs notes forthrightly that "any idea . . . of enjoying salvation or being a Christian in isolation is foreign to the New Testament writings."[4] It is, in fact, God's purpose through the miracle of redemption to weld together a divided and estranged humanity into a living unity where differences of sex, race, nationality and position are all transcended in Christ (Col 3:11). The church as the company of redeemed is to be a pattern and pledge of the ultimate unity effected through the abolishing of all enmity at the cross (Eph 2:16).

Church fellowship is more than a demonstration of unity. It is one way God has ordained for the believer both to give himself to the Lord and fellow believers, and to get from them that which is necessary for spiritual edification. The gifts of the Spirit given to each member for the good of all are best expressed when met together. The full significance of the Lord's Supper as expressive of the unity of the body with the risen Lord takes place when all "come together . . . into one place (1 Co 11:20 ff.). Moreover, the frequent commands to mutual admonition and encouragement (cf. 1 Th 4:18; 5:11; Ro 1:12) cannot be accomplished in isolation.

4. Alan Stibbs, *God's Church*, p. 92.

For these reasons the Lord exhorts His people not to forsake "the assembling of ourselves together, as the manner of some is" (Heb 10:25). The record of the New Testament church also reveals the practice of gathering together: "And upon the first day of the week, when the disciples came together to break bread, Paul preached unto them" (Ac 20:7). Paul's instruction for behavior in the church at Corinth assumes their meeting together (1 Co 14:19, 28, 35), and he specifically mentions the problem of unrestricted tongues when "the whole church be come together into one place" (1 Co 14:23).

Whether participation in the assembly constitutes church membership may be open to question. However, it would appear that a participation in the sense of the New Testament, which requires sharing in the ministry of the church both in contribution and reception, is not unlike what is known as "church membership." Membership which requires "more or less" is not New Testament membership.

There is also a place in biblical church fellowship for believers to gather in groups smaller than the entire church. Encouragement for even "two or three" is given by Christ as He pledges answer to their united prayer when they assemble in His name because He is there (Mt 18:19-20). Small groups also lend themselves to the mutual exhortation and encouragement of believers in a way that can never take place when all are gathered together. Believers may learn to share their experiences and voice prayers in informal meetings where they would not in the total church. The experience of the faithful in Malachi's day should also be that of the church: "Then they that feared the Lord spake often one to another: and the Lord hearkened, and heard it" (Mal 3:16).

Qualifications of membership. Regeneration is the prime requisite for membership in the church. Members of the church of God are identified as "them that are sanctified in Christ Jesus . . . that . . . call upon the name of Jesus Christ our Lord" (1 Co 1:2). This requirement stems from the fact that the church is an organism and not an institution. It is the fellowship of those who participate with Christ in vital union, who are "by one Spirit . . . baptized into one body" (1 Co 12:13). Only those joined to Christ can be members of His church.

The record of the early church makes it clear that only the saved were admitted into membership. It was those "that gladly received" Peter's word on the day of Pentecost who "were baptized: and the same day there were added unto them about three thousand souls" (Ac 2:41). "And the Lord was adding to their number day by day those who were being saved" (2:47, NASB). "And believers were the more added to the Lord" (5:14). It would appear from the evidence of the New Testament that membership necessitates an understanding of the essentials of the gospel and a profession of its reception resulting in regeneration, thus precluding infants from church membership.

The necessity of baptism for membership is a much-disputed point. It is certain that no rite makes one a member of the body of Christ and therefore it does not join one to the church as an organism. The early church, however, did practice baptism as an initiatory rite into the visible congregation. It was the symbol of the spiritual transaction which united the person with Christ in the saving events of the death and resurrection of Christ.[5] That this was the practice of the church is evident from the record of Acts: "They that gladly received his word were baptized" (2:41). When the people of Samaria received the word "they were baptized" (8:12). The Ethiopian eunuch (8:38) and Cornelius (10:48) were also baptized immediately following their conversion, as was also the apostle Paul (9:18). Bruce states plainly that "the idea of an unbaptized Christian is simply not entertained in NT."[6]

While the New Testament teaches a regenerate church membership and only those in Christ are in the church as His living body, it is possible for some unsaved individuals to gain entrance into the local congregation. Jude refers to certain men who had "crept in unawares" (Jude 4). Peter likewise speaks of "false teachers among you" (2 Pe 2:1), and Paul warned the Ephesian elders of "grievous wolves" entering in among them (Ac 20:29), reminiscent of Christ's warning of "false prophets, which come to you in sheep's clothing, but inwardly they are ravening wolves" (Mt 7:15). The exhortations for self-examination to see "whether ye be in the faith" (2 Co 13:5) would also suggest the possibility

5. See discussion of baptism.
6. F. F. Bruce, *The Book of the Acts*, p. 77.

that some in the church were not genuine believers. God alone can know the heart of man, but the realization of the possibility of false profession requires the church to do all possible to make the issue of the necessity of the new birth crystal clear.

Transference of membership. The New Testament reveals several methods used in the reception of believers by new congregations. One was the letter of commendation sent from the church or from well-known leaders (Ac 18:27; Ro 16:1; Col 4:10; 2 Co 3:1-2). Personal introduction by a member of the church was also practiced in the case of Barnabas with the newly converted Paul (Ac 9:27). The Scripture does not indicate that all transfers followed these patterns, and it is probable that many were received into new churches simply through confession of their faith and experience of regeneration.

GOVERNMENT OF THE CHURCH

The church must have some form; in fact, it always does. The question remains as to which form is prescribed in the Scriptures. Some argue that the method of organization and the officers of the church are not prescribed. "No particular structure of church life is divinely ordained."[7] They maintain that as different forms of secular government serve different peoples, so it is with the church. "Any form . . . which the Holy Spirit can inhabit and to which He may impart the life of Christ, must be accepted as valid for the church. As all forms of life adapt themselves to their environment, so does the life of Christ by His Spirit in the church."[8] Support for the freedom of form is sometimes taken from the fact that Christ Himself gave no specific directions concerning the government of the church. However, this is answered by the fact that the church was not in existence at that time, and that He did promise to give additional truth through the coming Holy Spirit.

The New Testament, recording as it does the life of the church from its inception through the apostolic period, presents a cer-

7. Donald G. Miller, *The Nature and Mission of the Church,* p. 82.
8. Ibid. Davies also states, "The Church in the New Testament can assume many forms, and is not limited to any one particular form which is peculiarly the expression of its very being" (W. D. Davies, *A Normative Pattern of Church Life in the New Testament: Fact or Fancy?* p. 14).

tain amount of variety in church forms, due at least partially to
the transitional nature of this period. Despite this fact, most
interpreters have seen at least some basic elements of church governmental form prescribed or hinted in the biblical record. Three
major types of government have been suggested and practiced
among churches: episcopal, presbyterian, and congregational.

EPISCOPAL

Definition. The episcopal form of government is government
in the church by bishops. The name is derived from the Greek
term for bishop, *episkopos,* meaning "overseer." This form of
government maintains a threefold ministry of the church: bishops, presbyters (or priests) , and deacons. The essential concept
of this government is that the right to consecrate other bishops
and ordain priests and deacons belongs only to the bishop. This
provides for a succession of bishops and their rulership over the
two subordinate ministries.

The succession of bishops is sometimes traced back to the
apostles and thus termed "apostolic succession." Others, denying
that any continuous line can be traced all the way back to the
apostles, prefer simply the term "historic episcopate," while still
others, such as the Methodists, practice government by the bishop, with no claim of historic succession. Along with the Methodists, episcopalianism is found primarily in the Orthodox,
Anglican, and Roman Catholic churches. The latter, with its
addition of the pope who speaks with infallible authority *ex
cathedra,* is sometimes called monarchial.

Evidence. It is generally agreed that a third office of bishop,
distinct from presbyters, is not found in the New Testament, the
two terms being used synonymously for one office.[9] Nevertheless,
as Lightfoot points out, "History seems to show decisively that
before the middle of the second century each church or organized
Christian community had its three orders of ministers."[10] The
position of a single bishop or monepiscopacy is clear in the writings of Ignatius, whose lifetime certainly overlapped that of the
apostle John. As an example of many extravagant statements

9. See pp. 206-8.
10. Lightfoot, p. 186.

concerning the prestige of the bishop, he urges his readers to "do all things in unity, under the bishop presiding in the place of God, the presbyters in the place of the Council of the Apostles, and the deacons . . . who are entrusted with the service (*diakonia*) of Jesus Christ."[11]

To account for the historical fact of the lack of a third office in the New Testament, episcopalians argue that while the office itself is not seen in the New Testament it is a development of certain features already evident in the New Testament church. The main antecedent of this office is seen in the position of James in the church at Jerusalem. Paul refers to him as an "apostle" (Gal 1:19) and one of the "pillars of the church" (Gal 2:9). At the important Jerusalem council involving apostles and elders, he presides, summing up the discussion and rendering his judgment in the matter (Ac 15:13 ff.). His preeminence on this occasion is supported by other references where he is obviously named as the leader of the church (Ac 12:17; 21:18).

An examination of his relation to the other leaders of the church reveals, however, that he is more the presiding officer among a group than an authority over them. Coming to the Jerusalem council, Paul and Barnabas are received of "the church, and of the apostles and elders" with no mention of James (Ac 15:4). Following the expression of judgment by James, it was the decision of "the apostles and elders with the whole church" to send a delegation carrying letters back to Antioch with Paul and Barnabas (v. 22), letters which are described as "decrees . . . ordained" by them (Ac 16:4).

There is no question of the prominent position of James, but it is far from a monepiscopacy of later years. His ascendancy is rather to be accounted for by his unusual reputation for holiness which earned him the surname, "the Just," and the tradition that his "knees had become callous like a camel's" from praying.[12] More important even than his holy character was the fact that he was the nearest male relative to Christ, a fact that was especially important in a Jewish society concerned with family solidarity.

11. E. M. B. Green, *Called to Serve: Ministry and Ministers in the Church*, p. 43; cf. also the statements cited by Leon Morris in *Ministers of God*, pp. 96-97.
12. Eadie, *Commentary on the Epistle to the Galatians*, p. 98.

It is not without significance that Paul calls him "the Lord's brother" (Gal 1:19).[13]

The ministry of Timothy and Titus as authoritative figures involving several churches is also viewed as precedent for the episcopacy. However, their service to churches covering a considerable area makes it impossible to identify their position as a bishop, for the bishop appears in the early church, particularly in Asia Minor, to be confined to a certain locality.[14] Furthermore, no titles are given to them, and no provision is made for the continuation of their particular position, which would be the case if they were initiating an office of bishop.

The reference to the appointing of bishops certainly has reference to elders and not their successors (cf. Titus 1:5, 7). Their function is better explained as temporary representatives of the apostle Paul, helping in the establishment of missionary churches (1 Co 4:17; 1 Th 3:2; Phil 2:19-23; 2 Co 8:23). After their ministries to particular churches, they return to the apostle (cf. 2 Ti 4:9, 21; Titus 3:12).

Whether or not the positions of James and Timothy and Titus were actually taken by the early church as the link between apostolic superintendence and that of the later bishop, this office does gradually appear around the turn of the first century, first in Asia Minor, and a generation later in the West. Appearing first as more or less a headship among equals, it develops into a position of independent supremacy during the second and third centuries.[15] Instrumental in bringing this about were the needs of the church. The bishop provided a unifying factor amid churches of diversified character, many of which were suffering persecution. As an authoritative doctrinal voice, he was also a safeguard against heretical intrusions. And finally, there was the practical need for someone to represent the churches of one locality in communicating with others. According to Episcopalians, these needs were met through the guidance of the Spirit by the establishment of this form of government.

Apostolic succession. The concept of apostolic succession has

13. Green, pp. 45-46.
14. Theodor Zahn, *Introduction to the New Testament,* 2:34.
15. Lightfoot, pp. 234 ff.

been understood in several ways.[16] In the face of Gnostic heretics who claimed a secret tradition handed down from the apostles, Irenaeus appealed to the open and public succession of the bishops in centers founded by the apostles. True apostolic teaching was transmitted only through these. Others view the bishops as successors in function, for they carried on some of the work of the apostles, including leadership and responsibility for the purity of doctrine. A third concept of succession is the succession in doctrine whereby continuity depends on maintaining apostolic doctrine. Still another understanding is succession by ordination. The apostles ordained bishops as their successors; these, in turn, ordained successors, and so on until the present. Only those within this succession constitute the legitimate ministers and can exercise a valid ministry or the valid celebration of the sacraments.

There is no question but what the teaching of the apostles is to be continued through the ministers of the church. Paul expressly instructs Timothy to commit the teachings that he has received to others who will likewise pass them on. Thus, there is to be a succession of apostolic teaching. The same continuity is true for the function of the church leadership. This was handed over by the apostles, who also functioned as elders (1 Pe 5:1-2; 2 Jn 1-2) in the appointment of local elders (Ac 14:23; 20:17 ff).

An apostolic succession, however, whereby the apostles ordained others to succeed them as the only valid ministers, is not found in the New Testament. Several facts argue against this concept:

1. The absence of instructions for succession. In the original commission of the apostles there is no provision for any successors (Mk 3:14 ff.), nor are any instructions given subsequently to that end. This is most conspicuous by its absence, since the Old Testament, which had a divinely ordered ministry, contained explicit instructions concerning its establishment and continuity.

2. The absence of early historical succession. In agreement with the absence of instruction is the lack of any mention of the transfer of the apostolic office in the New Testament record. When Paul charges the elders for the care of the church at Ephesus there is no hint of a transfer of any authority of office (Ac 20:17, 28). The same is true in the case of Timothy and Titus, where

16. Morris, pp. 92-93.

succession could most logically be expected to appear. There is no evidence that the apostle ordained them as successors to his office. The New Testament shows the elders and bishops taking the place of the apostles, but precisely as elders and bishops and not apostles. They succeed apostles, but in a fundamentally different position.[17]

Contrary to the concept of a valid ministry as limited to those in a succession of ordination, the New Testament gives no indication that apostolic commissioning was indispensable for the ministry. In many instances quite the opposite appears. There was certainly a ministry in Rome and Antioch before the arrival of any apostle, and the church at Philippi is well established with the ministry of bishops and deacons (Phil 1:1), having been only a tiny group of believers when the apostle left (Ac 16).

Historically the doctrine of succession by ordination does not appear for some time after the New Testament church. Although Ignatius writes very early recognizing the episcopate, he has nothing to say about succession. The *Didache* also upholds congregational church government, instructing the local churches to appoint their own bishops and deacons (15:1). Monarchical succession is first found in Irenaeus' writings at the end of the second century. But even here there is no doctrine of the *transmission* of grace or authority by ordination, only a sequence of ministry. It is not until the third century that the doctrine of succession through ordination comes into being, and that, according to Lindsay, by lawyers of the Latin Church who sought to connect the growing authority of the church with the apostolic authority in much the same way that the government of the emperors from Augustus to Diocletian was said to be the prolongation of the old Republican constitution.[18]

3. The uniqueness of the apostolic office. The absence of successors to the apostles is due to the uniqueness of their office; it could not be transmitted. Directly commissioned by Christ Himself, the disciples were sent forth as His representatives with His authority. The words of Christ on the occasion of the first mission of the twelve, "He that receiveth you receiveth me" (Mt 10:40), are indicative of their regular ministry following the

17. Cullmann, p. 78.
18. T. M. Lindsay, *The Church and the Ministry in the Early Centuries*, p. 279; cf. W. Telfer, *The Office of a Bishop*, p. 119.

resurrection. Then they go forth as the authoritative spokesmen of Christ (Mt 28:18-20; Ac 1:8) bearing witness along with the Holy Spirit who inspires them and leads them into truth (Jn 15:26-27; 14:26; 16:12-15) which is nothing less than the teaching of the risen Christ Himself (cf. Jn 16:12 ff).

This unique function necessitates qualifications only found in the apostles of Christ's time. They must bear direct witness to the resurrection (Ac 1:22) and receive their commission and teaching ultimately from Him. It is on this latter basis that Paul lays claim to his apostolate. His gospel was not received of men but "by the revelation of Jesus Christ" (Gal 1:11-12). The teaching of the apostles was thus the norm of the church and its foundation (Ac 2:42). It was through their words that later generations would believe on Christ (Jn 17:20). This uniqueness of the apostolic authority was later manifest in the establishment of the canon which made clear a line of demarcation between apostolic doctrine and later ecclesiastical writings.[19] Thus it is evident that the apostolic office was by its very uniqueness not transferrable.

4. The priesthood of all believers. The imposition of an essential ministry for the conveyance of grace to the church does serious harm to the doctrine of the priesthood of the believers according to which all members of the church have the same direct access to God and His grace. The direct relationship of the believer to Christ is also involved in His rulership of the church, including all of its members. C. S. Hendry states the issue clearly: "When the episcopate (with or without the pope) is thus placed on the side of Christ over against the church and assigned the exclusive function of re-presenting the gospel to the church, who re-presents the gospel to the bishop? If the pope is the vicar of Christ to the world, who represents Christ to the pope?"[20]

The doctrine of succession makes the church dependent upon the ministry, when in reality the living Christ through His Spirit indwells the total church corporately. The gifts of ministry, like all other gifts, exist for the sake of the church that it corporately might do the work of the ministry (Eph 4:12).

In the final analysis it is the church which is to carry on the

19. Cullmann, pp. 87-98.
20. C. S. Hendry, *The Holy Spirit in Christian Theology*, p. 61.

apostolic mission of the proclamation of Christ (Mt 28:19 ff.). Thus the entire household of God succeeds the apostles as the building erected upon a foundation, and not only those gifted for the ministry (Eph 2:19-20). The Holy Spirit, who ministers the teachings of Christ and works through each member, is the true Vicar of Christ in His church (Jn 14:16, 26; 16:7, 13).

PRESBYTERIAN

Definition. The presbyterian form of church government consists in the rulership by the elders (*presbuteros*) as representatives of the church. The local church is governed by the session, which is composed of ruling elders elected by the membership, with the teaching elder or minister as presiding officer. The next highest-ranking body is the Presbytery, which includes all the ordained ministers or teaching elders and one ruling elder from each local congregation in a given district. Above the presbytery is the synod, and over the synod is the general assembly, the highest court. Both of these bodies are also equally divided between ministers and laymen or ruling elders.

Although both classes of elders, teaching and ruling, have equal authority, a distinction is usually maintained between their ministries, making the teaching elder the principal order. Teaching elders are ordained by other ministers, while ruling elders are ordained by the local congregation. Furthermore, while the ruling elder assists in the government of the church, the ministry of the Word and sacraments belongs to the teaching elder. It is of utmost importance, however, according to Presbyterianism, to maintain the parity of ministers. They are of equal ministries and there is no third order of ministry above them.

Evidence. The New Testament presents clear evidence that the care of the church was committed to elders.[21] They are seen, along with the apostles, leading the affairs of the church at Jerusalem (Ac 15:4, 22-23). Their qualifications concerned the ability to rule (1 Ti 3:4-5) and the references to rulers in the church undoubtedly apply to elders (1 Th 5:12 f.; Heb 13:17). The extent of authority invested in elders as representative rulers is not explicitly stated. It does appear that there are certain issues ultimately decided by the whole church (Mt 18:15-17).

21. See the discussion on the function of the elders, pp. 210-14.

There is also indication of a distinction of ministries among elders. Some who labored in teaching are singled out from the other ruling elders (1 Ti 5:17). It is questionable, however, whether this reference is sufficient to establish a distinct ordination for certain presbyters and the limiting of the ministry of the Word and sacraments to them. All bishops or elders are to be apt to teach (1 Ti 3:2; cf. Titus 1:9).

The scriptural basis for authoritative representative bodies above the local church is sought primarily in the event of the Jerusalem council (Ac 15:1-35; 16:1-4).[22] Here, following dissension and disputation in the church at Antioch over the place of circumcision in salvation, Paul and Barnabas, along with certain others, were sent to the apostles and elders at Jerusalem to discuss the question (15:1-2). A decision was announced by James and accepted by the group. Letters were carried back to Antioch concerning the outcome (15:19-30). These decrees were subsequently imposed by Paul upon other churches (16:4). This principle of representation and central authority is said to have developed into various district organizations as the administrative and judicial needs demanded.

While the Jerusalem council does present an example of an interchurch discussion and agreement, it does not clearly establish an authoritative organizational structure over the local church. In the first place, it is evident that the decision of the Antioch church to go to Jerusalem was purely voluntary. There is no evidence that Jerusalem had any organizational authority which demanded their coming. Second, when the events preceding the council are carefully observed, it will be seen that Paul and Barnabas went not as inferiors to receive the correct doctrine from Jerusalem, but rather because of their disputations with those who had come from Jerusalem (Ac 15:1). They could not accept their doctrine nor could they believe that it was the theology of the church at Jerusalem. Paul was not in doubt concerning the gospel which he had received by revelation (Gal 1:12);

22. The responsibility of giving relief aid to the Jerusalem church (1 Co 16:1-2) cannot be construed as indicative of any position of supremacy of this church or of an ecclesiastical organizational structure. It involved, rather, the responsibility of fellowship in the body of Christ (1 Co 12:26) and perhaps the recognition by the Gentile believers of the debt owed to those who have ministered spiritually to them (1 Co 9:11).

but rather than condemn the church at Jerusalem for heresy in the teaching of these that had come from Judea, he was convinced that his doctrine was the same as that held by the church at Jerusalem. In this confidence he went to Jerusalem for the purpose of demonstrating the unity of the true apostolic teaching. Undoubtedly, respect for the Jerusalem church and its leading "pillars" (Gal 2:9) contributed also to the convening of this council. But this respect in no way necessitated the council out of organizational supremacy.

If organizational structure is not evident, cooperation among churches in a recognition of their basic unity certainly is. The Jerusalem council forbids an absolute independence in attitude and practice among local congregations. This is further supported in the New Testament by the practice of interchurch relief (1 Co 16:1-3) .

CONGREGATIONAL

Definition. The congregational form rests the authority of the church in each local church as an autonomous unit, with no person or organization above it except Christ the Head. Emphasis is also upon the democratic structure of the church whereby the ultimate authority is vested in the members themselves. This does not preclude ministers elected in recognition of their divine gifts to serve as leaders, but their authority rests in their relation to the congregation and is generally less extensive in practice than either the episcopal or presbyterian ministers. In the ultimate sense, officers have no more ecclesiastical authority than any other member. Each has but one vote on any issue.

There is no fixed pattern of office among congregational churches, although there is general agreement that there are two types of ministers. Sometimes these are expressed in a plurality of elders who exercise the general oversight of the church and deacons who have a ministry of service. More generally there are the pastor and deacons, in which case the deacons are also concerned with the oversight of the congregation.

Ordination is generally not regarded as giving a man special status to do what laymen must not do. Rather, in ordination a man is "set apart to do what laymen may indeed do if need be; but he is set apart to give full time and energy to the work of

God, having received God's own call to do so, and in the confident hope that his ministration will be the more effective because of his calling, his gifts and his training."[23]

Evidence. Considerable scriptural evidence is advanced for the investment of authority solely in the local church as a democratic body.

1. The authority of the local church. The New Testament presents no church organization above the local church.[24] While the apostles and their emissaries appear to exercise a certain authority in a plurality of churches, there is no evidence that the permanent offices of bishop or elder and deacon have any jurisdiction outside of a local congregation.[25] This autonomy of each congregation is evident in the practice of the New Testament church.

a. Church discipline. The ultimate authority for discipline rests with the church itself. The failure of other means of reconciliation results in the matter coming before the local church as the final court beyond which there is no higher appeal (Mt 18:15-17). Paul himself, although giving directions for the excommunication of a member, calls upon the church to execute discipline rather than doing it himself (1 Co 5:5; cf. 2 Th 3:6, 14-15).

b. Election of officers and delegates. The local church approved the suggestion of the apostles and chose the seven men to serve (Ac 6:3-5). Although the congregations are not mentioned in the appointment of elders by the apostles and their representatives (Ac 14:23; Titus 1:5), the procedure may well have been like that of choosing the seven men in Acts 6. The qualifications for office given to the church at large imply its responsibility in selecting officers.[26] The church also sent out and received

23. A. R. Vine, *The Congregational Ministry in the Modern World*, ed. H. Cunliffe-Jones, p. 10.
24. This is explicitly recognized by Louis Berkhof, *Systematic Theology*, p. 590; E. J. Forrester, "Church Government" in *The International Standard Bible Encyclopaedia*, 1:655.
25. "Each congregation represented the whole Church of God in its own area; its offices had sufficient commission when they had its appointment. The bishops or elders are local ministers. . . . Like the synagogues the churches are democratic in character and apparently autonomous. Unity is expressed in the practical help of one part of the Body for another" (George Johnston, *The Doctrine of the Church in the New Testament*, p. 96).
26. Hermann W. Beyer, "episcopos" in *TDNT*, 2:617.

messengers (Ac 11:22, 14:27; 15:3-4; 2 Co 8:19; 1 Co 16:3). Although in the case of the Jerusalem council it appears that the deliberation was carried on by the apostles and elders (Ac 15:6), the church listened and approved the decision (vv. 12, 22-23, 25). The decision was likewise received by the entire church at Antioch (v. 30). In all of these important actions there is no hierarchy which rules by its own authority.

c. Responsibility in doctrine and practice. The responsibility of maintaining true doctrine and practice is directed toward the entire church. This is not to say that those elected by the church do not in a special sense bear this obligation. But the final obligation rests with the church. It is to test the spirits (1 Jn 4:1), for every believer is anointed by the true Spirit (1 Jn 2:20, 27) and able to discern truth. The exercising of ministries is subject to the approval of the church which must "prove all things" (1 Th 5:21). Similarly, the ordinances are given to the church: "For I have received of the Lord that which also I delivered unto you" (1 Co 11:23). The church is therefore the final custodian of the apostolic doctrine and ordinances, not a special clergy or any governing body above the local church.

2. The democracy in the local church. The Scriptures point not only to local church autonomy but to a basic democracy as the form of local church government, all members having equal rights and responsibility. As has been noted previously, this does not preclude ordered ministries of leadership. But their authority derives from the Lord of the church through the acknowledgment of the congregation. The headship of Christ, the universal priesthood of the believers, and the practice of the early church all argue for a democratic form of government.

a. The headship of Christ. The doctrine of the headship of Christ to the church means that He is in living vital contact with each member. As there is no mediating organ in the physical body to carry out the functions of the head among the members of the body, so there is no special ministry between Christ and the members of the church. Where any two or three are gathered together in His name, Christ is in their midst (Mt 18:20).

The recognition of the headship of Christ means that the Ruler of the church is in heaven. "Since Christ rules, there are no rulers. There are indeed persons to whom official duty has been allocated. . . . But this differentiation of the gifts of grace (*charismata*) does not create any differences in jurisdiction or rank."[27] These gifts of ordered ministries, including leadership, are among those given to the church as a whole (1 Co 1:7), and therefore subject to the church as the body of Christ, each member of which is equally indwelt of the Spirit (1 Co 6:19) and taught of God (1 Th 4:9).

The direct relation of the church to the lordship of Christ is evident when the entire membership is charged with the responsibility of maintaining order (1 Co 14:40). This is implied also in the exhortations to unity of mind and action (Ro 12:16; 1 Co 1:10; Phil 2:2-4). These "are not mere counsels to passive submission, such as might be given under hierarchy . . . ; they are counsels to cooperation and harmonious judgment."[28] The whole church also bears the responsibility for purity in doctrine and practice. Contending for the faith is the duty of all the "sanctified" (Jude 1, 3). The letters of Revelation 2 and 3 are ultimately the words of the Spirit to the churches (Rev 2:7, 11, etc.). Responsibilities imply authority to carry them out, thus arguing for the final authority of the church as a whole.

b. The priesthood of believers. Because all believers comprise the priesthood of the New Testament church (1 Pe 2:5, 9), no particular group may be interposed between any believer and God. The humblest believer has direct access into the throne room of God along with the minister (Heb 10:19-22). This equality before God appears to demand a democratic form of government.

c. The practice of the New Testament church. In viewing the authority of the local church, we discover that not only was each church organizationally autonomous, but this authority rested with the people who elected ministers and chose their own delegates and messengers. Discipline likewise was executed by the whole church (2 Co 2:6-7).

Relationship between local churches. Local church autonomy according to the New Testament does not mean isolation or absolute independence from other churches. No church government is biblical which fails to recognize the unity of the church.

27. Emil Brunner, *The Christian Doctrine of the Church, Faith, and the Consummation, Dogmatics,* 3:43.
28. A. H. Strong, *Systematic Theology,* p. 904.

As the eschatological community, the church is the place where the Spirit is at work to bring about that unity of mankind intended by God and destined to take place in the future age.

This bond of unity is expressed both in common faith and practice as well as cooperative endeavors. Corinthian believers were to see themselves united "with all that in every place call upon the name of Jesus Christ" who is "both their's and our's" (1 Co 1:2). All the churches had a common faith (Eph 4:5; Titus 1:4; Jude 3; 2 Pe 1:1) and shared the apostolic letters (Col 4:16; Gal 1:2). God-given teachers were received in all churches (Ac 18:24-28; 1 Co 16:12; Ro 16:3; 3 Jn 5-8), and cooperation in discipline was expected (2 Jn 9-11). Unity of faith and purpose is further evident in the thanksgiving expressed for the faith and love of one church toward other churches (1 Th 1:7-9; 4:9-10; 2 Th 1:3-4; Ro 1:8; Col 1:4). Furthermore, this unity necessitates seeking counsel and understanding between churches, as evidenced in the Jerusalem council (Ac 15). There were common customs and practices of worship (1 Co 11:16; 14:33, 36), and a spirit of unity was conveyed in salutations from church to church (1 Co 16:19; Ro 16:16; Phil 4:22).

Besides the cooperation evident in the unity of faith and practices, churches aided one another materially (1 Co 16:1; Ro 15:26). They supported missionary activity among the churches, both materially and spiritually (2 Co 11:9; Phil 4:15; 1 Co 16:6; 2 Co 1:16; Ro 15:24). All of the practices of cooperation among the churches are voluntary and yet are obligatory because of the unity of the body in Christ.

CONCLUSION

The biblical data presents a basic congregational form of church government with local autonomy and a basic democracy. It is evident, however, that no detailed and full-orbed organizational pattern is presented in the New Testament. Rather, the governmental structures provide basic principles of church order which may be adapted for different requirements. Thus there is flexibility for various programs such as the Sunday school which are nowhere explicitly detailed in Scripture.

The biblical picture of the nature of the church and its government yields two primary principles which must underlie any church organization. The first is stated by Davies when he writes, "The ultimate New Testament criterion of any Church order . . . is that it does not usurp the Crown Rights of the Redeemer within His Church."[29] No person or group can purport to stand for Christ over against the body which is under the immediate headship of Christ. Nor does any organizational practice which fails to recognize the mind of Christ through the indwelling Spirit, no matter how closely patterned after the New Testament structure, qualify as biblical church government. The second indispensable feature of any biblical church order is the recognition of the unity of the church. Although distributed geographically in local autonomous churches, the church is finally one under the headship of Christ. It is a oneness in multiplicity. No church organization must be allowed to hinder the realization of the one fellowship of all believers in Christ.

THE DISCIPLINE OF THE CHURCH

The discipline of the church rests upon the fact that God Himself disciplines His children. No true believer is without the chastening hand of God. "For whom the Lord loveth he chasteneth, and scourgeth every son whom he receiveth" (Heb 12:6). God disciplines His own directly concerning matters of their family relationship to Him. But He has also ordained mediate discipline by the church concerning those affairs that concern the life and walk of the corporate household of faith.

THE BASIS OF DISCIPLINE

Divine holiness. The basis of all discipline is the holiness of God, which both demands it and is the goal toward which it strives in believers (Heb 12:11). As the temple of God, the church is a place of holiness, even as the temple of old of which the psalmist wrote, "Holiness becometh thine house, O LORD, for ever" (Ps 93:5). In loving grace God has joined Himself to mankind in the very sanctuary of the heart of members of the church. But He comes as the Holy One, demanding the reflection of His character within His temple: "Be ye holy; for I am holy" (1 Pe 1:16). The church must therefore be on guard lest "the leaven of malice and wickedness" enter that temple and

29. Davies, p. 21.

defile that which has been sanctified by the sacrifice of Christ
(1 Co 5:6-8). Failure to discipline evidences a lack of awareness
of the holy character of God.

Discipline is demanded not only because the church is God's
but because it is God's witness to the world. It is the vehicle
God has chosen to make known His name and glory during this
age. What the world sees in the church is its conception of God,
and only a clean church can bring the world to glorify God
(1 Pe 2:12).

Divine command. The discipline which is implied by the
nature of the church is directly commanded by her Lord. Instructing His disciples concerning the future church, Christ outlined the procedure of discipline, concluding with its divine
authority: "Whatsoever ye shall bind on earth shall be bound in
heaven; and whatsoever ye shall loose on earth shall be loosed
in heaven" (Mt 18:18). The church exercises discipline with
the authority of heaven, for it is the Lord in their midst who
judges. Indirectly through the apostles also, Christ commands
the church to discipline on numerous occasions (1 Co 5; Titus
3:10; 2 Th 3:6-15; 1 Ti 5:20; Gal 6:1).

Practice of the church. The New Testament records several
instances of obedience to the divine command in the practice of
disciplining those who brought harm to God's people. Instruction
was sent by the apostle Paul to the church at Corinth for the
excommunication of the incestuous man. The same discipline
was extended to Hymenaeus and Alexander for blasphemy
(1 Ti 1:20).

PRACTICE OF DISCIPLINE

Scope of discipline. While discipline is enjoined for the purity
of the church, it must be practiced with great care. The apostle
has much to say concerning the sin of the people in the church at
Corinth, involving divisiveness, immorality, and disorderly conduct, yet he only instructs discipline against one man. The same
limited practice is evident throughout the New Testament. No
attempt is made to make the church sinless through the exercise
of church discipline for every deviation. The Scripture does not
explicitly state the criterion by which an offense is worthy of discipline. It would appear from the instances mentioned that dis-

cipline concerns those who clearly have a harmful effect upon the congregation in one way or another.

Categories of offense requiring disciplinary action include difficulties between members (Mt 18:15-17; 1 Co 5:5-6), disorderly conduct (2 Th 3:6-15), divisiveness (Ro 16:17-18; Titus 3:9-10), and gross sins (1 Co 5:1-13; 1 Ti 5:20). It is important to note that, along with the sins of immorality, Paul includes covetousness, idolatry, abusive speech, drunkenness, and swindling as sins deserving discipline (1 Co 5:11). Finally, false teaching is also cause for church discipline (1 Ti 1:20; cf. 2 Ti 2:17-18). This is implied also in the Lord's rebuke of the church at Pergamos for not putting away those among them who held false doctrine (Rev 2:14-16). It is obvious from the scriptural examples that discipline for erroneous teaching concerns fundamental doctrines of the faith and not lesser differences of interpretation. Care must be taken not to exceed the warrant of Scripture on this matter.

Procedure of discipline. Disciplinary action begins with the recognition of offense. This is sometimes difficult, for the self-consciousness of imperfection makes every believer hesitate to point out sin in another's life. Nevertheless, the Scriptures give indication that such action is necessary on occasion. As with leprosy in the congregation of Israel, there were clear and unmistakable signs evidencing the disease; and when these were present, immediate action had to be taken.

In the case of individual offense the offended party is first to seek private reconciliation with the offender (Mt 18:15). If this fails, witnesses are to be included in a second attempt so that when it comes before the church it will be established (vv. 16-17). Initiatory action involving public offenses against the whole body, although not explicitly stated, should normally be taken by the spiritual leaders of the church, following Paul's instructions that the "spiritual" are to restore those overtaken in a fault (Gal 6:1). These initial contacts provide opportunity for the repentance of the offender and forgiveness. If, on the other hand, they are not heeded, this first step constitutes warning of further action which will be taken and also gives occasion for serious rebuke (cf. 2 Ti 4:2; 1 Th 5:12-14).

If further action is necessary, it is to be taken by the whole church. The case that is not settled in private is to be told to the church (Mt 18:17). The Corinthian believers were to be "gathered together" to take action against the offending brother (1 Co 5:4-5), which is termed "punishment . . . of many" (2 Co 2:6. It is also the Thessalonian and Roman churches, and not simply certain ones in them, that are to take action with regard to those unruly and schismatic in their midst (2 Th 3:6-15; Ro 16:17). Although Paul speaks of exercising certain disciplinary acts on his own in the case of Hymenaeus and Alexander (1 Ti 1:20), this action was probably executed by the church, similar to the incident at Corinth.

The act of the congregation when rightly taken in disciplining one of its members is in reality the act of the church at large represented in a particular locality. The discipline of one church should therefore be respected by other churches. For, in the final analysis, all true disciplinary action is the exercise of authority by the Lord of the church. The Corinthian discipline was "with the power of our Lord Jesus Christ" (1 Co 5:4*b*), and similar authority is seen in the reference to the heavenly ratification of the disciplinary act and the presence of Christ in their midst (Mt 18:18-19).

Since the church as a body disciplines, restoration is also an act of the congregation. The "many" who discipline must "forgive him, and comfort him," and confirm their "love toward him" (2 Co 2:6-8).

Forms of discipline. Scripture presents several disciplinary measures which may be taken, depending upon the nature of the offense. Those who walk disorderly are to be warned or admonished (1 Th 5:12, 14). This includes not only discipline by the leaders but also a mutual discipline exercised by all the members. In addition to the admonishing it may be necessary to withhold fellowship from those who do not respond in obedience (2 Th 3:6, 14). This does not yet involve excommunication, but rather an abstaining from association or intimate fellowship with him, which would indicate to the offender that his action had caused a rupture of harmony (v. 14; cf. 1 Co 5:11). He is yet to be counted as "a brother" (v. 15), but one who needs to be put to shame that he might be restored to fellowship (v. 14).

Should the offender persist in his sin even after the admonition and withdrawal of fellowship, the final step of discipline is excommunication. The severity of this step is indicated in Paul's instruction concerning the man at Corinth: "Deliver such an one unto Satan for the destruction of the flesh, that the spirit may be saved in the day of the Lord Jesus" (1 Co 5:5; cf. 1 Ti 1:20). In the words of Christ, "Let him be unto thee as an heathen man and a publican" (Mt 18:17b).

Since the sphere outside the church is the realm of Satan (1 Jn 5:19; cf. Col 1:13; Eph 2:12), to deliver someone unto this realm is to put him out of the church, cutting him off from all Christian privileges. But this discipline was more than simple privation; it was "for the destruction of the flesh." This phrase has had two interpretations.[30] One which was current in the early centuries understood "flesh" as the lusts of the lower nature. But it is difficult to see how turning a person over to Satan would effect the destruction or the conquering of evil desires. It is better to take "the flesh" as a reference to the physical nature. Thus Satan is the instrument in God's hand by which God inflicts some type of physical punishment. This corresponds with the physical effects of divine judgment upon those who profane the Lord's Supper (1 Co 11:30). Here, as in the case of the incestuous man and Hymenaeus and Alexander, the discipline was intended for spiritual gain so that the offenders would be ultimately found among God's people (1 Co 11:32; 5:5; 1 Ti 1:20). No mention of physical infliction is made in the disciplinary instructions given by Christ (Mt 18:17). Therefore, it is not necessarily the inevitable concomitant of excommunication, but remains in the sovereign hand of God to use as He will. The final act of the church in discipline can only be that of excluding the offender.

Attitude in discipline. The procedure of discipline from the initial confrontation, even including the final step of excommunication, is to be performed in love and humility. As we have seen, it is in reality the Lord of the church executing discipline by His Spirit through His people. As He deals in love and grace with His sons even when they sin, seeking to heal and restore rather than destroy, so the purpose of all discipline must be to win

30. G. W. H. Lampe, "Church Discipline and the Interpretation of the Epistles to the Corinthians" in *Christian History and Interpretation: Studies Presented to John Knox,* ed. W. R. Farmer, C. F. D. Moule, and R. R. Niebuhr, pp. 349-51.

back the erring. The apostle writes the Galatians, "Brethren, if a man be overtaken in a fault, ye which are spiritual, restore such an one in the spirit of meekness; considering thyself, lest thou also be tempted" (Gal 6:1).

The "spiritual" will manifest the fruit of love, long-suffering and gentleness in discipline. Paul's own attitude toward the Corinthian case expresses the heart of the "spiritual" in discipline: "For out of much affliction and anguish of heart I wrote unto you with many tears; not that ye should be grieved, but that ye might know the love which I have more abundantly unto you" (2 Co 2:4). The apostle rebuked the Corinthians because they were "puffed up" and had "not rather mourned" over the sin in their midst (1 Co 5:2). Grief over the devil's success, sorrow for the disgrace to the congregation, and mourning for the soul of the sinner who has been overwhelmed with sin and guilt, are the motives for disciplinary action.[31]

Humility must also accompany discipline, for no marking of sin in a brother can fail to remind all believers of their own frailty (Gal 6:1). Nor can it fail to evoke concern from the church regarding its possible failure toward the erring one, to pray for him and set before him an example of godliness.

Above all, effective and true discipline can only be carried out in an attitude of prayer. The Lord clearly establishes the authority of the church to discipline upon His presence among those praying in His name: "If two of you shall agree on earth as touching any thing that they shall ask, it shall be done for them of my Father which is in heaven. For where two or three are gathered together in my name, there am I in the midst of them" (Mt 18:19-20). The church has the right to pass judgment on its members only because it is the body where Christ dwells and promises to reveal His will through prayerful seeking.

Finally, discipline in the name of Christ must include readiness to forgive. It can never rejoice in punishment which brings sorrow beyond that which produces repentance. Paul reminds the Corinthians concerning the one disciplined that they "ought rather to forgive him, and comfort him, lest perhaps such a one should be swallowed up with overmuch sorrow" (2 Co 2:7; cf.

31. R. C. H. Lenski, *The Interpretation of St. Paul's First and Second Epistle to the Corinthians*, p. 208.

2:5-11; 7:10-13). To leave him in Satan's realm after he had repented would let Satan exceed the limits of his appointed task and allow him to gain a victory (2:11).[32]

EFFECT OF DISCIPLINE

The exercising of church discipline is designed to have a two-pronged effect both on the individual offender and on the church.

The effect upon the individual. As God's direct discipline is always for "our profit" (Heb 12:10), so church discipline is remedial in purpose. In each instance of discipline mentioned in the New Testament, this intent is evident. Christ spoke of gaining a brother (Mt 18:15; cf. 2 Th 3:15). The incestuous man was disciplined so "that the spirit may be saved" (1 Co 5:5), and Hymenaeus and Alexander, "that they may learn not to blaspheme" (1 Ti 1:20). Those in opposition are to be corrected with the motive that God may "give them repentance to the acknowledging of the truth" (2 Ti 2:25).

While restoration is the ultimate goal, the more immediate consequence of discipline upon the individual is the experience of shame (2 Th 3:14) and sorrow (2 Co 2:7). Paul warns against excessive punishment which produces "overmuch sorrow." Nevertheless, there is a necessary "godly sorrow" which works a "repentance to salvation" never to be regretted (2 Co 7:10).[33] While this speaks primarily of the sorrow of the Corinthians over their sin in failing to exercise discipline which required the strong rebuke of the apostle (cf. vv. 8-9), it is also applicable to the one disciplined, who also sorrowed (cf. 2:7). There is a "sorrow of the world," a self-pity over the painful consequences of sin and the shattering of worldly attachments, but how much better it is to experience that disciplinary sorrow of God in con-

---

32. Lampe, p. 354.
33. On the question of whether it is the "repentance" or "salvation" which is "not to be repented of," Hughes notes, "The Vulgate, Theophylact, Ambrose, Augustine, Hervcius, Meyer, Bengel, Alford, Hodge, and others connect it with *sōtērian* [salvation]; but the majority of commentators, and also the English versions, are more likely to be correct in connecting it with *metanoian* [repentance]. We would suggest, however, that it is more saitsfactory still to take it as qualifying the whole phrase *metanoian eis sōtērian* [repentance unto salvation]. This sense may be aptly conveyed by the use of hyphens: 'repentance-unto-salvation which is not to be regretted'" (Philip E. Hughes, *Paul's Second Epistle to the Corinthians*, pp. 271-72, n. 11).

trition over sin against Him. Although it produces sorrow now, church discipline, like the discipline of the heavenly Father, "afterward . . . yieldeth the peaceable fruit of righteousness unto them which are exercised thereby" (Heb 12:11).

Effect upon the church. Disciplinary action also has an effect upon the church as a body. As Achan's sin prevented Israel from victory against her enemies (Jos 7:13), so sin in the church gives occasion for the enemies of God to blaspheme (Ro 2:24; cf. 1 Ti 6:1). The removal of sin restores the honor of God and enables the testimony of the church to shine brightly in the world.

Discipline also protects the church from further decay, for sin which is allowed to remain spreads its infectuous disease like a cancerous growth, and the health of the entire body is destroyed. The Corinthian church gloried in their acquiescent attitude toward the sin in their midst, but the apostle sharply rebuked them for it, reminding them that " a little leaven leaveneth the whole lump" (1 Co 5:6). It is the duty of the church for its own preservation as the temple of God, to discipline sin, no matter how difficult it is to do so at the time.

Finally, the execution of discipline has the beneficial effect of reminding all members of their own propensity toward sin and warning them of its consequences. Instructions concerning the sin of church leaders are applicable to all discipline: "Them that sin rebuke before all, that others also may fear" (1 Ti 5:20). The discipline of the Corinthian member brought a godly sorrow for sin to the whole church and, with it, the putting of their house in order. The apostle notes this effect, writing, "For behold what earnestness this very thing, this godly sorrow, has produced in you, what vindication of yourselves, what indignation, what fear, what longing, what zeal, what avenging of wrong! In everything you demonstrated yourselves to be innocent in the matter" (2 Co 7:11, NASB).

Church discipline in all its forms was given by the Head of the church for the health and welfare of the body. To avoid its practice when necessary for the sake of reputation or what is really a false unity can only lead to a sick and weak church life.

7

The Ministry of the Church

A FUNCTIONING ORGANIZATION demands that activities be carried on and responsibilities performed. In the Old Testament God appointed a ministry for His people. That ministry, as far as the people's religious life was concerned, was performed by the priesthood. God has likewise given a ministry to the New Testament church that it might accomplish that for which it was formed.

THE MINISTRY OF ALL MEMBERS

One of the foundations of Reformation truth was the concept of the priesthood of all believers. This not only has reference to the direct access of each member of the church to God through Christ the High Priest, but it also speaks of the ministry which each member of the church bears.

UNIVERSALITY OF THE MINISTRY

In sharp distinction to the official priesthood which existed to mediate between God and His people in Israel under the old covenant and among pagans, the church recognized only the mediatorship of Christ, in whom all members share equally. Consequently, there is no concept in the New Testament church of a special office whereby some members are sharply distinguished from others bearing a peculiar relationship to God. Jesus specifically prohibited His disciples from establishing class distinctions: "But be not ye called Rabbi: for one is your Master, even Christ; and all ye are brethren. And call no man your father upon the earth: for one is your Father, which is in heaven. Neither be ye called masters: for one is your Master, even Christ" (Mt 23:8-10).

All saints constitute "a royal priesthood" (1 Pe 2:9), they are made "priests unto God" (Rev 1:6; cf. 5:10). This means that

127

there is no sacred office of the sanctuary, but that all of the Christian life is to be sanctified in priestly service to God (Ro 12:1). The universal ministry of believers is also mentioned in 1 Peter 2:9, where the believer priesthood is to "proclaim the praise or mighty acts of God."[1] This is a technical phrase referring to the duty of one who has personally experienced the gracious power of God to publicly acknowledge that fact. As this was in the strictest sense an official act, all believers are engaged in the official ministry commanded by Christ.[2]

Not only in the common priesthood, but also in all metaphors used for the church, such as the flock, temple, body, vine and family, the ministry of Christ is fused with the ministry of His people as a whole. "In that single, corporate ministry every individual as a lamb or as a disciple has an essential share. Shareholders (*koinonia*) in the Spirit are shareholders in the manifold vocation that the Spirit assigns."[3]

The universality of the ministry is evident in the gifts of the Spirit given to each member in the church for the ministry. As the apostle declares, "The manifestation of the Spirit is given to every man" (1 Co 12:7; cf. vv. 7, 11, 18; 14:26; Eph 4:7, 16; 1 Pe 4:10). In reality, the ministry of the church is the ministry of the Spirit which is divided among the various members, each contributing his gift to the total work of the church.

The biblical viewpoint of the ministry provides no distinction between the "clergy" and "laity" as is often held. These terms came from the Greek words *kleros*, meaning "lot," and *laos*, meaning "people." But, in the Bible, God's *kleros* or lot, that is, the people that fall to Him as His own possession, are all believers (1 Pe 2:9), not just a small section. So also, God's *laos* or people includes all. Thus "all clergy are laymen, and all laymen are also clergy, in the biblical sense of these words."[4]

Furthermore, the Bible does not present any special work exclusively for certain officers. All could teach and contribute to the edification of the church in the public service (1 Co 14:26-

1. W. F. Arndt and F. W. Gingrich, *A Greek-English Lexicon of the New Testament and Other Early Christian Literature*, p. 105.
2. Ernst Käsemann, "Ministry and Community in the New Testament" in *Essays on New Testament Themes*, pp. 80-81.
3. Paul S. Minear, *Images of the Church in the New Testament*, p. 262.
4. Alan Cole, *The Body of Christ*, p. 40.

29). The fact that many in the gathering prophesied was the thing which convinced the unbeliever of God's presence (1 Co 14:24-25). No instructions are given as to who should administer the sacraments. It would appear from the incident of Philip and the eunuch (Ac 8:38) that baptism was not limited to certain officials, although undoubtedly it was normally performed by the recognized leaders of the congregation. If "breaking bread from house to house" (Ac 2:46) is a reference to the Lord's Supper, then the converts themselves did it.

The universality of ministry must not be construed to mean that there is no ordered ministry in the church. The gifts of the Holy Spirit include those designed to provide leadership and structure to the church. They serve, however, as those delegated by the church to perform certain functions in the name of the whole group. Two dangerous attitudes always present themselves in relation to church order. On the one hand, those appointed to leadership assume the position of lord over the flock rather than an undershepherd of Christ. The opposite attitude is similarly disastrous when the people refuse to recognize those appointed to serve among them as the leaders. While all believers are ministers with varied services, the Spirit has distributed the ministries in such a way that the body may function with order (1 Co 14:40).

NATURE OF THE MINISTRY

The one dominant concept of the ministry is that of service. Jesus both taught and lived the ministry of service which was carried on in the practice of the early church.

The ministry of Jesus. The ministry of the New Testament church is in reality the ministry of Christ. The church ministers because of what Christ has done for it; but, in another sense, it ministers as the continuation of Christ's ministry. Thus Paul speaks of that which Christ has wrought by him (Ro 15:18), and Peter reminds the elders that Christ is the chief Shepherd or chief Pastor (1 Pe 5:4), the Shepherd and Bishop of God's people (1 Pe 2:25). It is true that Christ performed a priestly ministry which cannot be emulated by the church in providing redemption through the sacrifice of Himself; nevertheless, the concept of ministry performed by Christ is to be carried on by the church.

The ministry of Christ was characterized by the theme of service. Jesus came as the Servant of the Lord in fulfillment of the prophecies found in the servant songs of Isaiah (42:1-4; 49:1-6; 50:4-7; 52:13—53:12). By word and deed Christ fulfilled the great themes of obedience, witnessing and suffering, climaxing His servanthood with the giving of His life for the world. According to His own word, he "did not come to be served, but to serve, and give His life a ransom for many" (Mk 10:45, NASB).

But Christ not only conceived of His own ministry as service; He made it clear that the same service was to characterize the ministry of His followers. Using His own ministry as the example, Christ instructed His disciples that the ministry does not consist in domination, but in service. In contrast to the world rulers who lord it over their subjects, Christ said, "But it shall not be so among you: but whosoever will be great among you, let him be your minister [*diakonos*, servant]; and whosoever will be chief among you, let him be your servant [*doulos*, slave]" (Mt 20:26-27).

This lesson of servanthood was indelibly imprinted upon the minds of the disciples by the act of Jesus at the Last Supper. Girding Himself with a towel, Jesus performed the work of a household slave in washing the feet of the disciples. To this vivid example, He added these instructions: "If I then, your Lord and Master, have washed your feet; ye also ought to wash one another's feet. For I have given you an example, that ye should do as I have done to you. Verily, verily, I say unto you, The servant is not greater than his lord; neither he that is sent greater than he that sent him" (Jn 13:14-16). According to Jesus, the glory of the ministry is not in terms of status but, rather, in service.

The ministry in the New Testament church. The same concept of service appears in the ministry of the New Testament church. Three words in particular describe the service of all New Testament believers. The first is *doulos*, which means quite simply, a slave, one who serves because he is subject to the will of another.[5] This expression is used primarily to denote the rela-

5. Werner Foerster, "doulos, sundoulos, doulē, douleuō, douleia" in *TDNT*, 2:261.

tionship of believers to their Lord. They are bondslaves of Jesus Christ (Ro 1:1; cf. Ja 1:1; Jude 1; Rev 1:1; 1 Pe 2:16). Voluntary subjection can be the only fitting response to the love of Christ who bought them for Himself. "For you have been bought with a price; therefore glorify God in your body" (1 Co 6:20, NASB).

Along with expressing the most absolute form of service to Christ, *doulos* also applies to service to men. Paul says, "We preach not ourselves, but Christ Jesus the Lord; and ourselves your servants for Jesus' sake" (2 Co 4:5). "I made myself servant unto all, that I might gain the more" (1 Co 9:19). Thus the ministry of members of the church is slavery both to Christ and to one another.

The ministry is also conceived as *leitourgos,* from which is derived the term *liturgy.* This word, which denoted among the Greeks the performance of a public service, came to be used in the Greek translation of the Old Testament as a technical term for priestly service to God. While the New Testament believer does not have a "liturgy" to fulfill in the Old Testament sense, for Christ has fulfilled it once and for all (Heb 8:2, 6; 9:21; 10:11), his ministry can be described by this term in the general sense of service to God and the church. The collection made by the Gentile churches for the impoverished saints at Jerusalem is *leitourgia* (Ro 15:27; 2 Co 9:12), as is also the giving of personal service (Phil 2:30). Paul's preaching of the gospel to the Gentiles is also done as a *leitourgos* of Jesus Christ (Ro 15:16). What is evidently to be understood as prayer and worship is described as ministering (*leitourgein*) to the Lord (Ac 13:2).

However, the most characteristic word to describe the work of the Christian ministry by far is *diakonia,* from which the term *deacon* is derived. The basic idea is the service of a table waiter, but it came to be used generally for service, commonly for menial tasks. The fitness of this word for the ministry of the believer is seen in its "special quality of indicating very personally the service rendered to another." It comes nearer to expressing the concept of a service of love than any of the other Greek terms for serving.[6]

By choosing the term *diakonia* to describe the work of the

6. Hermann W. Beyer, "diakoneō, diakonia, diakonos" in *TDNT,* 2:81.

ministry, the early church deliberately steered clear of the many alternatives which would have pointed toward the concept of "office" and distinction in rank. After an examination of the other possible word choices, Schweizer concludes that in *diakonia* "the New Testament throughout and uniformly chooses a word that is entirely unbiblical and non-religious and never includes association with a particular dignity or position."[7] Thus it can be applied to apostleship (Ac 1:17, 25; Col 1:25) as well as to all saints (Eph 4:12). It is the ministry of the word (Ac 6:4), of reconciliation (2 Co 5:18), of the new covenant (2 Co 3:6), as well as serving tables (Ac 6:1). All in the church serve in the capacity received individually from the Lord (Col 4:17).

MINISTRIES OF THE CHURCH

MINISTRIES AND GIFTS

The ministries of members of the body of Christ are infinitely varied. In Romans 12:6-8, Paul mentions gifts (*charismata*) of prophecy, service, teaching, exhortation, giving and ruling. Writing to the Corinthians in an extended discussion concerning the subject of gifts, he includes the longest list: "For to one is given by the Spirit the word of wisdom; to another the word of knowledge by the same Spirit; to another faith by the same Spirit; to another the gifts of healing by the same Spirit; to another the working of miracles; to another prophecy; to another discerning of spirits; to another divers kinds of tongues; to another the interpretation of tongues" (1 Co 12:8-10). The apostle then gives rank to some of the functions, repeating many of the gifts mentioned earlier and adding those of helps and governments: "And God hath set some in the church, first apostles, secondarily prophets, thirdly teachers, after that miracles, then gifts of healings, helps, governments, diversities of tongues" (1 Co 12:28). In Ephesians 4:11 the gifts are viewed as operating through gifted individuals which the ascended Christ has bestowed on His church: "And He gave some as apostles, and some as evangelists, and some as pastors and teachers" (NASB).

Differences in these lists of gifts evidence the fact that the apostle is not attempting to name all of the gifts but only major representative ministries found in the early church. These were

7. Eduard Schweizer, *Church Order in the New Testament*, pp. 171-76.

ministries of preaching and teaching the Word, ministries of leadership and administration, and finally, those that concerned the physical well-being of the body.

As has been noted, each member of the church has a ministry of some type. Each has a "manifestation of the Spirit" (1 Co 12:7). Some may share similar gifts but these would reveal themselves through different personalities in a great variety of ministries. Nor is there anything in Scripture prohibiting the thought of one person having more than one, producing the possibility of many combinations. No member, however, unites all of the gifts in himself. To do so would be attempting to make oneself a little Christ. Rather, each is to consider soberly or sensibly that particular ministry which God has given him and to make the best use possible of it (Ro 12:4-8). The point to be noted with all of the gifts is that they are "varieties of ministries" for the edification of the body (1 Co 12:5, NASB).[8]

The question of whether all of the gifts which were operative in the New Testament church are permanent ministries for the church age has been greatly debated, especially in recent years with the upsurge of the so-called charismatic movement. The advocates of this position argue that the Scripture nowhere states that some of these gifts are less permanent than others or that some were only for a particular period of church life. Referring particularly to the gift of tongues and other miraculous gifts, Brumback writes that there "is the total absence of *any definite declaration* by the Lord of His intention to cause tongues and other powers to cease shortly after the establishing of the church."[9] Also, reference is made to Romans 11:29, "the gifts and calling of God are without repentance," and to the promise of Christ in the disputed long ending of Mark (16:17-20) that miraculous "signs shall follow them that believe." In addition to this scriptural evidence, it is argued that the needs of the church for the full ministries of the Spirit make all the gifts

8. In his discussion of gifts in 1 Co 12, the apostle uses four interesting words for the various functions in the church. They are *pneumatika* (v. 1, "spiritual gifts"), functions assigned by the Holy Spirit; *charismata* (v. 4, "gifts"), a gift stemming from grace (*charis*); *diakoniai* (v. 5, "ministries," NASB), pointing to the purpose of gifts as service; and, *energēmata* (v. 6, "operations"), the active outworkings of the gifts.
9. Carl Brumback, *"What Meaneth This?"*, p. 61.

just as necessary today as at the beginning of the church. Any absence of them, it is concluded, is not due to God's withdrawal of provision but to the "lukewarmness and unbelief" of God's people.[10]

On the other hand, there is evidence which suggests that not all gifts were intended for the permanent life of the church. In the first instance, the ministries of apostles and prophets, ranked by the apostle Paul as first and second in one of the lists of gifts (1 Co 12:28; cf. Eph 4:11), are declared to be foundational to the church (Eph 2:20). Men with the authority of the apostles are not found in the church today. Rather the church is called to obey the doctrine of those unique ministers of the church, who laid the foundation in their inspired witness to Christ. Similarly, prophets, to the extent that they received direct revelation of God for the needs of the church during its infancy, are no longer with us.[11] The validation of the uniqueness of a foundation ministry is seen in the church's later closing of the canon, which specifically identified and distinguished that which was revealed normative doctrine from that which was built upon it. In the apostles and at least to some extent in the prophets, the principle of the temporary nature of some spiritual gifts is established; and the possibility of other first-century gifts being temporary is open to examination.

Secondly, and closely related to the first argument, is the fact that the miraculous sign gifts are linked with the unique foundational ministry. In his warning against the neglect of "so great salvation," the writer to the Hebrews identifies that salvation as that "which at the first began to be spoken by the Lord, and was confirmed unto us by them that heard him; God also bearing them witness, both with signs and wonders, and with divers miracles, and gifts of the Holy Ghost, according to his own will" (Heb 2:3-4). In this statement three different relations to the message are specified: (1) the Lord began to speak it, then there were (2) those ("them") who confirmed it to (3) the people ("us") of the early church. The signs and miracles are specifically related to the second group, the immediate circle around the

10. Donald Gee, *The Pentecostal Movement*, p. 10.
11. For a discussion of the meaning of these ministries and their foundational position, see pp. 82-83, 200-203.

Lord who confirmed His message, as God's authentication of their ministry. This special use of these gifts is confirmed by the apostle Paul's references to working "signs, and wonders, and mighty deeds" as "signs of an apostle" (2 Co 12:12), and to bringing the Gentiles to Christ through preaching the gospel accompanied by "mighty signs and wonders, by the power of the Spirit of God" (Ro 15:18-19). This is not to imply that only apostles worked signs, for the New Testament records the working of signs by others also (e.g., Acts 8:6) and no such limitation is implied in 1 Corinthians 12. But it is suggestive of the fact that the sign gifts were for this early apostolic era, during which the final word of God concerning the fulfillment of the promised salvation in Christ was not complete and its messengers still needed authentication.

The sign use of many of these miraculous gifts by the early church is in sharp contradiction to the use made of them by many contemporary advocates. For example, the Apostle Paul healed many as authentication to his ministry (see Acts 19:11 ff.) but did not—as evidenced in the cases of Timothy (1 Ti 5:23) and Trophimus (2 Ti 4:20), who both suffered illness—suggest this gift for the health of the saints; but it is often advertised for such today through healing ministries.[12]

Finally, the general cessation of miracles in the history of the church following the apostolic era substantiates the fact that not all the gifts were to be continued in the same way.[13] The rejection of this conclusion, by insisting that the unspiritual nature of the church caused the diminishing of these ministries and that the need of the church for them remained constant, is negated by God's use of miracles in biblical history. Instead of a record of continual miracle working among God's people, the Scriptures show that miracles were prominent in three main periods: the time of Moses, that of Elijah and Elisha, and the New Testament

---

12. For a good discussion of the gift of tongues along this same line, see Anthony A. Hoekema, *What About Tongue Speaking?*
13. For the classic examination of the historical evidence, see B. B. Warfield, *Miracles: Yesterday and Today, True and False.* He argues that the miraculous gifts were the credentials of the final summing up of the revelation of Christ and that all of the historical facts of the New Testament and the early church Fathers can be explained by relating these gifts to the apostles and to those who had them conferred upon them by, apostles (pp. 21-28).

era of Christ and the apostles. Men such as Abraham, David, and John the Baptist performed no miracles, according to our knowledge. Apparently, miraculous signs were used by God for authentication during certain epochs more than others.

On the basis of both the biblical and historical evidence, it seems most reasonable to conclude that certain of the spiritual gifts active in the early church are no longer given to God's people. This is not to circumscribe the Spirit's activity and certainly not to deny divine miracles. God can and has worked miraculously throughout the history of the church, but these miracles are not necessarily the manifestation of these early gifts. For the most part, the practice and theology today associated with the sign gifts bear little resemblance to the New Testament pattern.[14]

MINISTRIES AND "OFFICES"

The fact that all members have spiritual gifts to contribute to the edifying of the church and that these are all equally "ministries" does not, however, preclude distinctions among the ministries. Some of the gifts provided for a certain ordered ministry which may be termed "office" so long as they are not distinguished from ministries.[15] For the orderly operation of the church it was necessary that certain individuals be recognized as being endowed for certain regular ministries. However, the authority which these ministries might entail resided not in the position itself but in the God-given function to minister to the church. In recognizing such a ministry, the church as the Spirit-controlled body was recognizing the ministry of leadership provided by the Head.

THE ORDERED MINISTRIES

It is common to classify the ordered ministries as general and local. The former served the church at large while the latter related to the local church as permanent officers.

---

14. Cf. Hoekema.
15. New Testament ministries are never formally termed "offices." Rather, they are always noted in terms of function. In Ro 11:13, the word "office" (AV) is *diakonia*, "ministry." "The office of a bishop" in 1 Ti 3:1 is literally "overseership," while in vv. 10, 13 the words "use the office of a deacon" are the translation of only the verb "to serve."

GENERAL MINISTRIES

The general ministries consisted of apostles, prophets, evangelists and perhaps teachers (Eph 4:11). These ministries are not chosen by the church, as are the local offices, but are Christ-given ministries to the church which can only be recognized and regulated in the assembly. In this sense they are more properly "gifts" than "offices." Each of these ministries involves in some way the ministry of the Word. Some appear to be foundational in nature (Eph 2:20; 3:5), passing from the scene when the canon of revelation is complete, while others continue permanently in the church, being associated with the local offices.

Apostles. The apostles provided a special ministry in the early church, for they alone were directly appointed by Christ. The word *apostle* means basically a "sent one" or "messenger." While it can refer to an ordinary messenger, this is not the usual term for such, but denotes being sent on a special purpose. In the New Testament the additional idea of being sent with full authority is always present; in this case it is the authority of Christ.[16]

It is not easy to formulate a clear picture of the New Testament apostle. The name is applied first to the circle of the twelve as the original bearers of the New Testament message. That these had a special place of importance is seen in their names being written on the twelve foundations of the wall of the New Jerusalem (Rev 21:14).

But the name also was applied to Paul, who considered himself "not a whit behind the very chiefest apostles" (2 Co 11:5), and, to a wider circle, to the first missionaries or their most prominent representatives. This included Barnabas who with Paul was sent out from the Antiochian church (Ac 14:4, 14); James, the Lord's brother (1 Co 15:7); the lesser-known Andronicus and Junias (Ro 16:7; NASB); and others unnamed (1 Co 15:7).

Although the distinction cannot be found in the term or in explicit biblical estimations of the wider and narrower circles of apostles, the difference appears to rest on the basis of their apostolate. Barnabas, as one sent forth with the gospel, is called an "apostle," but he is never given the more precise description

16. Karl Heinrich Rengstorf, "apostolos" in *TDNT*, 1:421.

of an "apostle of Jesus Christ" which is found so often in the Pauline salutations. Thus it would appear that there were two categories of apostles, those sent specially by the church (2 Co 8:23; Phil 2:25; Ac 14:4, 14), and those who had been directly commissioned by the risen Lord. The apostle Paul rests his equality with the greatest of apostles upon the fact that he had "seen Jesus Christ" (1 Co 9:1) and had been commissioned to preach the gospel (Gal 1:16). The primacy of the narrower circle of apostles does not appear in the exercising of administrative authority in the early church. Rather, it is seen in the proclamation of the original authoritative message of the gospel.

As hearers of the original revelation, the apostles' function is necessarily limited to the foundations of the church (cf. Eph 2:20; 3:5; 2 Pe 3:2; Jude 17). "The apostles belong to the church's infancy and are given to bear a special witness. They do not represent a permanent element in the life of the church other than the witness they left behind, which is enshrined for us in the Scripture."[17]

Prophets. Frequently appearing with apostles in the early church and next in rank to them were the prophets (1 Co 12:28; Eph 2:20; 3:5; 4:11). These were individuals directly prompted by the Spirit to speak forth a message from God. Their revelations included both forthtelling and foretelling, with the emphasis upon the former. Only twice in the New Testament is a prophet seen predicting future events. Once Agabus predicted a coming famine (Ac 11:28), and later the same prophet foresaw the bondage of Paul before the apostle went to Jerusalem (Ac 21:10-11). The primary function of the prophets was to bring God's message to the early church for the purpose of edification (1 Co 14:3-4). This was done either through bringing new truth, or by giving insight into truth which was already known. Judas and Silas are seen as prophets exhorting "the brethren with many words" upon the occasion of bringing the decision of the Jerusalem council to Antioch. This action was probably characteristic of the prophets' function in the church.

It does not appear that they were used as the apostles to bring permanent revelation but, rather, a message from God to meet

17. Leon Morris, *Ministers of God,* p. 48.

the needs of the immediate situation of the church.[18] They therefore held an important place in the church, being foundational along with the apostles (Eph 2:20), although still subject to them (1 Co 14:37). Primarily through the order of prophets, the Spirit guided the church during the time when revelation was incomplete and the knowledge of the faith was yet very imperfect among the new converts. The ministry of the prophet as speaking inspired utterances from God gradually died out after the end of the apostolic age and the completion of the canon. Their place of exhortation was taken by the regular local ministry of pastor-teachers.

Evangelists. Only three references are found in the New Testament to the ministry of an evangelist. Acts 21:8 tells of Philip the evangelist, who is probably the one who preached throughout Samaria (Ac 8:4-8) and instructed the Ethiopian eunuch (Ac 8:26-40). Paul exhorts Timothy to "do the work of an evangelist" (2 Ti 4:5), and the office of "evangelist" is next to that of the prophet as one given to the church by the risen Lord (Eph 4:11).

As the name *evangelist* (*euangelistēs*) suggests, being related to the word translated *gospel* (*euangelion*), the evangelist was one who proclaimed the glad tidings of Jesus Christ more or less along the idea of a traveling missionary. The apostles who likewise proclaimed the gospel would have functioned as evangelists, but were superior in rank to the evangelists because of their apostolic position (cf. Ac 8:14 ff.; Eph 4:11). The ministry of the evangelist is not limited simply to the preaching of the salvation message to the unsaved. The church "stands" in the gospel (1 Co 15:1), and it is the criterion by which it lives (Phil 1:27; 2 Co 9:13). The work of the evangelist, therefore, also included the establishing of the church in the whole counsel of God. This activity as a church-planter has a continuing place in the ongoing of the church toward the fulfillment of the Great Commission, especially since the departure of the apostles.

Teachers. Mentioned third after the apostles and prophets in 1 Corinthians 12:28, and fourth after the apostles, prophets and evangelist in Ephesians 4:11, are the teachers. In Ephesians they are listed with pastors, signifying that as the pastor is responsible

18. C. E. B. Cranfield, *A Commentary on Romans 12-13, Scottish Journal of Theology Occasional Papers No. 12*, p. 29.

for feeding the flock, teaching would be part of his function. The mention of teaching separately (1 Co 12:28; Ac 13:1) implies that there were also teachers who were not pastors, as such, although teaching was probably most often a function of another office (cf. 1 Ti 3:2). The teachers, in contrast to the prophets who are directly inspired of the Spirit, "edify the congregation by means of their own clearer understanding."[19] Their function becomes increasingly important as the foundational prophets pass from the scene. Even as the missionary activity of the apostles passes over to the evangelist, so the prophetic work of edification is carried on by the teachers. It is perhaps because of this historical sequence, as well as their relative importance in the early church, that these last two ministries of evangelist and pastor-teacher come after that of apostle and prophet.[20] The ministry of teaching in the church carries with it grave responsibility, noted in the warning of James: "Be not many of you teachers, my brethren, knowing that we shall receive heavier judgment" (Ja 3:1, ASV).

LOCAL OFFICERS

The New Testament refers to two permanent officers in the local church.[21] The first is that of the bishop, elder or pastor which, as will be shown in the following discussion, all refer to the same office. Besides this office, which deals primarily with the governmental *oversight* of the church, there is the office of deacon, which concerns the ordered *service* of the church. There is no evidence that either of these two offices was ever held apart from a local church, nor did their sphere of authority extend beyond the assembly of which they were members and officers. Each church had its own elders and deacons (cf. Ac 20:17; Phil 1:1). That these are the only two offices of the church is seen in the fact that when Paul deals with the qualifications for church officers, only these two are mentioned (1 Ti 3:1-13; Titus 1:5 ff.). In the one salutation to a church in which the officers of the church are specially mentioned, "bishops" and "deacons" only

19. Karl Heinrich Rengstorf, "didaskalos" in *TDNT*, 2:158.
20. Ibid.
21. J. B. Lightfoot, "The Christian Ministry" in *Saint Paul's Epistle to the Philippians*, pp. 181 ff.; Edwin Hatch, *The Organization of the Early Christian Churches*, pp. 26 ff.; Morris, pp. 72 ff.

are noted indicating that these comprise the leadership of the church (Phil 1:1).

Identity of elder, bishop and pastor. The terms elder or presbyter, bishop and pastor all refer to the same office in the New Testament. That elder and bishop concern the same person is manifest by the following evidence both from the New Testament and from the early writings of the Fathers:

1. In Acts 20:17 Paul calls for the elders to meet him, but in speaking to them later he refers to these same officers as "over seers [bishops]" (v. 28).

2. In Titus 1:5 the apostle gives instruction for ordaining "elders" in every city. In subsequently listing their qualifications, he states, "A bishop must be blameless" (v. 7).

3. The same identification appears in the description of qualifications in 1 Timothy 3. After listing those for a "bishop" (vv. 1-7), he proceeds immediately to those for the office of a deacon. No mention is made of the elder, but later, in reference to the elder, he ascribes to him the functions performed by the bishop (cf. 1 Ti 5:17 with 3:4). Thus the two terms are apparently used for the same officers.

4. A similar identification is made by Peter if the reading of the Authorized Version is accepted. Speaking to the "elders" (1 Pe 5:1), Peter charges them to "feed the flock of God which is among you, taking the oversight [doing the work of an overseer or bishop]" (v. 2). Even if it is argued that this phrase is not in the original text, being omitted by the best Greek manuscripts, its inclusion later gives evidence that an early scribe could apply this function to the elders with no sense of incongruity.

5. In the formal salutation to the church at Philippi, Paul addresses "all the saints . . . with the bishops and deacons." It would be incredible for the apostle to overlook a third order of ministers, namely, the elders. It is much more probable that he was also speaking of the elders in the term *bishop.*

6. This identification continues beyond the New Testament writings. Clement of Rome, writing at the end of the first century, along with the *Didache,* represents the church's ministry by the biblical usage of "bishops and deacons." Although bishop and presbyter (elder) begin to be separated in the beginning of the second century, yet in the fourth century when the leaders

of the church began to examine the apostolic records more critically, the identity of the two was asserted by such distinguished scholars as Hilary, Jerome, Chrysostom and others. Lightfoot notes that "in every one of the extant commentaries on the epistles containing the crucial passages, whether Greek or Latin, before the close of the fifth century, this identity is affirmed."[22]

It is also possible to identify the bishop or elder with the term *pastor:*

1. In Acts 20:28 the elders are instructed "to feed" the church. This term (*poimainō*) means to act as a shepherd and is related to the term for pastor (*poimēn*), which signifies a shepherd. Thus the elders were to act as shepherd to the church or to pastor it.

2. The same instruction is given to the elders in 1 Peter 5:1-2. They are to "feed" (literally, "shepherd") the flock of God or function as pastors.

3. A further indication that bishop and pastor are joined together in the same office is the reference to Christ as "the Shepherd and Bishop of your souls" (1 Pe 2:25) .

The term *elder*, which meant first a senior, elderly man (cf. 1 Ti 5:1-3) , denoted—with respect to church office—the dignity and authority which were associated with mature spiritual experience and understanding. While *elder* thus signifies the dignity of the individual, *bishop* refers to the function of the elder. The word means literally "an overseer," coming from *epi*, "over," and *skopeō*, "to look or watch." Thus it refers to the position of one whose responsibility it was to watch over the church. The term *pastor* also refers to the function of the elder as a shepherd of the church. Although it occurs only once as a term for an officer of the church (Eph 4:11) , the work of a shepherd is spoken of as belonging to the office of an elder (Ac 20:28; 1 Pe 5:1-2) .

Origin of the elder. It is generally agreed that the church took over the office of elder from the organization of the Jewish synagogue, for over each synagogue was a board of the elders responsible for civil and ecclesiastical affairs of the Jewish communal life. Since Christianity was first regarded as simply a branch of Judaism that believed that Jesus was the long-awaited Messiah and, in fact, the congregations were called synagogues in Jewish

22. Lightfoot, p. 99.

areas (Ja 2:2, ASV), it is not surprising that their organization would be modeled after the Jewish pattern. Apparently the similarity was not exact because, along with the Jewish elders, the organization of the synagogue included a "ruler of the synagogue" who was responsible for public worship and had the task of presiding over it (cf. Lk 8:41). In the church this responsibility, as we shall see, is combined with that of the elder. Nevertheless, the take-over of this office from the Jewish structure explains how elders appear naturally without any explanation in the church and, as would be expected, first in Jerusalem, as suggested by Acts 11:30. Paul and Barnabas then appoint elders in every church on their first missionary journey (Ac 14:23), and they are found in Ephesus (Ac 20:17), throughout Asia Minor (1 Pe 5:1; cf. 1:1) and among the Jewish dispersion (Ja 5:14; cf. 1:1). Among the Gentile churches, the elders were frequently called bishops or overseers (e.g., Phil 1:1), a term which was commonly used for the office of supervision in the Graeco-Roman world.[23] However, *bishop* did not completely replace *elder*, even among Gentile churches (1 Ti 5:17).

Duties of the elder. Elders are charged with the general oversight and care of the church. Their functions include administrative, pastoral and instructional duties.

The administrative position of the elder is clear from the title *overseer*. As Christ cared for the souls of His people as their Overseer (1 Pe 2:25), so the elders as those under Him watch over those committed to their charge. They are those who "rule" (*proistēmi*, literally, "stand before") the church (1 Ti 5:17). Elders are also undoubtedly in mind when Paul writes to the Thessalonian believers "to know them which labour among you, and are over you [proistamenous] in the Lord" (1 Th 5:12). Again the writer to the Hebrews certainly refers to elders in the description, "them which have the rule over you" (*hēgeomai*, literally, to lead or guide (Heb 13:7, 17, 24). As such the elders "watch" over the souls of their people as "they that must give account" to the Lord of the church (Heb 13:17); they "take care of the church of God" (1 Ti 3:5).

This leadership is not that of "lording it over" the church (1 Pe 5:3), but, rather, it is patterned after Christ who taught His

23. Beyer, "episcopos" in *TDNT* 2:611-14.

disciples that their greatness would not be like that of the world, but rather a "leader" must be "as one who serves" (Lk 22:26, Berkeley).

Elders also had the pastoral care of the church. Peter exhorted the elders to "feed [*poimainō*, to tend] the flock of God which is among you" (1 Pe 5:2). Paul likewise told the Ephesian elders, "Take heed therefore unto yourselves, and to all the flock . . . to feed [*poimainō*, tend] the church of God" (Ac 20:28). The elder pastors the flock with the shepherd's heart toward his sheep, performing the many functions necessary for the care of the church. The shepherd leads the flock, guiding it in the path of righteousness. It is his duty also to protect the flock from grievous wolves that would destroy it (Ac 20:29). The faithful shepherd-elder does not act as the hireling, who is only motivated by money and flees when danger comes (Jn 10:12-13), but, like the good Shepherd, he is willing to sacrifice his all for the flock.

The guidance and protection are accomplished primarily through the ministry of the Word of God. Paul discharged his pastoral duties with the Ephesians by declaring to them all the counsel of God (Ac 20:27), admonishing each one with tears (v. 31). The importance of feeding the flock with the Word is seen in Jesus' words to Peter (Jn 21:15-17). Twice He instructs him to provide food for the sheep (vv. 15, 17), and once more the general word for *tend* is used (v. 16). In the spiritual care of the flock, feeding from the Word of God is of primary importance.

The pastoral duties of the elder also require the comfort and encouragement of those who are weak and the discipline of the erring. Although addressed to the "brethren" as the responsibility of all, the instruction of Paul is particularly applicable to the pastors of the church: "Admonish the unruly, encourage the fainthearted, help the weak, be patient with all men" (1 Th 5:14, NASB). The word "encourage" means "to speak to someone in a friendly way"[24] and carries the thought of exercising tenderness in counseling, and encouraging the fainthearted for the battle of the Christian life. Helping the weak signifies cleaving to them and not forsaking them in their difficult moments.

24. Gustav Stahlin, "paramutheomai, paramuthia, paramuthion" in *TDNT*, 5:817.

Paul also urged the Ephesian elders to "help the weak" (Ac 20:35, NASB). They were to minister, giving themselves to support those standing in any need. All of this is to be done with the attitude of "long-suffering to all."

Admonition is mentioned separately, specifically as the function of the leaders (1 Th 5:12). While the tone of this word "is brotherly, it is big-brotherly" with "the thought of blame to some wrongdoing which is being rebuked."[25] The shepherd must discipline the erring, yet with all tenderness, seeking their restoration and not their harm. The great apostle provides an example in his rebuke of the Corinthians: "I do not write these things to shame you, but to admonish you as my beloved children" (1 Co 4:14, NASB).

A third general function of the elder is that of instructing the church. This is naturally involved in leading and shepherding the church, yet considerable separate attention is given to the necessity of teaching by the elder-pastors of the church. For this office one must be "able to teach" (1 Ti 3:2, NASB). The teaching function is so closely related to the pastor's office that Paul terms it "pastor-teacher" (Eph 4:11).[26] It is true that some elders in the New Testament church labored "in the word and doctrine" more than others (1 Ti 5:17), providing the basis for the distinction commonly made between ruling and teaching elders. The latter are those worthy of special "honor" or remuneration, as the term often signifies and the context (v. 18) demands.[27] They are thus more full-time pastors than are the other elders. Nevertheless, every elder, whether "ruling" or "teaching," is required to know the Word and subscribe to it "that he may be able both to exhort in sound doctrine and to refute those who contradict" (Titus 1:9, NASB). This task of instruction required that the pastor-teacher faithfully pass on the tradition received from the apostles. No reinterpretation or reformulation of truth is considered, but rather faithfulness to the Word. "To teach rightly, a person only need to be 'reliable'—that is, he must hand

25. Leon Morris, *The First and Second Epistles to the Thessalonians*, p. 166.
26. Most commentators agree that the placing of both of these terms under one article signifies that both describe the same person.
27. Arndt and Gingrich, p. 825.

on the message that he has received, without leaving it for new ways of his own choosing."[28]

The office of the elder-pastor is not an easy task. It is described as toiling or laboring (Ac 20:35; 1 Th 5:12; 1 Ti 5:17). The Greek word *kopiaō* indicates not simply the issue of work, but the cost associated with it, a toiling which results in weariness. Paul constantly used this term to express his own pastoral and missionary activities among the churches (1 Co 15:10; Gal 4:11), and those of others (1 Co 15:58; 2 Co 10:15). Only divine love can provide the motivation for this self-sacrificing, laborious toil (1 Th 1:3).

Qualifications of the elder. The type of individual required for the office of elder is clearly outlined in the Scriptures. Qualifications are listed concerning his own personal character, his family, his relation to others both inside and outside the church, and his abilities.

Both lists of qualifications begin with the *general qualification* of blamelessness (1 Ti 3:2; Titus 1:6). The Greek words, although different in both instances, each carry the idea of being irreproachable. Not that such a person will never be reproached, but no just ground will be found for any criticism.

The *personal qualifications* demand that the elder be of high moral character. He is to be "the husband of one wife" (1 Ti 3:2; Titus 1:6). This probably does not mean that a single man cannot serve or that an elder cannot marry a second time even after his wife's death. Rather, taking the more literal rendering, "a one-wife husband," it requires that a man be a loyal husband living in a pure marriage relationship without adulterous relationships or attitudes (cf. Mt 5:27-28). In view of the moral conditions of the world at the time, this regulation was a necessary demand and signified a change of life.[29]

Additional qualifications listed in 1 Timothy 3, relative to what this officer must be in himself, require him to be "temperate" ("vigilant"),[30] that is, not given to excess in any area of

28. Schweizer, p. 80.
29. Cf. William Barclay, *The Letters to Timothy, Titus and Philemon*, pp. 88-90. For the different interpretations of "the husband of one wife," see Homer A. Kent, Jr., *The Pastoral Epistles*, pp. 126-30.
30. The quoted words through the sections on the qualifications of the offices are from the New American Standard Bible. Those in the parentheses are the rendering of the Authorized Version.

life, "prudent" ("sober") or sensible and of sound mind, and
"respectable" ("of good behaviour"), having his life well ordered.
The list in Titus 1 adds further that the elder be "not self-willed"
or "so pleased with himself that nothing else pleases him, and
he comes to please nobody."[31] He must also be "self-controlled"
("temperate") or master of himself, "just," giving men their due,
and "devout" ("holy"), performing his duty toward God. Both
lists further require than an elder be free from all covetousness
of money. He is to be "free from the love of money" ("not
covetous") and "not fond of sordid gain" ("not given to filthy
lucre"). His life must not be concerned with amassing material
things.

The *family life* of the elder is to be in accord with God's order
portrayed throughout the Scriptures. His children must be under
his control in all dignity to qualify him to lead in church affairs
(1 Ti 3:4-5). They should share the faith of their father and
adorn that faith with godly lives (Titus 1:6).

Certain characteristics also qualify an elder in his *relation to
others*. These may be classified as personal characteristics which
are involved in interpersonal relationships. The elder is not to
be "addicted to wine" (1 Ti 3:3, NASB; Titus 1:7). From the
literal rendering of the Greek, "not beside wine," this also came
to mean a quarrelsome person as a result of drunkenness. Closely
related is the prohibition of a "pugnacious" ("no striker") attitude or a "quick-tempered temperament" ("not soon angry").

In contrast to these negative statements, an elder must be
"gentle" ("patient") and "uncontentious" ("not a brawler")
toward others. His concern for people must express itself in
hospitality. The original word is literally "love of strangers."
This was particularly important in the early church, as there
were not many suitable accommodations for Christian travelers,
since most places were expensive, usually dirty, and immoral. In
addition, there were those believers who were destitute and flee-
ing persecution. Hospitality was the expression of the bond of
love in Christ and was enjoined upon all believers (Ro 12:13;
Heb 13:2; 1 Pe 4:9). Closely connected with this quality was
the requirement to be a lover of what is good (Titus 1:8). Some
have interpreted this to mean a lover of good men (AV), but it

31. Barclay, p. 269.

probably involves devotion to good whenever it is found. According to the interpretation of the early church, it denoted the "unwearing activity of love."[32]

While the foregoing characteristics relative to interpersonal relations would apply to the elder's deportment both with those in the church and those outside, the apostle specifically notes that the elder must have a good reputation among the outsiders. It is from these that converts must be won, and it is therefore necessary that especially the leaders of the church live in such a way that no charge of hypocrisy can be leveled against them, which would harm the testimony of the whole group.

Relative to the faith, the elder must not be a "novice" (1 Ti 3:6). The Greek word means literally "newly planted" and refers to the fact that the office of overseer is not for the new convert but demands spiritual maturation. The concept of thrusting a believer into such a position in order to encourage his maturing is prohibited. The necessity of Christian maturity is for the avoidance of pride which sudden exaltation could stimulate, resulting in his judgment, even as it did with the devil. Furthermore, the elder must be "able to teach" (1 Ti 3:2, NASB); he must be able to hold fast "the faithful word which is in accordance with the teaching, that he may be able both to exhort in sound doctrine and to refute those who contradict" (Titus 1:9, NASB). This ability requires that he be mature in sound doctrine himself and be able to use it.

The fact that two extensive lists of qualifications for the office of elder are recorded in the New Testament evidences God's concern over the leadership of the church and the necessity for care in choosing such leaders.

Number of elders. The evidence of the New Testament points to a plurality of elders in a church. Each time the term appears it is plural.[33] Paul and Barnabas ordained "elders in every church" (Ac 14:23, cf. Titus 1:5), and it was a group of elders that Paul called from Ephesus in order to give them his farewell (Ac 20:17). Again, in addressing the leaders of the church at

---

32. Walter Grundmann, "philagathos" in *TDNT*, 1:18.
33. This is true of subapostolic literature as well. It is not until the second century that the rise of a single bishop is found. Hatch, p. 82; E. M. B. Green, *Called to Serve: Ministry and Ministers in the Church*, pp. 42-50.

Philippi, the apostle mentions the "bishops and deacons" (Phil 1:1). If there were deacons (plural) here, there was also a plurality of elders. James also confirms this, instructing the sick to "call for the elders of the church" (Ja 5:14; cf. Ac 21:18; 1 Ti 5:17; 1 Pe 5:1).

The two exceptions to this plural use, upon close examination, do not refute this consistent pattern. From the singular "bishop" in 1 Timothy 3:2 and Titus 1:5-7 some have argued for the possibility of a single elder[34] or for a third office of a single monarchial episcopate over the elders.[35] The context, however, refutes this. Titus is told to ordain "elders in every city. . . . If any be blameless. . . . For a bishop must be blameless" (Titus 1:5-7). The singular is clearly used as a generic reference to the bishop as a type, and the same is true of 1 Timothy 3:1.[36] Proof of this interpretation is seen in the fact that Timothy was ministering in Ephesus (1 Ti 1:3) where, as has been noted, there was a plurality of elders (Ac 20:17). The singular use of elder in 2 John 1 and 3 John 1 may be explained by the fact that the early church took over the Jewish system of teaching or Tannaite elders whereby a famous rabbi such as Hillel was known in the absolute sense of "the elder." It is probable that John, author of these letters, had acquired a similar reputation in Asia and was known simply as "the elder." This same title of honor continued in the postapostolic church.[37] Thus, the reference here is not to a single-elder church but, rather, a noted elder. The apostle Peter, likewise, called himself an elder, but certainly not in the sense of being the single elder in a certain church (1 Pe 5:1).

It is doubtful also that the "angels of the seven churches" (Rev 1:20 ff.) are references to the pastors. One of the churches, that of Ephesus, is known to have had a plurality of elders (Ac 20:17). Furthermore, this would exalt the elder above the con-

34. A. H. Strong, *Systematic Theology*, p. 916.
35. A. M. Farrer in *The Apostolic Ministry*, ed. Kenneth E. Kirk, pp. 159 ff., cited by Morris, *Ministers of God*, p. 75.
36. Beyer, "episkopos" in *TDNT*, 2:617; cf. Schweizer, p. 85; Morris, *Ministers of God*, p. 73; Green, p. 39; Hatch, p. 82.
37. Green, pp. 39-40. John Stott derives added significance from the age expressed in the term "elder": "It would be particularly appropriate to the apostle who had outlived the other apostles" (*The Epistles of John*, p. 40).

gregation in the figure of a star compared with that of a lamp-
stand for the church (1:20, NASB). In the New Testament the
elder is always a member of the community of believers. As
"angels" (*angeloi*) elsewhere in the Revelation always refer to
real angels, and angels are also represented by stars (cf. Rev 9:1,
and probably 12:4), the angels of the churches are probably to
be understood as real angels representing the churches, corresponding in some way to the angels that are related to nations
(Dan 10:13, 20-21; 12:1).[38]

The plurality of elders does not necessitate that all be considered equal (cf. 1 Ti 5:17). It does, however, avoid the concept
of a single ruler of a congregation and distributes authority as
well as responsibility among several, thus corresponding to the
Jewish community from which the office of elder was adopted.

Appointment and term of office. Although the New Testament
nowhere gives explicit instruction on the method of choosing
elders, the evidence from the actual practice of the early church
indicates that they were chosen by the entire assembly. In the
appointment of seven for church service in Acts 6:1-6, the apostles
instructed the community as a whole to "look ye out among you
seven men" (v. 3). The congregation then "chose" the seven
(v. 5) and presented them to the apostles for appointment to
their office (v. 6). The same procedure was probably followed
in the appointment of elders by Paul and Barnabas for the
churches on their first missionary journey (Ac 14:23). "Ordained,"
in agreement with the original etymological import of the Greek
word, means "elect by raising hands," but it can also simply mean
"appoint, install," without reference to the manner of selection.[39]
Since the action is that of Paul and Barnabas, it must refer primarily to the appointment of the elders to their office. However,
it would appear that the use of this word, along with the clear
precedent of the selection of the seven (Ac 6), suggests that the
method of appointment was by the selection of the church.[40]

---

38. Gerhard Kittel, "angelos" in *TDNT*, 1:86-87; R. H. Charles, *A Critical
    and Exegetical Commentary on the Revelation of St. John*, 1:34; Light-
    foot, pp. 199-200.
39. Arndt and Gingrich, p. 889.
40. H. A. W. Meyer, *Critical and Exegetical Handbook to the Acts of the
    Apostles*, p. 275.

Although a different word is used by Titus in the appointment of elders (Titus 1:5), this method of appointment could well apply here also.[41]

Selection of leaders by the church's vote is further suggested by other instances of collective activity in selecting individuals for specific duties. Those traveling with the apostle Paul to aid in taking collections for the suffering Jews in Judea were "chosen of the churches" (2 Co 8:19; cf. 1 Co 16:3). The church as a congregation sent Paul and Barnabas to the Jerusalem council (Ac 15:2-3), and when they arrived at Jerusalem they were received by the church and the apostles and elders (v. 4). At the conclusion of the meeting it was the decision of the "apostles and elders with the whole church, to send chosen men . . . to Antioch" (v. 22). While the subject of the sending of Paul and Barnabas in the first mission to the Gentiles is unclear, it seems best to view it also as an action of the entire church (Ac 13:1-4). Hort notes, "The members of the Ecclesia itself are bidden to set Barnabas and Saul apart; and it is the members of the Ecclesia itself that dismiss them with fasting and prayer and laying on of hands, whether the last act was performed by all of them, or only by representatives of the whole body, official or other."[42]

The manner in which Paul refers to the Ephesian elders as having been placed in that responsibility by the Holy Spirit (Ac 20:28), with no reference to any appointment by himself, also suggests that this was done by the Spirit through the community.[43] This would be in accordance with the pattern of the New Testament that, outside of the apostles who were appointed directly by the risen Christ, the Lord of the church speaks through the church as a whole, each member being indwelt by His Spirit.[44]

The length of term for the elder is nowhere stated in the biblical record. It would appear then that each congregation could use its own discretion. In a small congregation the same individuals may serve for a lengthy time, perhaps through re-

41. An alternative explanation to church selection in these two instances is that these are cases of newly formed churches requiring special appointment by the apostles and their emissaries. Cf. Schweizer, p. 190; F. J. A. Hort, *The Christian Ecclesia*, p. 146.
42. Hort, p. 64; compare Ac 6:6 on the change from the congregation to its leaders.
43. Ibid., p. 100.
44. Schweizer, pp. 189-93.

election, while in a larger congregation this responsibility may more profitably be passed around, as there may be many who meet the qualifications. Even though the title *elder* may be retained for an individual following his term of office, it must be remembered that his authority is applicable only for the term elected, and then only in the congregation of his election and not in other churches.

Response of the congregation to the elder. Not only does the elder have an obligation to the congregation, but the congregation also bears responsibilities toward its leaders. Paul beseeches the brethren at Thessalonica to "know" those over them (1 Th 5:12). The word "know" has the idea of appreciating their true worth.[45] They were also to "esteem them very highly" (v. 13), which signifies that they were to regard them as particularly important,[46] and this was not to be done unwillingly, but rather, "in love." The writer to the Hebrews exhorts his readers to obey their leaders and submit to them (13:17).

This attitude is stated broadly in 1 Timothy 5:17 as honoring the elders. Here "double honor" involves not only respect and obedience, but tangible remuneration, as the following context indicates. It is not that the word "honor" when used of material support denotes pay or wages, but rather "honor" which expresses itself in material remuneration when needed.[47] It is evidence of *lack* of honor for a church to fail to support adequately those which are called to devote themselves entirely to spiritual leadership. This responsibility to support the ministry is insisted upon again and again by Paul, although he himself did not request it (cf. Gal 6:6; 1 Th 2:6, 9; 2 Co 11:7 ff.; Phil 4:10 ff.; 1 Co 9:11).

The honor of elders signifies also that they must not be hastily charged with wrongdoing: "Against an elder receive not an accusation, but before two or three witnesses" (1 Ti 5:19). By the very nature of their office, elders are often exposed to misrepresentation and unjust criticism. These must be rejected, for honor would express itself in trust. If sin is proven, however, they are to be rebuked "before all, that others also may fear"

45. Morris, *The First and Second Epistles to the Thessalonians*, p. 165.
46. Friedrich Buchsel, "hēgomai" in *TDNT*, 2:907.
47. William Hendricksen, *I-II Timothy and Titus, New Testament Commentary*, p. 181.

(v. 20). The public nature of their office demands public discipline.

The respect which a qualified leader deserves in the church is finally seen in the exhortation to "remember them which have the rule over you," referring to those who had died (Heb 13:7). Their godly lives and ministry were to be an example to follow and a continuing source of encouragement in the life of the people.

DEACONS

Meaning. The term *deacon* comes from the Greek *diakonos,* meaning "servant." When it occurs in Greek prose literature, it generally denotes a servant or a slave within the household whose duty consists of waiting on his master at the table and sometimes doing marketing for him.[48] The term along with its corresponding verb, *diakoneō,* "to serve," and noun, *diakonia,* "service," is used very generally throughout the New Testament to denote service of various kinds. Christ came "to minister" (Mk 10:45) and is a "minister of the circumcision" (Ro 15:8). It is used of the ministry of Paul and other apostles (1 Ti 1:12; 2 Co 3:6; 6:4; Eph 3:7); of Apollos (1 Co 3:5); of Timothy (1 Ti 4:6); and others who performed service in the church (Ac 19:22; Col 4:7). It also refers simply to general service in the church (1 Co 16:15). Because of this wide nontechnical usage, it is difficult to clearly distinguish instances referring to the office.[49] But it is obviously an office in 1 Timothy 3:8-13, where qualifications are listed, and also in Philippians 1:1, where mention is made of "the bishops and deacons." Apparently the term progressed from its general meaning of service to its usage as applied to a special church ministry.

Origin of the deacon. The origin of the office of deacon is not clearly stated in the New Testament, nor does there appear to be any antecedent to this office of the church in the Jewish community, as in the case of elders. The synagogue did have an attendant called the Chazan, but his function was confined to the ministries

48. Hort, p. 204.
49. The Authorized Version renders *diakonos* as "minister" 20 times, "servant" 7 times, and "deacon" 3 times.

of worship.[50] There were also collectors of alms, but neither service provides a prototype for the New Testament deacon.[51] Nor can its source be traced to the Gentile world.[52]

The question of whether the appointment of the seven men to serve tables (Ac 6:1-6) constitutes the origin of this office is disputed.[53] Several arguments may be advanced for viewing these as the first official deacons:

1. While they are not specifically called "deacons," a form of the word is used twice in the passage to describe their work (v. 1, "ministration"; v. 2, "serve"), although it should be noted that this term is also used for the "ministry of the word" by the apostles (v. 4).

2. Their responsibility of serving in the area of the temporal needs of the church corresponds with our earliest knowledge of the task of deacons.

3. The prominent position given by Luke to this incident suggests that he is drawing attention to the creation of a new office. This is in contrast to the incidental first mention of elders in 11:30 as they do not represent a new office. It also fits Luke's method of writing Acts to give certain representative instances.[54]

4. Tradition beginning with Irenaeus holds these seven men to be the first deacons. Using this passage as a guide, it became the practice some centuries later to limit the number of deacons to seven, necessitating the order of subdeacons where additional help was needed.

5. The exacting spiritual qualifications for the seven men (Ac 6:3) correspond to those listed for the deacon (1 Ti 3:8-13).

6. Finally, if Acts 6 is not the record of the inauguration of deacons, then we have no indication of the start of this new office. Prior to this incident the term *diakonos* was employed only in a general sense, but in subsequent times it acquired a technical sense. The only biblical data to account for this change is the event of Acts 6.

50. When this attendant is mentioned in the New Testament, the Greek word is not *diakonos*, but an entirely different word, *hupēretēs* (Lk 4:20).
51. Beyer, "diakoneō, diakonia, diakonos" in *TDNT*, 2:91; Hort, pp. 209-10; Lightfoot, pp. 189-90.
52. Beyer, "diakoneō, diakonia, diakonos" in *TDNT*, 2:91-92.
53. For a discussion of both positions, see Morris, *Ministers of God*, pp. 82-86.
54. Lightfoot, p. 188.

On the opposite side, several facts are raised against understanding the seven men to be the first deacons:

1. They are never called "deacons" in Acts 6, and later, when Philip is mentioned, he is not called "the deacon" but "the evangelist" (Ac 21:8). This, however, is inconclusive, for being a deacon would not seem to prohibit one from also being an evangelist, or a great witness like Stephen (Ac 6:8; chap. 7).

2. Not only does Acts 6 not say that this is the institution of a new permanent order, but it appears to describe a purely temporary measure dealing with a particular situation.[55] This is said to be supported by the fact that later it is the elders at Jerusalem who receive the famine-relief supplies sent from the church at Antioch (Ac 11:30). It should be noted, however, that nothing is said of the distribution of these, which well may have been delegated to deacons.

3. The seven men of Acts 6 appear to rank next to the apostles, thus holding a position of much greater importance than later deacons. Their importance is seen in the subsequent ministries of Stephen and Philip. Still, the fact that they serve with the apostles does not necessarily indicate that they are different from the subsequent officers who serve under the bishops or elders, for possibly the apostles functioned as elders at this early time in Jerusalem.

While the New Testament does not explicitly connect the office of deacon with Acts 6, it seems most reasonable to see the seven men at least as prototype deacons. Hort is probably correct when he says that "the Seven at Jerusalem would of course be well known to St. Paul and to many others outside Palestine, and it would not be strange if the idea propagated itself. Indeed analogous wants might well lead to analogous institutions."[56]

Duties of the deacon. The seven men of Acts 6 were appointed to the ministry of the relief of the poor in the church. Theirs was a practical service designed to free the apostles for the ministry of the Word and prayer. Whether these men actually

---

55. Supporting the idea of a temporary measure is Beyer's suggestion that the seven were appointed to look after the Hellenistic widows who were probably barred from the common meals by the strict Jewish attitude to the law and purity. See his "diakoneō, diakonia, diakonos" in *TDNT*, 2:85.
56. Hort, p. 209.

served as deacons or not, this scene corresponds to what is known of the function of a deacon in other biblical references and early extra biblical pictures of church life. In Philippians 1:1 the apostle Paul includes the deacons in his address. Since this letter was written at least partially as a thank-you letter for the contribution given by the Philippian church, it is possible to see the "bishops and deacons" mentioned as the organizers of that collection, with the deacons assisting the bishops in the actual work of overseeing the collection.[57]

Among the requirements for the office of deacon (1 Ti 3:8-13) are those particularly appropriate for one serving in relation to material and financial matters among the people of the congregation. They must avoid greed, gossip and intemperance, vices which would be particularly tempting to one moving among the saints administering relief funds. The spiritual qualifications stated do not detract from this basic function, for in going from house to house they would have opportunities for ministries to the inner man as well. Without ceasing to be dispensers of alms, they could also become ministers of the Word.[58]

In subsequent time we find the deacons functioning in this same practical service. According to Justin Martyr, the offerings were received and blessed in the general meetings of the church by one officer, but they were distributed among the people by others known as deacons. These, as in the New Testament, are always closely related to the bishops or elders.[59]

The evidence, although somewhat scanty in the New Testament, indicates the office of deacon was primarily concerned with material ministries of the church, specifically distribution of relief to the poor. This corresponds well with the term chosen to designate this office, denoting service in general and table-waiting in particular. The New Testament church was concerned not only with spiritual needs of its members, but with their material needs as well. Undoubtedly this visible evidence of brotherly love did much to manifest the reality of Christ to those outside. In addition, the early church pictures the deacons as assisting the bishops in various administrative and liturgical functions,

57. Beyer, "diakoneō, diakonia, diakonos" in *TDNT*, 2:91.
58. Lightfoot, p. 190.
59. Hatch, pp. 49-50.

especially in administering the Lord's Supper. So it would appear reasonable to conclude that the general function of the deacons is the performance of various services of a practical nature in the church, relieving the elders of burdens which might interfere with their ministry of spiritual oversight.

Qualifications of the deacon. Along with the elder, the Scriptures present explicit qualifications for the deacon, concerning his personal character, his family, and the Christian faith (1 Ti 3:8-13). The ability to teach as well as explicit qualifications concerning hospitality and general contact with others, including non-Christians, are not considered because these are not part of the general work of deacons. On the other hand, the standards mentioned are equally high for the deacon as for the elder, and in certain cases the expressions are stronger.

Personally a deacon must be dignified ("grave," AV). The term denotes a seriousness of mind and character which should characterize his whole service. He is a minister for the whole congregation and must do so with the proper dignity and decorum, not lightheartedly. Then there are several qualifications specifically relating to his task of handling funds and moving among people. He is not to be "double-tongued," that is, he must not tell one person one thing and another something different. Such a characteristic was of vital importance to one who knew the problems of different members. He must also be one "not addicted to much wine" and "not fond of sordid gain" (v. 8, NASB). Both of these requirements are expressed in stronger terms than in the case of bishops (cf. v. 3), undoubtedly because deacons would be exposed more to temptations along these lines.[60]

With respect to the faith, the deacon must be one who holds to "the mystery of the faith with a clear conscience" (v. 9, NASB). While nothing is said, as in the case of bishop, that the deacon must be able to teach, the deacon must nevertheless know the truth of the Christian faith and live in acordance with it, having a pure or clean conscience. He must be spiritually right so that along with material relief he might also bring spiritual encouragement (cf. Ac 6:3).

The deacon, as the elder, must not be a neophyte in Christian

60. Donald Guthrie, *The Pastoral Epistles*, p. 84.

experience. Before serving as a deacon he is to be "tested" (proved). The use of the present tense does not suggest a specific test or trial period, but rather the constant observation which would lead to a reputation of proven character and maturity in the Christian life. The apostle makes it very clear that church offices are not to be used for the purpose of promoting maturity.

Finally, *the family life* of the deacons must also be in order. They must be "husbands of only one wife, and good managers of their children and their own households" (1 Ti 3:12, NASB). The demand for these qualifications for both elders (vv. 2, 4-5) and deacons shows the importance of the home in the New Testament. Probably with the deacons this requirement is not so much to manifest rulership ability as it is the nature of the deacon's Christian walk. "No place is more indicative of a person's real Christian character than his home. At home sham and all pretense are dropped, and a man can be seen for what he is."[61]

Number of the deacons. All of the testimony of the New Testament and early church points to a plurality of deacons in each local church (Phil 1:1; 1 Ti 3:8; Ac 6:1-6). Although some in early church history advocated the number seven, based on Acts 6:1-6, it seems doubtful that a fixed number was intended for all churches, because varying sizes and conditions would create varying needs for the ministry of deacons.

Appointment and term of office. It is evident from the account of Acts 6 that the seven men appointed for service were chosen by the congregation itself (Ac 6:3, 5). With no evidence to the contrary, this would support the practice of each local church electing the necessary number of deacons needed to fulfill this ministry among the congregation. The term of office is nowhere stated; but, as with the elder, a definite term would be in order, allowing more to serve in this capacity and also making it easier to remove the inactive or unworthy members.

Honor of the deacon. Not being in a capacity of leadership or instruction, no direction is given as there is with the office of elder, concerning the response of the congregation to the deacons. It is clear, however, that this is a ministry of dignity and honor. After listing the qualifications, the apostle adds, "For they that have used the office of a deacon well [literally, served well] pur-

61. Kent, p. 140.

chase to themselves a good degree, and great boldness in the faith which is in Christ Jesus" (1 Ti 3:13). The word "degree" means literally "a step" and has been interpreted by the Roman and Anglican churches to mean a step in promotion to a higher office, making the office of deacon the stepping-stone to the priesthood. But the remainder of the verse concerning spiritual blessing, as well as the previous instructions, would seem out of place if the primary aim of the deacon's office were preparatory to that of bishop or priest. It is more natural to understand it as the gaining of a good standing or respected reputation in the church and perhaps also with reference to God in the judgment. The deacon who serves well will also gain for himself "boldness" or confidence in the Christian faith through the consciousness that he has done his best in the strength of God. This confidence in turn will evoke even greater service.

DEACONESS

The office of deaconess. There is a difference of opinion as to whether the New Testament church had an office of deaconess. The Scriptures in question are Romans 16:1, where Paul refers to Phebe as "a servant [diakonos] of the church which is at Cenchrea," and 1 Timothy 3:11, where in the context of the qualifications for deacons, women are mentioned.

Against seeing Phebe as an official deaconess is the fact that while *diakonos* is used for deacon in some instances, it is more commonly used for any type of ministry. As it is obvious from Romans 16:2 that she ministered to the saints, she could be called a *diakonos* without making her an official deacon.[62] Against seeing the women of 1 Timothy 3:11 as deaconesses is the fact that the verses preceding and following refer to deacons. This leads some persons, with the Authorized Version, to view them as the wives of deacons.

But there is much evidence to support the interpretation that these women are deaconesses rather than deacons' wives and, if so, then Phebe is probably to be considered among them.[63]

1. The term used, which may be translated "wives" if the context so demands, also may be rendered "women" (cf. NASB).

62. John Murray, *The Epistle to the Romans*, 2:226.
63. Kent, pp. 140-41.

With no possessive pronoun accompanying it, and no Greek article which might be used in a possessive sense, there is no grammatical justification to link them to the deacons of verses 8-10. Since the form *diakonos* was used for both men and women, it was necessary to use the term "women" to distinguish the woman deaconess from the preceding deacon.

2. The term "likewise" (*hōsantōs*) appears to indicate a transition from one class to another as evidenced in its use to introduce the subject of deacons after the discussion of elders. "A bishop . . . must be blameless. . . . Likewise [*hōsantōs*] must the deacons be grave. . . . Even so [*hōsantōs*] women must be grave" (vv. 2, 8, 11; cf. 2:9; Titus 2:3, 6) .

3. It would seem strange to state qualifications for the deacons' wives when no such requirements are given for the wives of elders, although they have the more important role.

4. There was an order of deaconesses in the early church according to the letter of Pliny, the governor of Bithynia, about A.D. 112. In his report to the Emperor Trajan, he indicates that he tortured two Christian handmaidens who were called deaconesses.

From the above arguments it seems reasonable that in this passage dealing with church officers the apostle was laying down the requirements for women who served as deaconesses. The rather casual insertion in the context of deacons probably indicates that they were not as prominent as the men, but were to be considered as belonging to the same ministry. The strong separation between the sexes in the East would have made the service of women indispensable for certain tasks within the church, and order would demand that certain ones be appointed for these ministries.

Duties of the deaconess. The deaconess of the early church was concerned with those areas of service that could best be served by a woman. Indicative of their functions is the summary given in the Syrian *Didascalia* from the late third century. They were to assist at the baptism of women, especially in the art of anointing and "to go into the houses of the heathen where there are believing women, and to visit those who are sick, and to minister to them in that of which they have need, and to bathe those who have begun to recover from sickness."[64] Deaconesses undoubtedly also served the poor and the orphans, and provided hospitality for strangers. Thus while the New Testament prohibits women from assuming the role of leadership in the church (1 Ti 2:11-12; 1 Co 14:34), they do appear as having a significant ministry in the church along with men in the subordinate auxiliary role of the diaconate.

Qualifications of the deaconess. The requirements for a deaconess closely follow those laid down for the deacon (1 Ti 3:11). As the deacon, she must be dignified ("grave"), serving in seriousness of mind and character. She must not be slanderous. This terms describes one "given to fault finding with the demeanor and conduct of others, and spreading . . . innuendos and criticisms."[65] The noun form is used as a name for the devil, who slanders and accuses God; thus, as Kent notes, the deaconess must not be a "she-devil" as she circulates among the congregation in performance of her duties.[66] This prohibition for the deaconess parallels that of the deacon to be "not double-tongued" (v. 8). Further, the deaconess is to be temperate ("sober"). While undoubtedly used in the metaphorical sense to characterize all of life, this qualification perhaps has specific reference to the excessive use of wine in correspondence to the deacon as one not "addicted to much wine" (v. 8, NASB). Finally, the deaconess must be absolutely reliable, "faithful in all things" (v. 11). This covers with brevity in general terms the prohibition against fondness for dishonest gain expressed for the deacon.

The gospel of Christ brought a new dignity to women in ancient times, not only giving them personal equality before God, but a share in the ministry. The New Testament reveals that godly noble women who met these requirements were invaluable to the service of the church.

ORDINATION

The concept of ordination to church office does not play a major role in the New Testament. This paucity of references

---

64. M. H. Shepherd, Jr., "Deaconess; KJV Servant" in The *Interpreter's Dictionary of the Bible,* 1:786, citing the Syrian *Didascalia,* ed. Connolly, pp. 146-48.
65. W. E. Vine, *An Expository Dictionary of New Testament Words,* 4:39.
66. Kent, p. 142.

makes it impossible to establish a full-orbed procedure practiced in the early church. However, there is evidence of a solemn rite marking the setting apart of individuals to specific church functions.

THE FACT OF ORDINATION

Ordination is never directly stated with reference to the offices of the church in the New Testament. The Authorized Version uses the term "ordain" with reference to elders in Acts 14:23 and Titus 1:5, but neither of these instances concerns the act of ordination. The first reference uses the Greek word *cheirotoreō*, which has the idea of choosing or appointing, as seen in the reference to the brother "who was also chosen of the churches to travel with us" (2 Co 8:19). While in both cases the individuals may have been "ordained" to the work for which they were chosen, the rite is not involved with the word. In Titus 1:5 the Greek verb is simply *kathistēmi*, meaning in this usage, to appoint (cf. Mt 24:47, "make him ruler over all his goods").[67]

There are, however, several instances where the New Testament indicates a special act of ordination whereby certain ones are set apart to a specific function in the church. In Acts 6:6 the seven men chosen by the church were set before the apostles who "when they had prayed, they laid their hands on them." Paul and Barnabas are likewise sent forth as missionaries by the church at Antioch with fasting, prayer, and the laying on of hands (Ac 13:3). Hands were also laid on Timothy by the elders (1 Ti 4:14) and the apostle Paul (2 Ti 1:6). In all probability these have reference to the calling and appointment of Timothy to the ministry of missionary service with the apostle at Lystra (Ac 16:3). Finally, there is the disputed reference of Paul's injunction to Timothy: "Lay hands suddenly on no man, neither be partaker of other men's sins" (1 Ti 5:22). The context of bringing a charge against an elder and the injunction against partiality with respect to rebuking elders (vv. 19-21) suggests that the laying on of hands was the symbolic act of blessing by which the penitents were received back into the fellowship of the church after sinning. To do this before the sinner was truly

67. The use of "ordain" in 1 Ti 2:7 in reference to the apostle Paul as a preacher also refers simply to his appointment (Greek, *tithēmi*).

repentant would be to partake in his sins.[68] Against this interpretation, however, is the fact that this practice is not found elsewhere in the New Testament church or "for quite a long time later."[69] Therefore, it is probably a reference to ordination, which also fits the context well. One who hastily lays hands upon the unqualified is viewed as partaking in the sins of the one ordained.

PROCEDURE OF ORDINATION

In the ordination of the New Testament there is no procedure outlined for the call of the church and the examination of a candidate by an ordaining council or for various steps leading to ordination such as licensure. Different methods have been devised to implement what is stated in the New Testament concerning the ministries and their relation to the church. The candidate for ordination must first be assured of his own call to the ministry (1 Co 9:16; 1 Ti 1:12), and then be recognized by the church as one so called.

In the case of Timothy, his call and endowment for the ministry were marked for all by God through the utterance of inspired prophets (1 Ti 4:14; cf. 1:18). As Fairbairn notes, "This prophecy . . . is to be viewed as the distinct enunciation of God's will in respect to Timothy's qualifications . . . and the formal designation of him by the presbytery was the churches' response to the declared mind of God."[70] Subsequent to the prophetic era, recognition still must come through the Spirit of God using the qualifications for the ministry expressed in the Word (1 Ti 3:1-13; Titus 1:5-9). It is also important to note that it is not simply knowledge or the completion of a prescribed course of studies, but the sovereign call and equipping of God which are the preconditions of ordination.

The actual act of ordination consisted of the laying on of hands. In the references to this act where more detail is given, it is preceded by prayer (Ac 6:6) and fasting and prayer (Ac

---

68. Hort, pp. 214-15; Walter Lock, *A Critical and Exegetical Commentary on the Pastoral Epistles,* The International Critical Commentary (Edinburgh: T. & T. Clark, 1936), p. 64.
69. Morris, *Ministers of God,* p. 79.
70. Patrick Fairbairn, *Commentary on the Pastoral Epistles,* p. 189. This is probably similar to the speaking of the Holy Spirit through the prophets concerning the missionary task of Barnabas and Paul (Ac 13:1-2).

13:3; cf. 14:23). Thus it is evident that ordination is not magic, but an outward sign of a spiritual work of God.

In the New Testament the act of ordination is performed by the elders (1 Ti 4:14), the apostle Paul (2 Ti 1:6, probably in conjunction with the elders in 4:14), the apostles (Ac 6:6), and the prophets and teachers (Ac 13:1-3). In each instance the act of ordination was performed by the leaders of the church acting on behalf of the church itself, indicating that the church as a whole is the final ordaining body through which the Holy Spirit directs in the appointment of ministries (Ac 6:1-6). This is clear when in Acts 13:3 hands were laid on Paul and Barnabas not by their superiors but by their equals or inferiors as representatives of the church.

SIGNIFICANCE OF ORDINATION

Ordination is the recognition by the church of those whom God has called and equipped for a regular ordered ministry in the church. That it does not confer authority or spiritual gifts is evident from the fact that these are given sovereignly by God (1 Co 12:11, 18; Eph 4:7, 11). In the case of the seven men, they were equipped for the task before the laying on of hands, being previously "full of the Holy Ghost and wisdom" (Ac 6:3).

The significance of the ceremony of laying on of hands stems from its use in the Old Testament. There it was used with the bestowal of blessing (Gen 48:14; cf. Mt 19:15), and in the sacrifice where the hands of the offerer were laid on the head of the victim before it was slain (e.g., Ex 29:10; Lev 1:4; 4:4; Num 8:10). More closely related to New Testament ordination is the imposition of hands by representatives of the other tribes upon the tribe of Levi at their dedication (Num 8:10), and especially Moses doing the same upon Joshua as his successor (Num 27:18, 23; Deu 34:9).

It is obvious that in neither of the latter cases was there any transference of power. Both were equipped by God for their work, as is evident by the fact that the "spirit of wisdom" was already upon Joshua before the laying on of hands. Rather, there is in all of these uses the fundamental meaning of identification and representation. The laying on of hands by the church leaders is an act by which the whole church identifies itself in solidarity with those who are ordained as one with them in their ministry. The ordained are the members appointed by God to a representative ministry which leads the body in its corporate ministry (Eph 4:12-16).

While the act of ordination is the acknowledgment by the church of its God-appointed ministers, it is never the basis for their ministry. Paul reminds Timothy of his ordination, but not for the reason that the church should acknowledge him for this. Rather, he is to be followed because of his model character and his service through the exercising of the gift of ministry (1 Ti 4:12-14). The apostle also authenticated his apostleship primarily by his ministry among the churches (2 Co 3:1-3).

THE RECIPIENTS OF ORDINATION

In the New Testament churches, ordination was not reserved only for the elders, but included also those appointed to service in Acts 6 as well as Paul and Barnabas, who were sent as missionaries from Antioch. In the latter instance the laying on of hands was not for recognition of the church office, for Paul and Barnabas were already ministering among the churches. It was, instead, the recognition and identification of the church in the call of God to this new service as missionaries. It therefore appears that ordination was practiced for any who were called to the ordered ministry of the church and other important special service.

8

The Worship of the Church

WORSHIP IS CENTRAL in the existence of the church. The words of the apostle Paul that God has chosen and predestined sons unto Himself in Christ "to the praise of the glory of his grace" (Eph 1:4-6) suggest that the ultimate purpose of the church is the worship of the one who called it into being. Peter likewise calls the church "an holy priesthood, to offer up spiritual sacrifices, acceptable to God by Jesus Christ" (1 Pe 2:5). This worship involves proclaiming "the excellencies of Him who has called you out of darkness into His marvelous light" (v. 9, NASB).

In forming the church as a worshiping community, God has through the Scriptures given instruction both as to the nature and forms of true worship.

THE NATURE OF WORSHIP

MEANING OF WORSHIP

The English word *worship* comes from the Anglo-Saxon *weorthscipe* (*weorth,* "worthy," "honorable"; and *scipe,* "ship"). This later developed into *worthship,* and finally, *worship.* It means "to attribute worth" to an object. To worship God is thus to ascribe to Him the supreme worth to which He alone is worthy. The Scriptures nowhere give a definition of worship, but its meaning may be determined from the terms employed and from passages describing its character.

Terms of worship. The primary New Testament word for worship is *proskuneō,* which denotes the act of bowing or prostrating oneself in submissive lowliness and deep reverence. The prominence of the physical act in this term is evident in that it demands the presence of visible majesty before whom the worshiper bows. As such it is very common in the gospels when Christ was visible and again in Revelation when the exalted Lord once more appears. Apart from Acts 24:11, where it refers to the worship of God in the temple, the only instance of its use in the early church is in 1 Corinthians 14:24-25, where the unbeliever, overwhelmed by the presence of God manifest through the unmasking of his heart through the prophetic ministries in the church service, falls down before God in worship of absolute subjection.[1] Although the lack of the visible presence of Deity restricts the use of this word for church worship, the inward attitude of submission and humble respect remains a vital part of all true biblical worship.

The next most frequently used term is *sebomai* and its various cognates. Derived from a root meaning "fear," it involves a reverence which stresses the feeling of awe. Along with the related terms, *sebomai* is used frequently to express New Testament "worship" (Ac 18:7, 13) and the "godliness" or "piety" of the believers (cf. Ac 3:12; 2 Pe 1:3; 3:11; 1 Ti 2:10; 1 Ti 5:4).

A third important and highly significant concept involved in New Testament worship is expressed by the word *latreuō* and its synonym *leitourgeō*. Both of these terms signify the rendering of service; the latter, however, because it was the express term for priestly functions, is not used nearly as often in relation to the church, for here there is no special priestly group. Because all are priests, it can be used for the service of God of all believers, whether in prayer (Ac 13:2-3), giving (Ro 15:27; 2 Co 9:12), or in the ministry of the gospel (Ro 15:16). All these are acts of service in the worship of God. It is of interest to note that this word stands behind our word *liturgy* with its connotations of priestly acts and clergy-laity distinction, in complete contrast to its use for the life of service of all believers in the New Testament. This "liturgical" sense came about in the fourth century with the application of the Old Testament priestly ministry to the Christian clergy.[2]

The word *latreuō*, denoting the religious conduct of people generally, is more commonly used for the service of the church into which all may enter. It likewise describes actions of the total life, including the worship of praise and prayer (cf. Rev 7:15; 22:3), but even more, the total manner of life which is pleasing to God. The "reasonable service" (*latria*) of believers

1. Heinrich Greeven, "proskuneō" in *TDNT*, 6:765.
2. H. Strathmann, "leitourgeō—leitourgos" in *TDNT*, 4:215, 229.

is the living sacrifice of themselves which "consists in the fashioning of their inner lives and their outward physical conduct in a way which plainly distinguishes them from the world and which corresponds to the will of God" (cf. Ro 12:1-2) .[3]

Although the graciousness of salvation prohibits any thought of service in a meritorious sense or of conferring a benefit on God, these terms, as Moule notes, "still present a salutary bulwark against slovenly or supine conceptions."[4] Christian worship is the work of life as service to God.

Character of worship. True worship is the sincere expression of devotion to God. As such, it can only issue from the depths of one's innermost being. In the ritual of the Old Testament, God had already made it clear that only those sacrifices accompanied by a disposition of heart commensurate with their meaning were acceptable to Him. Such a heart would demonstrate itself in outward obedience of life (Is 1:10; Ho 6:6; Amos 5:12 f.) . That genuine worship involved the inner being is seen also in the fact that prayer and praise were in themselves considered the essence of sacrifice (Ps 51:17; 69:30 f.; 141:2) . With the shadow of Old Testament types fulfilled in Christ, the New Testament accentuates worship as the response of one's whole being to the reality of God revealed in Christ. No longer is there an offering of an animal; it is now the offering of oneself that is clearly demanded.

This worship is described by the apostle Paul as "reasonable" service (Ro 12:1) . "Reasonable" (*logikos*) , which is usually rendered "spiritual" in the New Testament (cf. 1 Pe 2:2, ASV) , signifies an act belonging to the inner aspect of man, his spirit or mind. But it is evident from the use of this term for the presentation of the whole self that Paul is not simply describing worship as consisting of inward motions or feeling. The offering of self not only must stem from the highest reason within man but it is the only "reasonable" worship consistent with an understanding of "the mercies of God" (Ro 12:1) . As Cranfield notes, the "intelligent, understanding worship . . . which is consonant with the truth of the Gospel, is indeed nothing less than the offering of one's whole self in the whole of one's concrete living,

3. Strathmann, "latreuō, latria" in *TDNT*, 4:65.
4. C. F. D. Moule, *Worship in the New Testament*, p. 80.

in one's inward thought, feelings and aspirations, but also in one's words and deeds."[5]

A new reality of worship in the realm of the spirit was also taught by Jesus in His reply to the question of the Samaritan woman at the well concerning the proper location for worship. Although He acknowledged the truth of God's revelation through the Jews, and therefore the validity of the true traditional worship at Jerusalem, Jesus transcended the question, revealing a new characteristic of worship: "An hour is coming, and now is, when the true worshipers shall worship the Father in spirit and truth. . . . 'God is spirit; and those who worship Him must worship in spirit and truth'" (Jn 4:23-24, NASB).

In calling for worship "in spirit and truth," the Lord is stating more than worship from the heart, for, as has been seen, this was already the characteristic of true worship in the Old Testament. Nor is the spirituality of God a new revelation (cf. Is 31:3). Christ is speaking of the new reality of worship which comes with Him. It is a Messianic statement. God as life-giving Spirit now confronts man directly in Christ rather than in the shadows of the typical forms. True worship can only take place as one is in the realm of this life-giving Spirit and is vitalized and motivated by Him.

This worship "in spirit" is also "in truth," the two concepts being closely related.[6] Worship "in spirit" is based upon the revelation of God in Christ who is the "true God" (1 Jn 5:20). The contrast is not so much truth as opposed to falsity, but truth as reality and finality in contrast to the worship under the old covenant which involved preparatory shadows (cf. Jn 1:17). True worship thus takes place only in Christ, for in Him one is in the supernatural life of the Spirit and in the truth.[7]

Because the New Testament believer enjoys the fullness of God's reality through the indwelling presence of Christ by the

---

5. C. E. B. Cranfield, *A Commentary on Romans 12-13, Scottish Journal of Theology Occasional Papers No. 12,* p. 14.
6. Neither in v. 23 nor in v. 24 is the preposition "in" (*en*) repeated before "truth," signifying a close relationship between the terms. Cf. A. T. Robertson, *A Grammar of the Greek New Testament in the Light of Historical Research,* p. 566.
7. See C. K. Barrett, *The Gospel According to St. John,* pp. 198-200; Edwyn Hoskyns, *The Fourth Gospel,* pp. 244-45; Eduard Schweizer, "pneuma, pneumatikos" in *TDNT,* 6:438-39.

Spirit, worship takes place on the highest level of personal relationship. The approach to God through the material rites and
physical acts gives way to the "substance," the reality in the person of Christ (Heb 8:5; 10:1). True worship is thus a direct
communion of persons from the depth of their beings.

Such personal worship does not rule out physical acts, for the
body is the expression of the person. But these are changed from
acts of service at altars of bronze and stone to acts of love in the
sanctuary of human life and need (Ja 1:27). Nor are outward
forms, although greatly minimized, completely eliminated, which
is evidenced in baptism and the Lord's Supper. But only as these
are expressions of a vital personal devotion can they be avenues
of true worship. The essence of worship may thus be summed
up as the giving of oneself completely to God in the actions and
attitudes of life.

THE WORK OF GOD IN WORSHIP

Certain basic principles underlie the biblical doctrine of worship. These correspond to the work of God in dealing with all
of His creation. Worship is directed toward God, mediated
through Christ, and performed in the power and inspiration of
the Holy Spirit.

Directed toward God. That which makes worship to be worship is the centrality of God. All activities, whether performed
in private or in public meetings, are only worship as they are
directed toward God. Although the worshiper will be blessed in
his own life through the experience of worship, the primary
object of worship is not the subjective experience but the ascription of glory to God. For participants "to evaluate the worship
service in terms of how it 'lifted them up' or gave them 'a good
feeling' or 'inspired' them . . . is to substitute what someone has
called 'subjective affection' for 'objective trust.' "[8]

Since it is the fact of God which transforms human activity
into worship, the nature of the God worshiped determines the
meaning of worship.[9] Biblical revelation portrays God as the
Creator and Redeemer of life. As Creator and Sustainer of life,

8. Donald G. Miller, *The Nature and Mission of the Church,* p. 107.
9. For a brief but comprehensive survey of the character of God as the
object of worship, see Ralph P. Martin, *Worship in the Early Church,*
pp. 12-17.

the worshiper recognizes Him as the source of his total being. "With thee is the fountain of life: in thy light shall we see light" (Ps 36:9). "In him we live, and move, and have our being" (Ac 17:28). He "daily loadeth us with benefits" (Ps 68:19) and is the Giver of "every good gift and every perfect gift" (Ja 1:17). Even in heaven the adoration of the creative and sustaining power of God is a theme of worship in the anthem of the four living creatures and the twenty-four elders: "Thou art worthy, O Lord, to receive glory and honour and power: for thou hast created all things, and for thy pleasure they are and were created" (Rev 4:11).

While God evokes worship as the Creator and Sustainer of all things, it is the manifestation of His love and grace in redemption which is the dominant theme of New Testament worship. The writers of Scripture burst into doxologies of praise over God's saving act which brought a "living hope" (1 Pe 1:3) and "all spiritual blessings" (Eph 1:3). The unspeakable gift of God's Son (2 Co 9:15) and His deliverance from darkness into light are the inspiration for the believers' worship of thanksgiving in the church (Col 1:12-13) and of the citizens of heaven (Rev 5:9-14).

Because God in His creative and saving acts has given Himself to man, worship can only be the response of faith to what has been done. There can be no thought of gaining God's favor or making amends through worship. Rather, all worship is the acknowledgment in praise and adoration of God for what He has already given. Man has nothing to offer but that which was first bestowed upon him. Worship thus initiates with God and ends upon Him to the praise of His glory.

Mediated through Christ. The principal teaching of the New Testament is worship toward God as Father through the Son. He is the one who has provided access through the veil into the heavenly sanctuary by "a new and living way . . . that is to say, his flesh" (Heb 10:20). He has entered heaven as the eternal, living High Priest to bring His people with Him. "Incorporate in His humanity our humanity now enters the presence of God."[10] Although personally unworthy, the worshiper is "accepted in the

10. Moule, p. 71.

beloved" (Eph 1:6) and urged to enter with "confidence" (Heb 10:19, NASB), drawing near "in full assurance of faith" (v. 22; cf. Eph 2:18; Ro 5:2). Through union with Christ the believer-priest is thus able to offer "spiritual sacrifices, acceptable to God" (1 Pe 2:5b). The mediatorship of Christ is the avenue of all prayer, for it is in the name of Him who Himself cried, "Abba Father," that the believer is able to address God as His loving Father (Jn 16:23-27).

The High Priestly ministry of Christ in worship must not be understood as taking place only in heaven, detached as it were from the worshiping church on earth. He is also present with His body as it worships. "Where two or three are gathered together in my name, there am I in the midst of them" (Mt 18:20; cf. 28:20). There is no true worship but that which takes place in fellowship with Christ.

For this reason all the components of New Testament worship are designed to lead worshipers to an awareness of His presence.[11] Not only prayer was offered in the name of Jesus, but new converts were baptized in His name (Ac 2:38). The communion table was the "Lord's Supper" through which His death was recalled and proclaimed, and His future coming anticipated (1 Co 11:20-26). Participation meant acknowledging His presence as "the communion of the body of Christ" (1 Co 10:16b). He is the subject of confessions of faith (Ro 10:9; 1 Co 12:3), and the early creeds (e.g., 1 Co 15:3-5), and hymns of the church (1 Ti 3:16; Phil 2:6-11).[12] Especially was Christ present as His Word was read and proclaimed in the church (Col 3:16).

Although Christ is primarily the Mediator of worship, He appears on rare occasion as the object as well. Stephen cried out in his martyrdom, "Lord Jesus, receive my spirit" (Ac 7:59). This is especially noteworthy in comparison to the Lord's own prayer: "Father, into thy hands I commend my spirit" (Lk 23:46). Similarly, Paul addresses the Lord directly on the Damascus road, "Lord, what wilt thou have me to do?" (Ac 9:6). Most significant is the prayer expressed in the transliteration of the Aramaic original "Maranatha," "Our Lord, come" (1 Co 16:22;

11. Martin, p. 130.
12. For a discussion of these forms of worship see ibid., pp. 39-65.

cf. Rev 22:20).[13] The fact that the Aramaic form was taken over even by the Greek-speaking Christians evidences the importance of this sentiment in the early church. Finally, Christians are identified as those who "call upon the name of Jesus Christ our Lord" (1 Co 1:2; Ac 9:14, 21; cf. Ac 2:21; 22:16; Ro 10:12 f.). The form of these words is a Hebraism for the Old Testament worship of God in calling upon the name of Jehovah (Gen 4:26; 12:8; 2 Ki 5:11).[14]

Thus, while God the Father remains the ultimate and principal object of New Testament worship, the early believers who with Thomas saw in Christ their Lord and their God could not help but adore Him as the Lamb who is "worthy . . . to receive power, and riches, and wisdom, and strength, and honour, and glory, and blessing" (Rev 5:12).

Performed in the Spirit. The worship of the church is finally empowered by the dynamic of the Holy Spirit. The way to the Father, while opened by Christ, is entered by the believer in the power of the indwelling Spirit (Eph 2:18). Therefore, Paul says, "We . . . worship God in the Spirit" (Phil 3:3).

His influence in worship pervades every form. By Him the lordship of Jesus is acknowledged (1 Co 12:3), as He alone can make the presence of Christ a reality in the worshiping community. Prayer is offered "in the Spirit" (Eph 5:18; Jude 20) and by the Spirit through us as He "maketh intercession for us with groanings which cannot be uttered" (Ro 8:26-27). He also gives spiritual understanding of the Word of God in order that its truth may be acknowledged in the worship of praise and obedience of life (1 Co 2:10-16; 1 Jn 2:27).

It is evident from the teaching of the New Testament that genuine worship begins with God and ends upon Him. With all things, worship also is "of him, and through him, and to him, . . . to whom be glory for ever" (Ro 11:36). Through His grace, the believer in worship is given the honor to reflect that glory.

13. It has been suggested that the use of *Maranatha* with the Lord's Supper in the early church (*Didache*, 10:6) evidences its meaning as a confession of the exalted Christ's presence ("our Lord is present") in the church, especially at the Lord's Supper. Linguistically the Aramaic form allows for the indicative as well as the imperative. Cf. K. G. Kuhn, "maranatha" in *TDNT*, 4:471-72.
14. W. F. Adeney, "Worship (in NT)" in *A Dictionary of the Bible*, ed. James Hastings, 4:943.

TIME AND PLACE OF WORSHIP

Our examination of the New Testament words for worship revealed that they were used for the believer's total life which is lived to the praise and glory of God. Thus, worship is not restricted for New Testament priests to certain cultic practices performed at certain places on specified days. It was an everyday affair. But, in addition to the worship of each day in the normal routine of life, the church met together for fellowship in worship and as such required a certain order.

The time. The earliest picture of the church meeting for worship shows believers gathering together daily in the temple (Ac 2:46; cf. Lk 24:53). This practice apparently did not continue long, for no further mention is made of such daily assembly. Instead, the established time of worship came to be the first day of the week (Ac 20:7; 1 Co 16:2). It is probable that many of the Jewish believers continued to worship on the Sabbath.[15] And from the wide observance in the subapostolic church of the Passover and Pentecost, along with references to these events in the biblical record of early church life (Ac 20:6, 16; 1 Co 16:8), it also seems likely that Christians continued to celebrate these festivals for some time. The Passover being fulfilled in Christ (1 Co 5:7), and Pentecost in the coming of the Holy Spirit, these ancient Jewish observances were pertinent to the heart of Christian truth. However, the observance of any special day was never imposed upon the church as a binding obligation. Each person was to be persuaded in his own heart concerning days as long as his practice of observance or nonobservance could be done conscientiously toward God (Ro 14:5-6). To insist upon keeping days and seasons as a legal requirement is placing oneself under the bondage of the law from which Christ has redeemed the believer (Gal 4:9-10; cf. Col 2:16).

It has been suggested that worship on the first day began by simply lengthening the Sabbath worship through the night until the next morning.[16] Be that as it may, by marking out the

15. The Sabbath remained in Jewish society as the only free day for worship, while in Gentile society there was no weekly free day, but only pagan festivals at irregular intervals.
16. H. Riesenfeld, "Sabbat et Jour du Seigneur" in *New Testament Essays, Studies in Memory of Thomas Walter Manson*, ed. A. J. B. Higgins (Manchester: Manchester U., 1959), pp. 210-16; cited by Moule, p. 16.

first day for Christian worship the church established a deliberate distinction from Judaism. On this day Christ had risen from the dead and appeared to His disciples. The church was founded on the fact of a risen Lord, and it was only fitting that the first day be "the Lord's day" (Rev 1:10). Although later the symbolism of the heathen sun cult was recognized as symbolic of the resurrection, and the term *Sunday* was used in Christian circles, the significance of the day in the early church gained its meaning totally from the reality of the risen Lord.

Outside of establishing the first day as the time of worship and acknowledging its significance as "the Lord's Day," the New Testament lays down no regulations concerning its observance. Even as the New Testament believer-priest offers his total life in sacrifice to God, so no one day belongs to the Lord to the exclusion of the others.

The place. As with the time of worship, the early Christians did not immediately cut themselves off from Jewish places of worship. Thus we find them frequenting the temple, even as Christ had done during His earthly ministry (Mk 14:49), praying and teaching the doctrines of Christ (Ac 2:46; 3:1; 5:42). It appears that they also attended the synagogue, for Saul sought to purge the synagogues of those that believed on Christ (Ac 22:19).[17] But, along with attendance in accordance with their Jewish customs, there arose, above and beyond these, distinctive Christian assemblies. In Acts 1:13 followers of Christ are already seen praying together in the upper room. Later they are seen "breaking bread from house to house" (Ac 2:46; cf. 5:42)[18] and gathering to pray in the house of Mary, the mother of Mark (Ac 12:12).

The practice of meeting in homes evidently became the established the pattern, for we hear of the church in a house (Col 4:15; Ro 16:5; 1 Co 16:19; Phile 2). The use of specific church buildings did not appear before the end of the second century. Despite the fact of the use of homes, the emphasis on assembling together precludes our thinking of only a few people. The unity of the

17. The reference to "your synagogue ["assembly," AV] (Ja 2:2, ASV) probably indicates an assembly of Jewish Christians. At least the possessive "your" suggests Christian direction.
18. The Greek *kat' oikon* may be equally translated "at home" (Oscar Cullmann, *Early Christian Worship*, p. 10) or "by households" (F. F. Bruce, *Commentary on the Book of Acts*, p. 81).

church in worship and edification depends on gathering together in "one place" (1 Co 11:20 ff.; 14:23). The writers of the epistles also obviously expected their letters to be read before the whole congregation (Col 4:16; 1 Th 5:27). Thus, the homes in which churches met must have been capable of accommodating a considerable group. Nevertheless, the large congregations which subsequently developed with church buildings and continue in our day are in marked contrast to the New Testament churches. The implications of this change for the unity of the church, its fellowship in worship, and mutual edification are certainly worth considering.[19]

EFFECT OF WORSHIP ON THE CHURCH

While biblical worship is always founded upon God, originating in His grace and directed toward His glory, it also has a purpose for the life of the church. The apostle Paul clearly specifies this goal when he exhorts the Corinthian church, "Let all things be done unto edifying" (1 Co 14:26*b*). All manifestations of the Spirit in the worship at Corinth were designed to build up the total community of believers. This took place through the growth of individuals, but that which was done only for self-edification was wrong (1 Co 14:4). Upbuilding of the congregation involves a mutual interrelationship of individuals edifying one another (1 Co 12:7; 14:3-5, 12, 17, 26). It takes place as each member ministers the gift bestowed to him by the Spirit for the benefit of the body. Each believer must view himself as in the service of Christ for the edification of the body, both receiving from others and contributing to them.

Edification must not be thought of only in terms of morality or emotional uplift. Rather, it aims at a fullness of growth in the total life of faith through the ministry of the Word in its various applications of exhortation, encouragement and comfort (1 Th 5:11; 1 Co 14:3), and especially in the practice of love (1 Co 8:1; cf. 12:31—13:13).[20]

19. For a provocative study of church worship which bears on this problem, see Schweizer, "Worship in the New Testament," *The Reformed and Presbyterian World* 24 (Mar. 1957):196-205.
20. Otto Michel, "oikodomeō" in *TDNT*, 5:140-42.

THE FORMS OF WORSHIP

The New Testament does not outline proceedings of the worship service of the early church. Nevertheless, glimpses of what took place as believers met together do appear. These forms of worship reveal a richness commensurate with the freedom and fullness of the Spirit's operation in the church. There is no monotony of routine in the biblical expression of worship.

JEWISH ANTECEDENTS

Having sprung from Jewish soil in its acknowledgment of Jesus as Lord and acceptance of the Old Testament as its own Scriptures, the church in worship naturally found antecedents in Jewish forms.

The worship of the Jews involved both the temple and the synagogue, and each had its influence on the early church. The central feature of temple worship was the sacrificial cultus, although prayers were also offered there. For sacrifices to continue in the church would contradict one of the major themes of New Testament truth that Christ Himself offered the perfect sacrifice in fulfillment of the old covenant sacrifices (Heb 9:23-28; 10:11 ff.). Although the disciples are seen praying in the temple, there is no mention of their offering sacrifices. Nevertheless, the theology of the sacrifices remained as the temple language was used to explain the work of Christ and the new position of believers. These were now spiritualized to express the new reality of personal relationship with God in the Spirit. The believer himself (1 Co 6:19) and the church are now the temple of God (1 Co 3:16-17; Eph 2:21-22). All members of the church are priests who offer their entire life every day as well as community worship on Sunday as "spiritual sacrifices" unto God. Thus, while the language of the temple sacrificial system is retained, the old typical forms have no place in the worship of the church.

The synagogue, on the other hand, provided the background for much of the pattern of church worship. This is due not only to the fact that the central forms of temple worship were outmoded, but also to the greater impact of the synagogue in Jewish experience. The vast majority of Jews scattered throughout the empire had never seen the temple and even for those in Palestine their local synagogue was more real than the temple in Jerusalem.

As the core of the early churches was the Jewish believers, the impact of the synagogue was naturally felt.

Three main elements made up the worship of the synagogue.[21] A note of corporate praise opened the service, which then included prayers and the reading and exposition of the Scriptures. This latter element gave the synagogue its distinctive ethos as "the house of instruction." Along with prayers of praise and thanksgiving, the response to the Word of God's grace included the practice of charity toward the poorer members of the community. All of these forms were taken over into the pattern of New Testament worship. In addition, the church from the beginning created new forms of worship expressive of its new faith, so that Maxwell can say, "Christian worship, as a distinctive, indigenous thing, arose from the fusion, in the crucible of Christian experience, of the synagogue and the Upper Room."[22]

THE WORD

Centrality of the Word. The importance of the Word in the midst of the church appears in the report of the early believers that they were "continually devoting themselves to the apostles' teaching" (Ac 2:42, NASB). As Israel's worship began with hearing God (cf. Deu 6:4), so church worship begins with listening to the voice of God through His Word, for it is in His Word that God comes to His people, to address them, and hold conversation with them. Through the Word the obedience of faith is engendered (Ro 10:17; Jn 17:20) and life is transformed (Jn 17:17; 15:3). So important is the Word to the church that growth in it is practically a synonym for growth of the church. "And the word of God increased; and the number of the disciples multiplied in Jerusalem greatly" (Ac 6:7; cf. 12:24; 19:20). For this reason the apostles were determined not to let any service take precedent over "the ministry of the word" (Ac 6:4). In the apostolic word, Christ had promised His own presence. Even as He had linked His authority to the word of the disciples during His earthly life, stating, "He that heareth you heareth me" (Lk 10:16), so the later apostolic teaching is nothing less than

21. Martin, p. 24.
22. W. D. Maxwell, *An Outline of Christian Worship*, p. 5, cited by Martin, pp. 26-27.

the "word of God" (1 Th 2:13). Schweizer goes so far as to say, "All that can be said realistically about the presence of Christ is said in reference to the Word, rather than to the Lord's Supper."[23] If the church would focus its worship upon God revealed in Christ, it must hear His Word. Cranfield does not overstate the case when he concludes that "this hearing of the Word of God, hearing what the Lord of the Church wants to say to his church in its actual situation, is the primary task of the church, the basic human action in worship."[24]

Use of the Word. The Word was heard in the worship service, both in public reading and preaching. In his instructions to the young pastor Timothy, the apostle Paul charged him to "give attention to the public reading of Scripture" (1 Ti 4:13, NASB). Although no specific mention is made of reading the Old Testament, the many references to its contents in the New Testament presuppose an acquaintance with it even by Gentiles, which could only come through a public reading in the worship service. Concerning the New Testament writings, the apostle expected his letters to be read publicly in the assembly (Col 4:16; 1 Th 5:27). Also the "reader" in Revelation 1:3 is surely a public reader for he reads to "hearers."

Scripture reading therefore plays a significant part in the worship service. It must never become routine or "a time for relaxation between the more serious activities of hymns and anthems . . . but the time for the greatest attentiveness."[25] The worship of God certainly means the honoring of His Word with attentive and obedient ears.

Preaching the Word was also a part of the service of worship (Ac 6:4; 20:7 ff.; 1 Ti 4:13; 2 Ti 4:2). In the sermon the preacher is not only proclaiming the Word but helping people to hear it through applying it to various needs of the congregation. It has well been said that the duty of the preacher is to so expound the Scriptures that in reality the Lord of the church is holding a conversation with His people. In order for this to take place it goes without saying that the sermon must be an honest attempt

23. Schweizer, "Worship in the New Testament," p. 200.
24. C. E. B. Cranfield, "Divine and Human Action," *Interpretation* 12 (Oct. 1958):392.
25. Ibid.

to explain the passage of Scripture and not use it for a platform on which to erect the preacher's thoughts or any other human ideas. No sermons preached in the early church are recorded in the New Testament. The excerpts of messages in Acts are all of a missionary nature designed for the conversion of unbelievers. The worship service, on the other hand, is primarily for the edification of the body, and hence the sermon also is directed largely to the believer. This does not mean, however, that the content is devoid of gospel. Although the apostolic epistles written to the churches are not sermons as such, their preaching and teaching in the churches was undoubtedly of a similar nature. In these the same gospel themes that occur again and again in the evangelistic messages of Acts are prominent. Central to the preaching of Acts are the facts of the death of Christ for man's sins in fulfillment of divine promise (Ac 2:22-23; 3:14-15, 18; 10:37-39) and His subsequent resurrection, which proves that He is the exalted Lord of all (2:30-36; 3:15; 10:40; cf. 1 Co 15:34). This great divine transaction is attested by the power of the Lord manifest in the church and the gift of the Holy Spirit (Ac 2:19-21; 3:12; 5:32). Finally, His coming again in power and glory as Saviour and Judge to bring this age to a close was preached (3:20 ff.; 10:42; 17:31) and an invitation to receive forgiveness of sins and the gift of the Holy Spirit was extended on the basis of repentance from sin and faith in Jesus as Lord (2:38; 3:19; 10:43; 17:30).[26]

In the epistles these basic themes are made the foundation to further progress in the Christian life. Sanctification is based upon the facts of conversion (cf. especially Ro 6:1-13; Eph 2:1-8; Col 2:6; 3:1 ff.). Thus it is necessary, because believers are still living in the flesh, to remind them over and over again of the grace which operated in their salvation. In hearing the gospel again the only difference between the church member and the unbeliever is that the former "hears afresh what he has already learnt before, and, in hearing, accepts again what he has already

26. Freedom in the use of these basic motives is obvious in the apostolic sermons as well as some difference in the approach toward Jews and Gentiles. To the Jew there was constant appeal to Scripture, while to the Gentile more use was made of general revelation. Cf. R. H. Mounce, *The Esssential Nature of New Testament Preaching*; Bo Reicke, "A Synopsis of Early Christian Preaching" in *The Root of the Vine*, Anton Fridrichsen et al., pp. 128-60.

learnt."[27] It is only on the basis of this renewed realization of salvation grace that transformation of life can occur, for it is the same grace which began the process which continues in its perfection (Phil 1:6). Not only does gospel truth remind believers of the love of God and His grace in providing salvation through Christ, but unbelievers who are considered to be present (1 Co 14:25) may also believe and be saved.

The typical epistolary style shows the priority of gospel truth followed by hortatory application to life (cf. Ro 12:1; Eph 3:1). The indicative mood provided the basis for the imperative, and the affirmation for exhortation. Attending to "exhortation" was part of the apostle's instructions for Timothy (1 Ti 4:13), and the epistles are replete with instructions in ethics and discipline. There is no preaching of truth which does not have its ramifications for living, nor are there everyday questions of life that do not have some relation to the truths of salvation. True "prophetic" preaching has not taken place until the Word has been made relevant and contemporary to the concrete situations of hearers.

The precise pattern of the ministry of the Word in the early church is difficult to ascertain from the New Testament. The lists of spiritual gifts include those of teaching, exhortation, evangelization and prophecy, all of which would be involved in a full ministry of the Word to the body. For the apostle Paul it is the gift of prophecy whereby the speaker ministers the authoritative word to the "edification, and exhortation, and comfort" which forms the primary role of causing the church to hear the Word (1 Co 14:3). The procedure was apparently quite flexible, with more than one individual taking part.

Paul was probably not writing only of the Corinthian church when he said, "When ye come together, every one of you hath a psalm, hath a doctrine, hath a tongue, hath a revelation, hath an interpretation" (1 Co 14:26). Apparently there was along with the sermon "room . . . for a perfectly free proclamation in the Spirit."[28] This naturally required a certain caution, for freedom always runs the risk of abuse. For this reason the apostle is careful to urge that spiritual discipline be exercised. All things must

27. Schweizer, *Church Order in the New Testament*, p. 226.
28. Cullmann, p. 21.

be critically examined, and only that which is good received
(1 Co 14:29; 1 Th 5:21).

A true worship of hearing the Word of God leads naturally
and inevitably to a response. Thus an essential part of the worship of the early church included speaking to Him in prayer
and uttering His praises in word and song.

Prayer in the New Testament is both private and corporate
public prayer in the church congregation. The importance of the
former is seen in the many instructions given by Jesus on individual prayer, and His severe warning against pretentious public
prayers. For Jesus Himself prayer "was not only an important
part of His life: it *was* His life, the very breath of His being."[29]
One cannot avoid the conviction that for the apostle Paul, too,
prayer was the all-important channel by which God wrought
His grace in the church and sustained His people. As with Jesus,
the apostle's life and breath consisted of incessant prayer (cf.
1 Th 1:2; 5:17).

That which was so vital to the experience of the individual
was also a part of the life of the church as believers joined together in united prayer. They "continued steadfastly . . . in
prayers" (Ac 2:42), whether in homes (2:46) or in the temple
(3:1). Exhortations and instruction for prayers enjoined in the
epistles were certainly meant for the assembled believers as well
as for individuals (Eph 6:18; Phil 4:6; Col 4:2; 1 Th 5:17; 1 Ti
2:1-2, 8).

The contents of prayer varied according to the situation. Yet,
certain basic elements are evident in the instructions and the
recorded prayers. Four primary words are used to describe
prayer: supplications, prayer, intercessions and thanksgiving (cf.
Phil 4:6; 1 Ti 2:1). Though these cannot be sharply distinguished
as distinct parts of prayer, but often simply contemplate prayer
from different aspects, they do provide a glimpse of the variety
of contents involved.

Supplication signifies a petition for a definite need in a concrete situation. Prayer is used more generally for reverent and
worshipful address to God. When used in contrast to supplica-

29. James S. Stewart, *The Life and Teaching of Jesus Christ*, p. 108.

tions, it may suggest the believer's general need of God and dependency upon Him for all good. Intercession is related to the verbal form meaning "to fall in with a person, to draw near so as to converse familiarly."[30] It signified, above all, freedom of access and became a technical term for petition offered to a governor or king. In several contexts, however, as probably in 1 Timothy 2:1 in contrast to the other words, it indicates "a confident interview which is 'in the interest of others,' " and thus has the meaning of intercession.[31] Thanksgiving expresses that element of gratitude without which no prayer is complete.

All of these different aspects are evident in the prayer life of the church. Specific prayer was made for guidance in the choice of a successor to Judas (Ac 1:24). When Peter was imprisoned, fervent intercession on his behalf resulted in his freedom (Ac 12:5, 12-17).[32] Intercession was also made for those outside the church, especially for God-appointed civil authorities (1 Ti 2:1-6). The mission of Paul and Barnabas was motivated and directed by the Spirit through prayer (Ac 13:1-3), enabling them to hazard their lives for the name of Christ (15:26). Paul's prayers are models of the worship of thanksgiving for God's goodness so bountifully received. But they also express worship in the confident laying of needs and petitions before Him, and the absence of anxiety in the assurance that He knows best and will answer according to His wisdom and mercy (Eph 1:15-19; 3:14; 1 Th 1:2-4).

Praise and thanksgiving were an essential part of prayer, but they were expressed in distinct ways as well. The reference first to "a psalm" in the assembly (1 Co 14:26) suggests that the dictum of the Talmud that "man should always first utter praises, and then pray" may have provided a pattern for some church worship services. The many doxologies extolling the "blessedness" (Ro 1:25; 9:5; 2 Co 11:31; Eph. 1:3) and "glory" of God (Ro 11:36; Gal 1:5; Phil 4:20; 2 Ti 4:18), which occur at the beginning as well as within and at the end of the New Testament

---

30. Marvin R. Vincent, *Word Studies in the New Testament*, 4:216.
31. William Hendricksen, *I-II Timothy and Titus, New Testament Commentary*, p. 92.
32. The word translated "without ceasing" means literally "in an outstretched manner" and refers to a "tension of the will" in resoluteness and fervency. Cf. Ernst Fuchs, "ekteinō—ektenēs" in *TDNT*, 2:463-64.

epistles, are expressive of what took place in the worship services.[33]

Above all, the church praised God in song. Even as God's people in the Old Testament found music a fitting instrument of praise, with many of the psalms being intended for use in congregational worship (e.g., Ps 24, 118, 134, 145), so the church expressed its joyful enthusiasm in the Spirit through singing. The hymnody of the church undoubtedly included selections from the Old Testament Psalter as the believers began reading them through Christian eyes. It is probable that the hymn sung by Jesus and His disciples after the Lord's Supper is a reference to the second half of the *Hallel* of the Passover festival (Ps 115-118). James' encouragement to sing psalms in times of cheerfulness may refer to David's psalms (Ja 5:13). The nature of the songs of Paul and Silas in their imprisonment at Philippi is not stated, but under duress their minds could easily have turned to familiar portions of the Old Testament Psalter. The hymns of Revelation also are a combination of Old Testament phrases (cf. Rev 15:3-4).

But the creative Spirit was active in song in the New Testament as well as the Old. The "psalms and hymns and spiritual songs" (Col 3:16; Eph 4:19) are admittedly difficult to distinguish sharply. The usual suggestion is to the effect that "psalms" has reference to use of the Old Testament Psalter. The "hymns and spiritual songs" on the other hand are products of the church's own spiritual experience. A hymn concerned the address of praise and glory to God while "songs" were songs of spiritual themes other than direct address to God. The latter term was used for any song, therefore the qualification "spiritual."[34] As indicated, a clear distinction is somewhat compromised by other uses of these terms. Paul and Silas were "hymning" to God in the Philippian prison very probably, as noted above, with psalms (Ac 16:25). The same word is also used for Christ and the disciples singing psalms (Mt 26:30). Thus a psalm sung in praise to God could also be a hymn. It is also possible that the Spirit produced what

33. Cullmann, pp. 23-24.
34. Richard Chenevix Trench, *Synonyms of the New Testament*, pp. 295-301.

is termed "psalms" in the New Testament church (cf. 1 Co 14:26).

At any rate, New Testament hymns and songs are evident in the Scripture, being denoted by their rhythmic form and style.[35] Generally accepted examples of early Christian hymnology are Ephesians 5:14 and 1 Timothy 3:16. Other passages suggested include Colossians 1:15-20; Philippians 2:6-11; Hebrews 1:3, as well as numerous references in the book of Revelation (5:9 ff.; 12:10-12; 19:1 ff.). It is difficult in many instances to specify clearly what is hymnodic and what may be another poetic form of praise. With reference to Acts 4:24-31, where there is a fusion of spontaneous praise, psalmody and petition, Moule concludes, "It is impossible to establish with any fixed certainty that this or that is an actual 'hymn' in the sense of a fixed composition often repeated in the same form," for the New Testament writing "welled up from a great fund of poetry and praise which was all of a piece with the common worship of Christian communities. And it is as hopeless to 'categorize' in such conditions as it is to represent a galloping horse by one 'still' from a motion picture."[36]

These glimpses of early church hymnody, as well as the mention of psalms, hymns and spiritual songs, indicate a variety of content. Hymns of praise to God in adoration of His own person and His great salvation in Christ should be a significant part of the worship of the church. Songs of personal experience and aspiration can also be worship, but they should not take precedence over the proclamation of the objective reality of God and the gospel. Worshipful music issues from the heart along with the voice. It is "making melody in your heart to the Lord" (Eph 5:19), "singing with thankfulness in your hearts to God" (Col 3:16, NASB). It is an act in which the worshiper enters wholeheartedly with the spirit as well as the mind (1 Co 14:15). There is the constant danger of using hymns simply for their tunes or functional variation in the order of service when neither the

---

35. The features which identify a hymn are "a lyrical quality and rythmical style, an unusual vocabulary which is different from the surrounding context of the letter in which the passage appears, some distinctive piece of Christian doctrine (usually associated with the Person and Work of our Lord Jesus Christ) and hints that this passage in question finds its natural setting in a baptismal or Communion service" (Martin, *Worship in the Early Church*, p. 48).

36. Moule, pp. 69-70.

mind or spirit is sincerely involved in what is sung, and thus that which has the form of worship turns out to be only meaningless lip service.

Worship in song both glorifies God and edifies the church. In singing, believers are "speaking to one another" (Eph 5:19, NASB).[37] The action contemplated is described by Eadie as "giving expression among yourselves, or in concert, to your joyous emotions in psalms and hymns and spiritual songs."[38] Evidence of the practice of early Christians in speaking to one another in song is given by Pliny, the Roman governor of Bithynia, in his letter written to Trajan the Emperor in A.D. 112. The believers of his province, according to Pliny, were in the habit of meeting on a fixed day before dawn and "reciting a hymn antiphonally to Christ as God."[39] Tertullian, toward the end of the second century, tells of the Christian love feast at which "each is invited to sing to God in the presence of the others what he knows of the holy Scripture or from his own heart."[40]

This "speaking to one another," which signifies basically "the use of the voice," is further elaborated as "teaching and admonishing one another" in the parallel passages of Colossians 3:16. The instructional benefit of hymns that were filled with God's truth is obvious. Fletcher of Saltoun's words, "Let me write a nation's ballads, and I care not who writes the nation's laws," are applicable to the theology of the church as well.

It is therefore of prime importance that the lyrics of hymns and gospel songs are expressive of biblical truth. The hymn in 1 Timothy 3:16 with its great doctrinal facts is an example of teaching while the function of admonition is evident in Ephesians 5:14 (NASB):

> Awake, sleeper
> And arise from the dead,
> And Christ will shine on you.

37. The pronoun "yourselves" in the AV (*heautois*) is not only reflexive, but here it indicates reciprocal action. Thus it is not "to yourselves" or "for yourselves" but "among yourselves" or "each other" as also in 4:32, "forgiving each other." Cf. Col 3:13,16.
38. John Eadie, *Commentary on the Epistle to the Ephesians*, p. 399.
39. *Epistle to Trajan* (x. 96), cited by F. F. Bruce, *The Epistle to the Ephesians* (London: Pickering & Inglis, 1961), p. 111.
40. *Apology*, 39, cited by ibid.

Nowhere is God's gift of music more appropriate than in the church at worship. The sound of singing reverberated in Israel of old, but especially in the fulfillment of the Messianic prophecies, joy and singing were to break forth among God's people (Is 35:1-2; 52:7-9; 54:1). The people who have received the promised salvation in Christ and the gift of the Spirit cannot but sing.

Another aspect of worship in the early church closely allied with hymnody was the recital of credal formulas. The overlapping of these is seen in the introduction to what is generally accepted as a hymn. "And by common confession great is the mystery of godliness" (1 Ti 3:16, NASB). Martin, following Bultmann, suggests that the confessions entailed short simple sentences like "Jesus is the Christ" whereas hymns represent longer statements of the person and work of Christ and are thus capable of division into stanzas.[41] The place of credal statements in the public service is not fully known, but in all probability confessions of the lordship of Christ (1 Co 12:3; Ro 10:9-10) and statements expressive of the basic faith of the church (e.g., 1 Co 15:3-5; Ro 4:25) were a regular part of worship.[42]

THE OFFERING

The response of God's people in worship takes place not only in word and song but in action. The Scripture has sharp rebuke for a religion of word alone. Without embodiment in act, love is a sham (Ja 2:15-17; 1 Jn 3:17-18). Thus the gathering together of the church was also the occasion for collecting the offering (1 Co 16:1-2). The basic principles for the acceptable worship of God in giving are clearly outlined in Scripture.

The motive. The dynamic of stewardship, as in all worship, is found in the prior giving of God. Christian giving can only be a response to God's grace. For this reason the apostle Paul is careful to set his instructions for the collection against the background of God's "unspeakable gift" (2 Co 9:15). The reception of the riches of salvation which came through the self-giving of Christ is the inspiration for stewardship (2 Co 8:9). This includes not simply the initial salvation and gracious redemption

41. Martin, *Worship in the Early Church*, p. 53.
42. Cullmann, p. 22.

from judgment, but the continual bounty of God's blessing in life. Paul reminds the Corinthian believers that they cannot outgive God, for He will never be debtor to man: "He which soweth bountifully shall reap also bountifully. . . . God is able to make all grace abound toward you; that ye, always having all sufficiency in all things, may abound to every good work (2 Co 9:6, 8; cf. Lk 6:38). The faithful steward can never overdraw his account.

Another motive for giving is the love of man which demonstrates itself in a concern for his needs. In reality this is not a second motive, but the outworking of a love for God. According to Christ, the love of one's neighbor is closely related to the love of God (Mt 22:34-40; cf. Lk 10:25-37). This love is exemplified in the merciful action of the good Samaritan in caring for the miseries of man. The apostle John likewise links the response to human need with the love of God: "We know love by this, that He laid down His life for us; and we ought to lay down our lives for the brethren. But whoever has the world's goods, and beholds his brother in need and closes his heart against him, how does the love of God abide in him?" (1 Jn 3:16-17, NASB).

The needs of men are never the primary purpose for giving; nevertheless, God is concerned with them, and a church in love with God will share that concern in the worship of giving. While the parable of the good Samaritan shows that no man is beyond the purview of help, it is especially fellow believers which the disciples of Christ are to look after, for ministry to the brethren is, in fact, ministry to Christ Himself (Mt 25:34-40).

The measure. The worship of giving begins with one's own self. Paul notes that believers who had ministered to his needs "first gave their own selves to the Lord, and unto us by the will of God" (2 Co 8:5; cf. Ro 12:1). Their giving of substance was the natural consequence of this self-sacrifice. Beyond this stewardship in which every believer can participate equally, the measure of giving is according to a person's ability. "For if there be first a willing mind, it is accepted according to that a man hath, and not according to that he hath not" (2 Co 8:12; Ac 11:29). Each is to give "as God hath prospered him" (1 Co 16:2).

The individual amount or proportion is to be qualified by liberality (2 Co 8:2; 9:11, 13; Ro 12:8, NASB), and such a liberality that it is sacrificial. It was under conditions of severe trial and "deep poverty," not affluence, that the Macedonian church gave generously to Paul (2 Co 8:2-4). Liberality in God's eyes does not depend upon the amount, but may be displayed by those with the least. The poor widow who cast her two mites into the treasury out of her "want" gave more than the rich who cast in " much" but out of "their abundance" (Mk 12:41-44). Christ's impoverishment for the riches of His people and His continual liberality in the supply of all needs (cf. Ja 1:5) are the example and incentive for the measure of Christian giving.

The manner. More important than the amount is the spirit in which the stewardship is performed. Indeed, the measure and manner of giving are usually linked together. The offering which is acceptable to God stems voluntarily from "a willing mind," "not grudgingly, or of necessity" (2 Co 8:11-12; 9:7). The Macedonian believers, the apostle wrote, were literally "begging us with much entreaty for the favor of participation in the support of the saints" (2 Co 8:4, NASB). Moreover, giving is to be marked by cheerfulness (2 Co 9:7), an act, as Hughes so aptly notes, in which "the giver finds real pleasure" and "quite literally an *exhilarating* experience."[43] Finally, those handling the collection must also be careful that all financial matters are open and honest "not only in the sight of the Lord, but also in the sight of men" (2 Co 8:21). Almost nothing so quickly ruins the reputation of a steward and brings dishonor on the Lord's name than the mishandling of church funds.

The method. The Scriptures teach that the practice of stewardship is to be carried on in a systematic manner. The apostle gave instruction that on the first day of the week each one "lay by him in store, as God hath prospered him" (1 Co 16:2). The discipline of regularly setting aside funds is a part of genuine Christian experience, and its association with the Lord's day, is indicative of its link with worship.

The reward. Aside from the blessing of God that attends obedience in every realm, the Scriptures note several specific rewards resulting from faithful giving. Through it the plight of others is relieved; but even more, it causes the recipients to glorify God in thanksgiving and prompts their prayer for the generous

43. Philip E. Hughes, *Commentary on the Second Epistle to the Corinthians*, p. 331.

givers (2 Co 9:11-14). As such it promotes *koinonia* among the people of God and demonstrates the unity of the church. The term *koinonia* indicates "fellowship or a sharing with someone or in something," "a participation."[44] It represents the relationship of unity, both of believers with Christ and with each other. In the use of this word for giving, the apostle signifies that the sharing of material means is an expression of genuine *koinonia* (Ro 12:13; 15:26; 2 Co 9:13; Gal 6:6). In the example of generous sacrificial giving, others are encouraged and stimulated to do likewise (2 Co 8:1-2; 9:2). It also increases the giver's ability for further giving (2 Co 9:8-10; Lk 6:38; Pr 11:24), as well as fruit that abounds to the giver's account with God (Phil 4:17; 2 Co 9:10).

In conclusion, it is well to remember that our worship of giving is the concrete expression of devotion to God in all areas. Praise for His gracious salvation as well as prayer for His will to be accomplished are classified as merely pious exercises unless they are accompanied by a willingness to share in that will and purpose in a way that costs. The offering is an indication of the total life of devotion.

CONCLUSION

This brief glimpse at the worship of the early church, along with baptism and the Lord's Supper which are considered in the next chapter, reveals a wealth of variety in the expression of the Christian life in the early church when believers met together. One cannot help but feel that some of this expression is missing in many churches today and that to some extent Cullmann deserves attention when he asserts that "the services of worship in the Protestant Churches of our own era are very much poorer, not only in respect of the free working of the Spirit, but also in respect of what is liturgical and especially in respect of what is aimed at in the gatherings of the community."[45]

44. Friedrich Hauck, "koinōnos, koinōneō, koinōnia, sunkoinōnos, sunkoi-nōneō" in *TDNT*, 3:797-98.
45. Cullmann, p. 26.

9

Baptism and the Lord's Supper

INTRODUCTION

AT THE HEART of the expression of the church's faith are the rites of baptism and Lord's Supper. Although church history reveals much controversy and misunderstanding related to these practices, they are clearly commanded by the Lord and so form a vital aspect of the life of the community which can be neglected only with impoverishment of the church. These rites are usually termed ordinances or sacraments. The term *sacrament* is derived from the Latin *sacramentum*, which was applied to anything sacred or consecrated. The immediate connection of this term with the rites of baptism and the Lord's Supper lies in the use of *sacramentum* in the Vulgate to translate the Greek *mustērion*, "mystery" (e.g., Eph 5:32, 1 Ti 3:16; Rev 1:20). It thus came to be used for anything that had a secret or mysterious significance. Augustine called it "the visible form of an invisible grace." For a long time it was loosely applied to the doctrines of Christianity as well as to many symbolic rites. Later its use was limited to those rites believed to be specifically imposed on the church by the Lord.

Because of the mysterious connotation of the term *sacrament* and the almost magical power associated with it, as when the Roman Church insists that the priest has power to convert the bread and cup into the actual blood and body of Christ, many prefer the term *ordinance*. Coming from the Latin, *ordo*, meaning "a row, an order," ordinance emphasizes the fact that these rites were ordained by the Lord, with no thought of them as actual conveyors of grace, but rather only as symbols. The word *sacrament* is used by many with this same meaning. Since neither term is used in the Scripture for these rites, all depends on the significance attached to the terms by those employing them.

On the basis that only those rites which can be shown in Scripture to have been instituted by Christ for the church are to be regarded as ordinances to be regularly practiced by the church, most Protestants recognize two: baptism and the Lord's Supper. To these the Roman Catholic Church has added confirmation, penance, extreme unction, holy orders and matrimony, for a total of seven. It is impossible, however, to demonstrate from the Scriptures that these additional practices stem from the command of Christ.

BAPTISM

THE INSTITUTION OF BAPTISM

The act of baptism finds its precedent in the baptism of John and Jewish proselyte baptism. Christian baptism, however, was not simply a continuation of these but was a different baptism performed at the command of Christ (Ac 19:3 ff.). Proselyte baptism concerned the purity of the individual before the law, and John's baptism of repentance was performed in anticipation of the promised breaking in of the Messianic kingdom. But baptism in the name of Jesus contained a new significance far beyond either of these two precedents. The coming of Christ was the fulfillment of God's promised salvation, and Christian baptism indicates participation in this completed salvation through faith in Christ.

Commanded by Christ. The command to baptize forms part of Christ's Great Commission to the church: "Go therefore and make disciples of all the nations, baptizing them in the name of the Father and the Son and the Holy Spirit" (Mt 28:19, NASB). Baptizing is a concomitant of the command to make disciples, even as teaching is in the following verses. The practice of baptism, along with the proclamation of the gospel by the apostolic church, thus rests directly upon the institution of Christ. That this command was not for the apostles alone is evident in the concluding words of the commission: "And, lo, I am with you always, even to the end of the age" (v. 20, NASB). The apostles did not live to the end of the age, but the church will exist until its Lord comes for her. It was therefore to the disciples as foundational representatives of the church for this entire age that the command to disciple all nations, baptizing and teaching them, was committed.

Practiced by the church. The practice of baptism was universal in the early church. Beginning on the day of Pentecost in response to Peter's invitation (Ac 2:38, 41), consistent testimony is given to the administration of baptism in the churches (cf. 8:12, 36-38; 9:18; 10:47; 16:14-15, 33; 18:8; 19:5). Bruce goes so far as to say that "the idea of an unbaptized Christian is simply not entertained in N.T."[1] When the apostles and others proclaimed the gospel they called for a decision which ended in baptism. Baptism, however, was clearly subordinate to the gospel, without which it would have no meaning. It is in respect to this subordination that Paul's word about baptizing only a few at Corinth is to be understood, and not as a minimizing of the practice (1 Co 1:14-17). Paul was authorized by Christ to be His special witness as an apostle by preaching the gospel, and he did not conceive of baptism as part of that special authorization. Anyone could baptize who knew the name of Jesus, for baptism was not in the name of any human minister.

MEANING OF BAPTISM

Baptism reflects the meaning of the gospel and the salvation it brings. Therefore, it is as rich in meaning as the saving work of Christ. This significance involves both a relationship with Christ and fellow believers in the church.

Identification with Christ. Christian baptism is baptism "in the name of Jesus Christ" (Ac 2:38; cf. 8:16).[2] In contemporary Greek usage the phrase "into the name" was a technical term of commerce meaning "to the account" of someone, signifying

1. F. F. Bruce, *The Book of the Acts*, p. 77.
2. The difference between the Trinitarian formula prescribed in Mt 28:19 and the references in the apostolic practice to baptism "in the name of Jesus" has evoked many explanations. Cf. T. M. Lindsay, "Baptism (Non-Immersionist View)," *The International Standard Bible Encyclopaedia*, 1:392. A possible solution is that of Bruce: "The longer expression in Matthew 28:19 (*cf. Didache*, 7:1), where baptism is to be 'into the name of the Father and of the Son and of the Holy Spirit,' is appropriate for 'disciples of all the nations' (*i.e.* Gentiles), turning from paganism to serve the living God, whereas Jews and Samaritans, who already acknowledged the one true God, were required only to confess Jesus as Lord and Messiah" (Bruce, p. 181, n. 32). A more probable interpretation is that the historical references in Acts are not meant to give a particular formula, but rather simply to indicate that the rite was Christian in distinction to Jewish, heathen, or John's baptism (cf. Ac 19:3-5). See J. A. Alexander, *Commentary on the Acts of the Apostles*, pp. 85, 419, 651.

ownership.[3] The Jewish meaning evident in rabbinical writings carried several ramifications, but the basic thought was "with respect to or regard to." The Semitic concept was probably more directly behind the baptismal use, signifying Jesus "as the one to whom the candidate is made over."[4]

Baptism is, therefore, first and foremost, identification with Jesus Christ. By this act the initiate indicated that he was entering the realm of Christ's lordship and power. But not only was the name of Christ pronounced over the baptized, but the baptized also called upon the name of the Lord (Ac 22:16). In doing so, he openly confessed in penitence and faith his submission to the lordship of Jesus (cf. Ro 10:9). It is, as Beasley-Murray aptly notes, the time when one who has been an enemy of Christ makes "his final surrender."[5] Baptism is therefore the sign of the working of the gospel in which God unites the believer to Himself through Christ, and the believer testifies to the subjective reality of that union in his life.

Identification with Christ is also identification with His great saving acts. The waters of baptism are thus related to washing or cleansing from the defilement of sin (Ac 22:16; Heb 10:22; 1 Co 6:11; cf. Ac 2:38). Even more often, however, in Scripture the baptismal act signifies the believer's death to the old life and his resurrection as a new creature in union with Christ. The apostle bases his appeal to a holy life on the fact that "we are buried with him by baptism into death: that like as Christ was raised up from the dead by the glory of the Father, even so we also should walk in newness of life" (Ro 6:4). Similarly, to the Colossians he writes, "having been buried with Him in baptism, in which you were also raised up with Him through faith in the working of God, who raised Him from the dead" (Col 2:12, NASB). Peter sees an analogy to baptism in the flood waters of judgment and death through which Noah was borne by the ark to a new life (1 Pe 3:20 f.). While cleansing from sin is the result of this participation with Christ, the salvation experience is, at its heart, the death of the old life and the resurrection to a new life in union with Christ. The importance of this under-

---

3. Albrecht Oepke, *"baptō, baptidzō"* in *TDNT*, 1:539.
4. Hans Bietenhard, *"onoma"* in *TDNT*, 5:274-76.
5. G. R. Beasley-Murray, *Baptism Today and Tomorrow*, p. 43.

standing and its significance in understanding baptism is emphasized by Moule when he notes that "as soon as Baptism is treated *chiefly* as a cleansing, the tendency is to interpret it as a cleansing from *past* sins, with the corollary that thereafter the baptized must keep himself clean. But as long as membership in Christ is treated as a new life . . . the supernatural, wholly divine agency is more prominent."[6]

Identification with the church. Identification with Christ is at the same time identification with His body, the church. Death and resurrection with Christ refer not only to union with Christ but to a unity of Christ composed of many members. "For as the body is one, and hath many members, and all the members of that one body, being many, are one body: so also is Christ" (1 Co 12:12; cf. Ro 12:4-5). One is not united to the Head without at the same time being united with the body. So Paul writes that all believers in Christ are made into "one new man" (Eph 2:15).

Since baptism signifies the inward reality of the participation into His body, it was the normal initiatory rite into the visible body. In this act the new converts were identified outwardly with the fellowship of believers (Ac 2:41). Not only is the individual transition from the old life to new life made public in baptism, but the transition from union with the world to that of the community of believers is proclaimed as well. In the rite of baptism the believer took his stand with the disciples of Christ.

It is significant that every baptism in Acts took place almost immediately following the confession of faith. This is seen particularly in the case of the Ethiopian eunuch who quickly asked, "What doth hinder me to be baptized?" (8:36) and in Peter's action with the household of Cornelius (10:47). The same was true with the Philippian jailor (16:33). The preaching of the gospel apparently contained the full proclamation of the redemptive work of Christ and the demand for a response of faith which included the commitment of life. To believe in Christ was to profess the reality of what was signified in baptism and the intention of living a new life. All who so confessed were baptized, and full instructions in Christian doctrine followed.

By this means new converts were immediately involved in the

6. C. F. D. Moule, *Worship in the New Testament*, p. 57.

full life of the community. Their new love was allowed expression in the exercise of their gifts and the witness of the community. The risk of those who were not genuine entering the church and thus harming the body was compensated by a strong spiritual discipline.

The practice of separating baptism from the commencement of the Christian life with its identification with Christ and His church loses the real significance of the act. It is more than simply being obedient to the command of Christ, for He related it to the act of becoming His disciple; and the later New Testament interpretation and practice fill it with the rich meaning of this event.

EFFICACY OF BAPTISM

The question of the effect of baptism has evoked different responses and consequently much controversy. In approaching this subject it must be said at the outset that any interpretation which makes the rite itself spiritually efficacious must be rejected. The Scriptures without equivocation teach that salvation with all of its concomitant blessings is through faith alone. In reaction to the *ex opere operato* doctrine of the Roman Church, whereby baptism is given the power to work the regeneration of an infant involuntarily, many have taught that it has only a symbolic significance. Baptism produces nothing except the blessing of being obedient to Christ.

However, examination of the New Testament reveals that baptism is often associated with effects and that these same effects are the blessings of faith.[7] On the day of Pentecost when the people asked what they could do in response to Peter's proclamation, he replied, "Repent, and be baptized . . . for the remission of sins" (Ac 2:38). Similarly, Paul was told to "arise, and be baptized, and wash away thy sins, calling on the name of the Lord" (Ac 22:16). To be sure, faith was involved in the response at Pentecost and also in Paul's conversion. But the close association of baptism with the spiritual effects of faith in the early church is evident in these instructions. Other effects associated with baptism include union with Christ (Ro 6:3-4; Gal 3:27; Col 2:12), the possession of the Spirit (Ac 2:38), and finally,

7. Beasley-Murray, pp. 27-41.

salvation itself in the statement of Peter that "baptism doth also now save us" (1 Pe 3:21).

But in all of these passages faith is either imputed or explicitly stated along with the act of baptism. Burial and resurrection with Christ are "through faith in the working of God" (Col 2:12, NASB). The gift of the Spirit is not only related to baptism but is based on repentance (Ac 2:38). In addition, these effects, like the forgiveness and cleansing of sin, are mentioned as the fruit of faith, without reference to baptism. John writes, "If we confess our sins, he is faithful and just to forgive us our sins, and to cleanse us from all unrighteousness" (1 Jn 1:9). Of the house of Cornelius, Peter testified that their heart had been purified by faith without any mention of baptism (Ac 15:9; cf. Eph 3:17; Gal 2:20; 3:2, 14). Even in Peter's difficult statement it cannot be construed that the water of baptism saves, for he has already said that we are "born again . . . by the word of God" (1 Pe 1:23). And in 3:21, after speaking of the salutary effect of baptism, he goes on to explain that baptism is "not the removal of dirt from the flesh, but an appeal to God for a good conscience" (NASB). The term *eperōtēma*, "appeal," has occasioned much discussion, with many preferring to understand it as a pledge.[8] But whether it refers to a prayer to God for a good conscience or, as is more probable, a pledge of loyalty from a good conscience, the real significance of baptism involves the inward response toward God.

From this brief review of the similarities of their effects it is evident that baptism and faith are closely related according to the Scriptures. It is this relationship which is the foundation for speaking of the effects of baptism. Christian baptism is conversion baptism. It formed in the New Testament the final act of the repentance-belief-baptism response to the proclamation of the gospel. Thus, although salvation is through faith, baptism as the expression of this faith was often joined to the reality. The sign and the reality symbolized were not separated but were seen together, as James Denney said, "Baptism and faith are but the

8. See Edward G. Selwyn, *The First Epistle of St. Peter*, pp. 205-6; R. E. O. White, *The Biblical Doctrine of Initiation*, pp. 232-34. For the meaning of a prayer see Heinrich Greeven, *"eperōtēma"* in *TDNT*, 2:688.

outside and the inside of the same thing."[9] For this reason the gifts of faith are also those of baptism, for baptism is nothing but faith embodied in act. As God always meets human faith with His act in bestowing the blessing promised in the gospel, so He acts in the expression of faith in baptism.

The relation between baptism and faith must never be construed, however, so as to make the rite *the faith* which brings salvation. Rather, in every biblical example the inward, saving faith precedes baptism and, in some instances at least, it is clearly manifest that the gifts of salvation are bestowed as the fruit of that faith prior to baptism. The many instances where faith alone is mentioned without baptism as the condition of salvation make it impossible to accept any doctrine of baptismal regeneration whereby baptism is necessary for salvation. The blessings of the gospel are received through faith. Nevertheless, when that saving faith goes on to be expressed in an objective manner through baptism, God uses this act to confirm the realities of salvation. The faith of the individual is strengthened as it is openly expressed, and the saving acts of salvation are sealed and ratified with additional force to the heart of the believer.

SUBJECTS OF BAPTISM

One of the major areas of disagreement over baptism concerns the proper subjects. All agree that since baptism indicates that the recipient bears some relationship to Christ and His church, in the case of those capable of making a rational voluntary choice, only believers are candidates for baptism. Many, however, believe that the children of believers by virtue of their relationship to their parents also bear a certain relationship to the salvation promises of the gospel even without personal faith. They are, in the words of Berkhof, "children of the covenant, and are as such heirs of the all-comprehensive covenant-promises of God."[10] The promises are granted to them in an objective and formal sense and become real in their subjective experience later through acceptance by faith. On this basis, large segments of the church have throughout history practiced the baptism of

---

9. James Denney, *The Death of Christ*, p. 185.
10. L. Berkhof, *Systematic Theology*, p. 638.

infants of believing parents.[11] It is impossible, however, to find this practice in the New Testament church or in the earliest records of subsequent church history. Much evidence can be adduced to the contrary that baptism is for believers only.[12]

Command to baptize. In the Great Commission the Lord charged His disciples to "go therefore and make disciples of all the nations, baptizing them in the name of the Father and the Son and the Holy Spirit, teaching them to observe all that I commanded you" (Mt 28:19-20, NASB). Since becoming a disciple involves faith, baptism as a concomitant is for converts. The participle "teaching" bears the same relation to the imperative "make disciples" as does "baptizing." Those who are baptized are to be taught, for the basic connotation of a disciple is a learner. It is difficult to understand how infants could be included in this instruction.

It is sometimes adduced that Peter's exhortation to baptism on the day of Pentecost included children. After saying "Repent, and be baptized every one of you," he adds, "For the promise is unto you, and to your children" (Ac 2:38-39). But the prior command to repent surely excludes those incapable of faith. "Children" is a reference to their posterity, to whom the opportunity of salvation certainly belonged, but the avenue of obtaining it was through repentance, even as it was for their parents.

Biblical examples of baptism. The consistent pattern of New Testament practice was hearing, believing, and being baptized. On Pentecost "they that gladly received his word were baptized" (Ac 2:41). When the Samaritans "believed Philip preaching the things concerning the kingdom of God, and the name of Jesus Christ, they were baptized, both men and women" (Ac 8:12). It is significant that with the specific mention of "men and women" nothing is said of their children. Philip's reply to the

11. For the position of infant baptism see G. W. Bromiley, *The Baptism of Infants;* Oscar Cullmann, *Baptism in the New Testament;* Joachim Jeremias, *Infant Baptism in the First Four Centuries;* John Murray, *Christian Baptism;* Dwight H. Small, *The Biblical Basis for Infant Baptism;* Pierre Marcel, *The Biblical Doctrine of Infant Baptism;* G. C. Berkouwer, *The Sacraments.*
12. For the position of believer's baptism, see Kurt Aland, *Did the Early Church Baptize Infants?* Karl Barth, *Church Dogmatics* 4:4 (Fragment); Beasley-Murray, *Baptism in the New Testament;* Alexander Carson, *Baptism in Its Mode and Subjects,* 5th American ed.; Johannes Warns, *Baptism;* R. E. O. White, *The Biblical Doctrine of Initiation.*

eunuch's request for baptism is straightforward: "If thou be-
lievest with all thine heart, thou mayest" (Ac 8:36-37). The
eunuch commanded the chariot to stop, and he was baptized (v.
38). Additional examples of believer's baptism in Acts include
Paul (9:18), Cornelius and those with him (10:44-48), Lydia
and her household (16:14-15), the Philippian jailer and his
household (16:32-33), Crispus, his house, and many Corinthians
(18:8), and the Ephesian believers (19:4-5).

The baptism (of "households" has been taken as strong evidence for infant baptism, as this expression is taken to include
all in the family. "Household" (*oikos*) is said to be a formula
adopted from the Old Testament cultic language, especially that
relating to circumcision, which includes small children as well as
others.[13] The conclusion of infant baptism on the basis of this
theological use of an *oikos* formula is questionable on several
counts.[14] The alleged use of *oikos* in the Septuagint, in the sense
of a ritualistic formula denoting especially little children, is relatively rare in respect to the total number of occurrences of *oikos*.
Even if such a meaning were found in the Septuagint, which is debatable, it is not demonstrable that this usage is carried over to
the New Testament. The overwhelming majority of the uses of
oikos relative to a family contain no theological aura but are
completely parallel to the secular Greek use since Homer, meaning simply "family" and "inhabitants of the house," with no
emphasis on infants (cf. 2 Ti 1:16; 4:19). Nowhere in connection with an *oikos* passage in the New Testament is a child or an
infant expressly named.

In the passages dealing with household baptism, not only are
no infants mentioned, but in several there is clear evidence that
those baptized were responsible believers. In the case of the
Philippian jailer (Ac 16:31-33), Paul's instruction for salvation
was, "Believe on the Lord Jesus Christ, and thou shalt be saved,
and thy house" (v. 31). Taken at face value, this statement could
be construed to mean that the decision of the man would effect
the salvation of his house. But the teaching of the Scriptures that
faith must be personal precludes such an understanding. The
implication is that the jailer and also those in his house must be-

13. Jeremias, p. 21.
14. For the following refutation see Aland, pp. 87-94.

lieve for salvation. This interpretation is validated by the following verse, which declares that the word was spoken not only to the head of the house but also "to all that were in his house" (v. 32). In response to the word, it is explicitly stated that the jailer "rejoiced, believing in God with all his house" (v. 34). In the parallel situation of Crispus it is similarly stated that he "believed on the Lord with all his house" (Ac 18:8). It thus appears conclusive that all who were baptized in the house of the jailer were believers.

The situation with the house of Cornelius is similar. The angel had informed Cornelius that Peter would come and tell him how he and his house could be saved (Ac 11:14). That only believers were involved in the group is evident from the report of the actual events. While Peter was speaking, the "Holy Ghost fell on all them which heard the word" (Ac 10:44). These same participants who had received the Spirit spoke in tongues and magnified God, an action which obviously eliminates infants. Apparently it was a group of adults, or at least those old enough to hear the Word, who gathered from several families for this occasion (cf. 10:27).

The nature of the participants in the baptism of Lydia's household is not explicitly stated (Ac 16:14-15). Nevertheless, the way in which Lydia is introduced would suggest that she is either unmarried or a widow; either case would render doubtful the presence of infants or small children. Not a word is said of a husband. Rather, she is introduced as carrying on a vocation, "a seller of purple, of the city of Thyatira." Her request for Paul and Silas to lodge in her house displays an independence hardly possible if a husband were in the background. Who the members of the household were is not stated, perhaps relatives or servants. But, at any rate, no mention is made of infants, and the account of baptism is best viewed as a compressed version of what took place in the longer reports of the Philippian jailer and Crispus.

The final mention of a household baptism is that of Stephanas (1 Co 1:16). Again there is no description given of those baptized, but the household of Stephanas is mentioned later in terms which can only refer to believers. They are called "the firstfruits of Achaia" who "have addicted themselves to the ministry of the saints" (1 Co 16:15). In other words, the household of Stephanas

202   *The Church in God's Program*

was serving the church. Furthermore, they were of such stature that, with reference to them, the apostle exhorts the Corinthian believers to "submit yourselves unto such, and to every one that helpeth with us, and laboureth" (v. 16). The strong implication is that they were adult believers.

The evidence of New Testament examples of baptisms, including those of households where indication is given of the occupants, shows a consistent pattern of hearing the Word, belief, and then baptism.

Significance of baptism. As already noted, baptism signifies both the response of faith on the part of the one baptized and the salvation act of God performed in response to faith. Both the human and divine acts symbolized are realities which cannot be true in those incapable of faith. The union of the sign and the thing signified in New Testament baptism would seem to make the baptism of infants long before their actual faith and experience of salvation meaningless.

The problem of the separation of baptism from faith is seen in the practice of confirmation which is maintained in one form or another by pedobaptists. Because of the recognition of the necessity of faith in the efficacy of baptism as opposed to the Roman doctrine of *ex opere operato* in which the power of the sacrament is said to be bound to the water, the evangelical pedobaptist is obligated to recognize the additional concept of confirmation as the event when profession of faith is made and the symbolism is made real. If confirmation is stressed, however, there is danger of establishing another sacrament for which there is no biblical authority. On the other hand, the minimizing of this confession of faith jeopardizes the principle of the necessity of faith for the efficacy of the sacrament. In the practice of confirmation it is evident that infant baptism is incomplete and must be consummated in a later act.

Baptism at its heart signifies the completed identification with Christ and His work in death and resurrection which can only correspond to faith. There is no other meaning in the New Testament which is applicable to infant baptism.[15]

15. The difficulty involved in trying to distinguish the efficacy of baptism as it applies to adults and infants is noted by Murray. His attempt to maintain the same significance for both in the following quotation appears to contradict the clear biblical principle of salvation by faith:

Witness of history. The earliest evidence from church history following the New Testament records points to believer baptism. Unambiguous testimony for the baptism of infants emerges only about the middle of the first half of the third century.[16] The nature of the testimony indicates that infant baptism was practiced at least in some areas at the end of the second century.

The earliest witness is Tertullian (*c.* 160–220), who in an entire volume devoted to baptism opposed the baptism of infants and young children. His polemic is directed against something new, which suggests that a significant tendency toward this practice was emerging in North Africa during his time. The next evidence, now favoring infant baptism, appears in the early part of the third century in a synodal letter of Cyprian dated shortly after A.D. 250, and in the writings of Origen from between approximately A.D. 231 and 250. A third witness is the so-called *Church Order* of Hippolytus (A.D. 235). The claim of Origen that infant baptism was a custom reaching back to apostolic times is seized upon by its proponents to indicate that the practice was therefore older than the writing of Origen and, in fact, was continuous from the New Testament church, although earlier evidence is missing.[17] It may be argued, however, that such an interpretation of the appeal of Origen to apostolic tradition "ignores the mentality and methods of Church Fathers engaged in controversy."[18] The detailed polemic of Origen, which he takes up against his opponents, shows that there were strong elements in the church which did not accept the practice of infant baptism. Aland's interpretation, therefore, seems equally plausible "that Origen's statements can be explained only on the as-

---

"The possession of the grace signified by baptism does not presuppose in the case of infants the exercise of intelligent faith and repentance: they are not yet psychologically capable of such. And the church cannot require intelligent and credible profession on their part. The accompaniments of the grace signified by baptism and the prerequisites for its administration differ in the respective cases. But it is a mistake to think that the import or signification differs. Baptism signifies union with Christ and membership in His body. It means this for both adults and infants. And so, in respect of efficacy, baptism is for infants precisely what it is for adults, namely, the divine testimony to their union with Christ and the divine certification and authentication of this great truth" (Murray, p. 90).

16. Aland, pp. 42-79.
17. Jeremias, pp. 66, 86.
18. Aland, p. 48.

sumption that this 'custom of the Church' in Palestine (and elsewhere) is not yet very old. . . . A beginning of this 'custom of the
Church' about the end of the second century leaves enough time
before A.D. 230-250 for the formation of a firm ecclesiastical usage,
and on the other hand it explains why the arguments against it
have not yet been silenced."[19]

Prior to the end of the second century and the beginning of
the third there is no evidence of infant baptism, although the
subject of baptism occurs frequently. The *Didache* (*c.* A.D. 100) ,
the most ancient document outside of the New Testament, contains over seventy rules for baptism but nothing about infants.
The requirement of instruction for baptismal candidates implies
that only believers were involved. *The Shepherd of Hermas* and
the *Letter of Barnabas,* both dated within the first half of the
second century, likewise contain statements that presuppose believer baptism. The writing of Justin Martyr, Tatian, and lesser
apologists have several references to baptism, but nothing which
suggests the practice of infant baptism. In his *First Apology*
(chap. 61) , Justin Martyr gives a detailed description of baptism
in which he instructs that only convinced Christians are to be
baptized.

Examination of the works of Irenaeus (born *c.* A.D. 140—150)
also yields no evidence for infant baptism. His statement in
Against Heresies (2, 22, 4) that Christ "came to save all through
means of himself—all, I say, who through him are born again to
God—infants, and children, and boys, and youths, and old men"
cannot be understood as a reference to infant baptism, as some
contend, if the context is taken into consideration. Immediately
prior to this statement, reference is made to the fact that Christ
through His development to manhood did not despise any condition of humanity, thereby "sanctifying every age by that period
corresponding to it which belonged to himself." This thought,
along with the sentence immediately following the reference in
question to the effect that Christ passed through every age from
infancy to adulthood that He might sanctify all humanity, indicates that Irenaeus did not have baptism in mind, but simply

19. Ibid., pp. 48-49.

the fact that Christ shared humanity completely and therefore was able to sanctify all.

Finally, Clement of Alexandria, who takes us up to about A.D. 200, leaves nothing concerning infant baptism although he does discuss both baptism and several passages of Scripture relating to "children" (e.g., Mt 21:16), which he regards as adult believers.[20]

In summary, the historical evidence reveals a considerable time between the New Testament writings and the first reference to infant baptism, a gap which is difficult to account for if it was the established practice from apostolic times onward. The fact that many references to baptism occur during this period make it doubly hard to explain the absence of references to infant baptism.

If the baptism of infants was, in fact, a later innovation in the church, the question may be raised as to why it was begun. In reply it might be said that history teaches that in matters of ritual it has always been easier for the church to add something than to take it away. "It is quite as easy," as Jewett notes, "to suppose that infant baptism would gradually commend itself in post-apostolic times, as it is difficult to suppose that it fell into disrepute in many places after it had been established by apostolic authority."[21]

A very plausible theological motive for the emergence of infant baptism is seen in the changing understanding regarding an infant's involvement with sin. Much evidence indicates that the early Fathers of the church considered infants to be innocent of guilt. Since the rite of baptism was early given the unscriptural efficaciousness of washing away sins, as soon as children were thought to be born with the taint of original sin, sharing in its guilt, their immediate baptism was a logical procedure. The probability of such a development underlying the beginnings of infant baptism is supported by the appeal of Origen in support of baptizing infants to the fact of the participation of newborn children in the stain of sin.[22]

20. Ibid., pp. 59-60.
21. Paul K. Jewett, "Baptism (Baptist View)" in *The Encyclopedia of Christianity*, 1:523.
22. For the belief of the early church regarding the relation of sin to newborn children and its effect upon the practice of baptism, see Aland, pp. 100-11.

The covenantal relationship. For most advocates of pedobaptism the covenantal concept is decisive for the question of the recipients of baptism. Since the covenant established with Abraham in the Old Testament is fulfilled in Christ, all those in Christ are thus related to Abraham and consequently partakers of the covenant promises (Gal 3:29). While certain administrations may change, the covenant upon which the promises of salvation in Christ are based is essentially the same in both the Old and New Testaments. Since the sign of the covenant in the Old Testament, namely, circumcision, was applicable not only to adults under the covenantal relationship but also to their children, it is argued that the same covenantal relationship applies to those born in the homes of New Testament believers. Moreover, the apostle Paul shows the fundamental identity in the concepts of circumcision and baptism when he compares the inner reality of baptism to circumcision made without hands (Col 2:11-13). Murray summarizes the view: "The basic premise of the argument for infant baptism is that the New Testament economy is the unfolding and fulfilment of the new covenant made with Abraham and that the necessary implication is the unity and continuity of the church."[23]

The fact of the all pervasiveness of the Abrahamic covenant as the foundation in which those in Christ participate cannot be disputed. Nor can it be denied that the symbolic significance of circumcision as the putting away of sinful flesh is analogous to baptism, even though this became a spiritual reality only in the later faith of the Israelite (cf. Deu 10:16; 30:6; Jer 4:4; 6:10; 9:25-26; Ro 6:4; Col 2:11-12). But the further conclusion drawn from these facts that the circumstances of circumcision apply exactly to baptism does not follow. It fails to reckon with the progressive development in the administration of the covenantal concept. In the Old Testament the covenant, while efficacious only to those of faith, nevertheless included all the physical seed of Abraham through Israel. One was of the seed of Abraham and so related to the covenant through physical birth. In the New

23. Murray, p. 48; cf. also Bromiley, *The Baptism of Infants,* and "The Case for Infant Baptism," *Christianity Today* 9 (Oct. 9, 1964):7; John Calvin, *The Institutes of the Christian Religion* 4, xvi, 24.

Testament, however, the emphasis is upon the fact that one is of the seed of Abraham by faith: "Know ye therefore that they which are of faith, the same are the children of Abraham" (Gal 3:7; cf. 3:9, 29). Under the old administration during the Mosaic dispensation one entered the covenantal relationship by natural birth, but under the new covenant, which is but the fulfillment of the Abrahamic promises, one enters the covenantal relationship by spiritual rebirth. The Scriptures nowhere refer to a remnant of the faithful within the new covenant as there was within the old covenant with its physical hereditary relationships. All in the new covenant are believers. The baptism of John in anticipation of the Messiah provides the transition to the new entirely spiritual significance. As a "baptism of repentance for the remission of sins" (Mk 1:4b) it carried a purely moral meaning and was administered to Jews who had already been circumcised. There is no evidence of any children incapable of repentance being baptized by John.

Although circumcision and baptism are analogous in their underlying spiritual significance, the fact that baptism was not considered by the apostolic church as simply replacing circumcision is evident in the deliberations of the Jerusalem council (Ac 15). The knotty question of the necessity of circumcision might have easily been solved with the explanation that baptism has now taken its place.

The reference to children being sanctified by the presence of a believing parent in the household (1 Co 7:14) is sometimes said to point to the fact that such children are within the pale of the covenant. Whatever else this sanctification signifies, this interpretation goes too far, for the unbelieving husband or wife is also said to be sanctified by their believing partner. If sanctification means covenantal relationship, then the unbelieving spouses are in the covenant and should be baptized along with the children.

The kingdom and children. Jesus' words concerning little children and the kingdom are used by pedobaptists to support the contention that children are included in the benefits of the covenant community: "Suffer little children, and forbid them not to come unto me; for of such is the kingdom of heaven" (Mt 19:14).

These children, however, do not appear to be newborn babes. The word used for children (*paidion*) sometimes refers to those capable of understanding and even of a child twelve years old (cf. Mt 18:2; Mk 5:39, 42). The fact that the disciples forbade them from coming to Christ would seem to indicate that the baptism of infants was not practiced either by them or John; otherwise they could easily have thought that the children were coming for baptism. This reference to children is obviously designed simply to teach the childlike humility and unpretentiousness necessary for all who would enter the kingdom, with no reference to baptism.

MODE OF BAPTISM

The rite of baptism has been administered in the church in three different modes: sprinkling, pouring or effusion, and immersion. It is contended by some, especially those who practice sprinkling or pouring, that the mode is not specified in Scripture, and that all methods are acceptable "as long as the fundamental idea, namely, that of purification, finds expression in the rite."[24] There is, however, evidence which points to immersion as the mode practiced in the New Testament church. This evidence centers around the meaning of the word *baptize* and the symbolic meaning attached to it in certain passages, along with the details surrounding biblical baptisms and the witness of church history.

Meaning of the word. Lexical authorities agree that the primary meaning of baptize is to dip or immerse. The word *baptize* is the transliteration of the Greek term *baptizō,* which is the intensive form of *baptō.* According to Thayer's *Greek-English Lexicon of the New Testament,* the term *baptizō* means "prop. *to dip repeatedly, to immerge, submerge.*"[25] W. F. Arndt and F. W. Gingrich give the basic definition of *baptizō* as "*dip, immerse,* mid. *dip oneself, wash.*"[26] Cremer in his *Biblico-Theological Lexicon of New Testament Greek* says it means "to immerse, to submerge."[27] Oepke supports this meaning in Kittel's *Theo-*

24. Berkhof, p. 629.
25. Joseph H. Thayer, *A Greek-English Lexicon of the New Testament,* p. 94.
26. William F. Arndt and F. Wilbur Gingrich, *A Greek-English Lexicon of the New Testament and Other Early Christian Literature,* p. 131.
27. Hermann Cremer, *Biblico-Theological Lexicon of New Testament Greek,* p. 126.

logical Dictionary of the New Testament when he defines *baptō* as "to dip in or under," and the intensive *baptizō* as "to immerse." He shows that it was used by secular writers for the sinking of a ship, for drowning, as well as metaphorically in the sense of being overwhelmed.[28]

This is not to say that baptize must always mean complete immersion and cannot on occasion refer to a washing of something less, but it would indicate that unless there is strong contextual evidence to the contrary the meaning of immersion should be given preference on the basis of lexical evidence alone. Calvin himself, although practicing sprinkling, acknowledged that the word *baptize* meant to immerse.[29]

Although *baptō* is used in the Septuagint, translating the Hebrew word meaning "to dip" and does not always imply complete immersion, it must be noted that the word *baptō* is not used for New Testament baptism, but rather, the intensive form *baptizō* is always found. Moreover, to rely heavily upon the cultic illustrations of the Old Testament is to ignore the additional significance of death and resurrection symbolized in Christian baptism but absent in the Old Testament rites.[30] Finally, the use of the verb *baptizō* for Jewish ritual cleansing (Mk 7:4; cf. Lk 11:38) probably refers to washing by dipping the hands in water.[31] The use of the word *niptō*, "to wash," for the washing of hands in the preceding verse (Mk 7:3) together with *baptizō* (v. 4) corresponds to the Jewish distinction between the pouring of water over the hands and that of dipping them into a quantity of water.[32] The following noun, *baptismos,* used for the washing

---

28. Oepke, 1:529-30; cf. H. G. Liddell and Robert Scott, eds., *A Greek-English Lexicon,* pp. 305-6.
29. Calvin, 4, xv, 19.
30. Oepke, p. 536, notes that the goal of the Jewish washings including proselyte baptism was "ritual purity. . . . There is no thought of any natural, let alone ethical, death and regeneration."
31. The variant reading, *rantidzō,* "to sprinkle," is found in some important manuscripts, but *baptizō* is preferable as the original, both on the basis of manuscript evidence and from what is known of Jewish rites.
32. Claus-Hunno Hunzinger, *"rantidzō"* in *TDNT,* 4:981, n. 23. On the other hand, Meyer, considering the preceding washing of the hands in v. 3, argues for a complete bath in v. 4. "The statement proceeds *by way of climax;* before eating they observe the washing of hands *always,* but the *bathing, when they come from market and wish to eat"* (H. A. W. Meyer, *Critical and Exegetical Handbook to the Gospels of Mark and Luke* [New York: Funk & Wagnalls, 1884]), p. 88.

of utensils, most certainly refers to their being dipped in water. Thus, while it cannot be proven mathematically that these uses demand immersion, they would definitely allow that meaning. The figurative references to Christ's baptism of death (Mk 10:38; Lk 12:50) and the baptism into Moses (1 Co 10:1-2) do not refute the meaning of immersion, for both speak metaphorically of being immersed or overwhelmed.

It is significant that the Greek language had terms for sprinkling, *rantidzō* and pouring, *epicheō* and *proschusis*. All of these are employed in the New Testament, but never for the act of baptism.

Biblical examples of baptism. Where details are given surrounding the actual baptisms recorded in the New Testament, they either imply immersion or allow for it.

Most scholars agree that John's baptism was by immersion. This is borne out by several indications in the gospel records. After stating that Jesus was baptized in the Jordan, the writer adds, "and straightway coming out of the water" (Mk 1·9-10). The prepositions *in* (Greek, *eis,* "into") and *out* (*ek*) do not necessarily indicate immersion, for in Acts 8:38-39 both Philip and the Ethiopian went into (*eis*) the water and came out (*ek*). But they do indicate that the participants did go into the water, which may be applicable to pouring but it is certainly not necessary for sprinkling. The additional note that John baptized "in Aenon near Salim, because there was much water there" (Jn 3:23, NASB) implies immersion.

Similarly, it was when the eunuch came by "a certain water" that he asked for baptism (Ac 8:36). Surely he was carrying sufficient water in his caravan with which baptism by sprinkling or effusion might have been administered at any time. Again, while details in every case are not given, those given would favor immersion as the mode practiced in the New Testament, and no recorded circumstances would preclude it in any instance.

Symbolism of baptism. As was noted in the discussion of the significance of the rite of baptism, it marks not only the act of submission to God on the part of the one being baptized, but also symbolizes the salvation act performed by God. While this includes cleansing through the washing away of sins, its basic meaning is that the putting away of sins is through death to the old life plus resurrection to newness of life. Baptism can be called a cleansing bath, but, in distinction to the many washings of the Old Testament system, it is a once-for-all cleansing through immersion into the sea of death. The reality symbolized in Christian baptism is therefore an advance over the reality pictured in the Old Testament ritual cleansings. This new radical transaction, which was brought about only with the death and resurrection of Christ and the believer's participation with him, is most adequately symbolized in immersion. Thus the apostle speaks of the believer's salvation as putting off the body of flesh by being "buried with him in baptism" (Col 2:12). The context indicates that the cleansing of the New Testament believer which corresponds to that symbolized in circumcision now takes place through death and resurrection with Christ. Similarly, Paul reminds the Romans that their baptism into Christ was a baptism into Christ's death. "Therefore we are buried with him by baptism into death: that like as Christ was raised up from the dead . . . even so we also should walk in newness of life" (Ro 6:4).

To be sure, the identification with Christ pictured in baptism also includes cocrucifixion, which is not symbolized in immersion. But it was His burial which signified the completeness of the Lord's death and the reality of the resurrection. For this reason it is mentioned in all four of the gospel accounts and as part of the kernel of the gospel story (1 Co 15:3-4). Moreover, in Romans 6 baptism is more closely linked with the statement of burial and resurrection than that of crucifixion.

Thus the central truths of salvation as codeath and resurrection are closely related to baptism, suggesting that in the mind of the New Testament believer these truths were pictured in the rite of baptism by immersion.[33]

Witness of history. The unanimous testimony of ancient history reveals that immersion was the normal mode of baptism in

33. A. Richardson suggests also that the figure of "putting on Christ" which is related to baptism (Gal 3:27) stems from the practice of the baptismal candidate putting on white robes. "Some such practice must have been necessary from the very beginning, since baptism was by total immersion in running water (cf. Didache (7.1-3; Heb 10:22)." (*An Introduction to the Theology of the New Testament*, pp. 346-47).

the early church. The earliest reference to baptism outside of
the New Testament, the *Didache* (*c.* A.D. 100), instructs that
(triple) baptism be performed in living water and, if that is not
possible, in cold water, and finally, if necessary, in warm water.
If none of these are available, pouring water three times on the
head would suffice, clearly implying that the normal practice was
by immersion. Incidentally, a different word (*ekcheō*) is used
for pouring, showing that *baptizō* does not mean "to pour." Although pouring was permitted in the case of a water shortage, and
sprinkling probably developed with the so-called clinical baptisms of those who were too sick to leave their beds, the ordination
of Novatian was opposed by some on the ground that no one
should be admitted to the clergy who "had been baptized in his
bed in a time of sickness."[34]

Immersion was in common practice throughout Christendom as
late as the thirteenth century, although effusion and sprinkling
had begun much earlier. The mode of immersion in triple form is
still retained by the Eastern Church, even for infants.

The evidence from history is succinctly stated by Fisher when
he concludes, "Baptism, it is now generally agreed among scholars,
was commonly administered by immersion."[35] To this testimony
of church history following the New Testament might be added
the historical precedents of the rite in the Jewish proselyte baptism and the baptism of John, both of which were administered
by immersion.[36]

The conclusion that baptism was commonly by immersion
would not seem to preclude all other modes from being legitimate baptisms. Even as baptism itself was the normal act of the
new believer, being closely related to conversion, it is obvious
that salvation did not depend upon it and that in circumstances
comparable to the salvation of the thief on the cross the rite of
baptism could not be performed. So it would seem that the basic
significance of baptism, namely, identification with Christ and
His saving work, might, if necessary, be signified through a mode
other than immersion, even as the early church provided. The

34. From a letter preserved by Eusebius which was written by Cornelius
    of Rome (A.D. 251). Cited by Jewett, p. 519.
35. George P. Fisher, *The Beginnings of Christianity*, p. 565.
36. For the practice of Jewish proselyte baptism, see Alfred Edersheim,
    The Life and Times of Jesus the Messiah, 2:745-47.

evidence points, however, to immersion as the standard practice of the New Testament church and the mode which most fully signifies Christian salvation.

THE LORD'S SUPPER

The second biblically ordained rite for the life of the church and by means of which the church worships God is the Lord's Supper (1 Co 11:20). It is also called communion, from the apostle's reference to the cup and bread as "the communion of the blood of Christ" and "the communion of the body of Christ" (1 Co 10:16). The concept of communion, however, concerns only one aspect of the total meaning of the rite. A similar restricted sense is involved in the term Eucharist, which is derived from the Greek word *eucharisteō,* the term used for the giving of thanks before partaking of the elements (Mt 26:27; 1 Co 11:24).

Because the elements became regarded as thank offerings, *Eucharist* became the most widely used expression for the supper in ancient times. The rite is also mentioned in the New Testament as the "breaking of bread" (Ac 2:42; 20:7) and the "Lord's table" (1 Co 10:21). The more comprehensive designations such as the "Lord's Supper" and the "breaking of bread" probably also included a reference to a meal which was eaten in connection with the bread and the cup after the pattern of the Last Supper. The Roman Catholic mass is not derived from the New Testament, but rather from the Latin, *missa,* from *mittere,* "to dismiss." Its use comes from the phrase *ite, missa est,* "Go, you are dismissed," which is addressed to the congregation by the priest toward the end of the service. From this reference to the concluding portion, it was extended to the whole rite during the fourth century.

INSTITUTION OF THE LORD'S SUPPER

Instituted by Christ. As with baptism, the Lord's Supper was instituted directly by the command of Christ and, in this case, by His example as well. On the night before His death, Christ gathered with His disciples to eat the Passover meal.[37] In the

37. The nature of the Last Supper is still strongly debated. The accounts of the synoptic gospels seem clearly to establish the meal as a Passover (cf. Mt 26:17 ff.; Mk 14:12 ff.; Lk 22:7 ff.). Certain references of John, however, are said to indicate that Christ died on the day of the

setting of this ancient feast held in remembrance of God's redemption of His people from the slavery of Egypt, Jesus turned
to the future and His imminent redemptive death, which was to
fulfill not only the Passover but all previous sacrificial rites. No
longer would His disciples look back to redemptive types; from
now on, they were to remember Him and His perfect, final sacrifice which was given for them. The account of the institution is
recorded by each of the synoptic writers (Mt 26:26-29; Mk 14:22-
25; Lk 22:17-20) and the apostle Paul (1 Co 11:23-26). The
comparison of the reports shows that those of Matthew and Mark
are very similar, while Luke has some elements in common with
these and others which are similar to Paul's account.

> And while they were eating, He took some bread, and after a
> blessing He broke it; and gave it to them, and said, "Take it;
> this is My body." And He took a cup, and when He had given
> thanks, He gave it to them; and they all drank from it. And He
> said to them, "This is My blood of the covenant, which is to be
> shed on behalf of many. Truly I say to you, I shall never again
> drink of the fruit of the vine until that day when I drink it new
> in the kingdom of God" (Mk 14:22-25, NASB).

> And having taken some bread, when He had given thanks, He
> broke it, and gave it to them, saying, "This is My body which is
> given for you; do this in remembrance of Me." And in the same
> way He took the cup after they had eaten, saying, "This cup
> which is poured out for you is the new covenant in My blood"
> (Lk 22:19-20).

> For I received from the Lord that which I also delivered to
> you, that the Lord Jesus in the night in which He was betrayed
> took bread; and when He had given thanks, He broke it, and
> said, "This is My body, which is for you; do this in remembrance
> of Me." In the same way the cup also, after supper, saying, "This
> cup is the new covenant in My blood; do this, as often as you
> drink it, in remembrance of Me" (1 Co 11:23-25, NASB).

There is basic agreement in all accounts, and although the explicit command, "Do this in remembrance of me," is included
only by Luke and Paul, who states it twice, there can be no ques-

Passover, requiring the supper to precede the Passover by twenty-four
hours (cf. Jn 13:1; 18:28; 19:14). For a discussion of the nature of
the Last Supper see Jeremias, *The Eucharistic Words of Jesus*, pp. 1-60;
A. J. B. Higgins, *The Lord's Supper in the New Testament*, pp. 13-23.
For a harmonization of the synoptic accounts with John's gospel see
William Hendricksen, *A Commentary on the Gospel of John*, 2:221 ff.,
401 ff.

tion but what Jesus expressed this imperative.[38] He desired that
His people "remember" Him continually during His absence by
partaking of the elements which speak of them sharing in the
fruits of His sacrifice of the new covenant. Note that Jesus does
not wait to give this rite until His postresurrection ministry but,
as with baptism, even before His death He sheds "the light of
victory over what at first still seemed to be an obscure and mis-
understood reality."[39]

Practiced by the early church. Based upon the institution by
the Lord, the early church from the beginning "remembered" the
Lord by observing this rite. Paul claims the Lord's authority for
the practice by stating, "For I have received of the Lord that
which also I delivered unto you" (1 Co 11:23). In these words
he is probably not claiming a special revelation received directly
from Christ, but rather, the delivering of a tradition which stems
ultimately from the Lord and with His authority.[40] The references
to the Lord's Supper are not as frequent as those to baptism, perhaps because of its secondary position "as only a reappropriation
and renewal of the definitive fact of Baptism"[41] or simply because
the New Testament does not often concern itself with the proceedings of the worship service of the assembled believers. Nevertheless, the evidence points to the recognition of dominical authority behind the supper and its regular practice in all the
churches.

Thus the church immediately after Pentecost was "breaking
bread" in fellowship (Ac 2:42, 46). These words refer to the
ancient Palestinian custom of breaking the bread with the hands
rather than cutting it, which action initiated the meal (cf. Jer
16:7, ASV; Lam 4:4).[42] Taken in themselves, the words need

38. Jeremias, *The Eucharistic . . .* , pp. 159-65.
39. Berkouwer, p. 196.
40. The words "received" (*parelabon*) and "delivered" (*paredōka*) are the
    technical terms for the transmission of tradition. The same language is
    used with respect to Paul's proclamation of the essentials of the gospel
    which he undoubtedly received from the earlier apostles (1 Co 15:3).
    Cullmann shows in an excellent discussion on tradition that this does
    not necessarily mean that the reference is to the historical Jesus, but
    rather that the exalted Lord Himself is present in the transmission.
    In this sense the tradition can be viewed as direct communication from
    the Lord without excluding intermediaries through whom the Lord is
    working. See Cullmann, "The Tradition" in *The Early Church*, pp. 67-
    68.
41. Moule, p. 47.
42. Johannes Behm, "klaō" in *TDNT*, 3:728-29.

not mean more than the inevitable preliminary to eating, but
their use in certain contexts points to a special significance of the
meal. In Acts 2:42, breaking of bread is one of four practices
characteristic of the infant church. Placed alongside continuance
in the apostles' doctrine, fellowship (*koinonia*), and prayers, the
breaking of bread most surely signifies the communion meal.
This is further substantiated by the attitude of exultation and
sincerity of heart which accompanied the eating (v. 46). Paul's
breaking of bread with the disciples at Troas on the first day of
the week also suggests the celebration of the communion (Ac
20:7, 11). The use of this terminology for the Lord's Supper is
apparent in the apostle's reference to the breaking of bread as the
"communion of the body of Christ" (1 Co 10:16*b*). From the
earliest time of the church, therefore, the sharing of the Lord's
table played a significant part in the worship and edification of
God's people as they met together.

The practice of the Lord's Supper in the early church raises the
question as to whether the New Testament gives evidence of two
different types of communion in the early church. On the basis
of the distinctive characteristics of the breaking of bread in Acts
and the Pauline interpretation of the Lord's Supper, the two-type
theory, generally associated with Hans Lietzmann, distinguished
between a primitive Palestinian fellowship meal and a sacramental Hellenistic Eucharist.[43]

The first was said to be characterized by an emphasis on fellowship and joy over the presence of the risen Christ and His imminent return with no thought of the proclamation of His death
and its sacrificial significance so prominent in Paul's writing.
According to the theory, the Palestinian fellowship meals were
inspired by the fellowship meals which the risen Lord ate with
His disciples (Lk 24:36-43; Jn 21:12; Ac 10:41; cf. also Ac 1:4,
NASB margin), while the later Pauline type was derived from
the institution of the sacramental bread and cup in the upper
room as claimed by the apostle in 1 Corinthians 11:23. Moreover, the cup referring to the wine which is prominent in Paul's
account is not mentioned in Acts.

Upon examination, however, the validity of this rigid distinction breaks down with regard to both the origin and content.[44]

43. Hans Lietzmann, *Mass and Lord's Supper: A Study in the History of
   the Liturgy,* trans. Dorothea H. G. Reeve, pp. 204-8.
44. Higgins, pp. 56-63.

The source of the apostle's concept of the communion as a remembrance of the death of Christ was a tradition which he received of the Last Supper. Likewise, it is inconceivable that the Last Supper shared with Jesus before His death was not also in the minds of the disciples when their table fellowship was renewed for a time with the risen Christ. In the case of the two disciples who talked unknowingly with Christ there can be no doubt, for it was as He broke bread and gave it to them that their eyes were opened to know Him (Lk 24:30-31).

The connection of the so-called Palestinian breaking of bread with the fellowship meals with the risen Lord goes back, therefore, to include the recollection of the Last Supper with its thought of the sacrificial death of Christ.[45] And although it was characterized by joy, there is no reason to believe that the remembrance of Christ's death was not present, for it was only through His sacrifice that the fellowship of His risen presence and the eschatological joy could have any substance. Likewise in the Corinthian church, which was founded by Paul, a joyful spirit evidently pervaded their worship, including the communion, even to the point of degenerating into excess and necessitating the apostle's correction. Thus, the celebration of the Lord's Supper in the early Palestinian church as well as the later Pauline mission churches shared a common origin in the Last Supper as well as the content of remembrance of the Lord's death and a joyful recognition of His presence and future coming.

MEANING OF THE LORD'S SUPPER

The meaning of the Lord's Supper is primarily summed up in the command of Christ, "This do in remembrance of me" (Lk 22:19; 1 Co 11:24-25). It is first and foremost a memorial rite of Christ and His redemptive death, even as the Passover was a remembrance of God's redemption of His people from the bondage of Egypt (Ex 12:14; 13:3, 9; Deu 16:3). Based upon a common participation in Christ and His salvation, there is also in the Lord's Supper a communion of believers in the unity of His body (1 Co 10:16). These two thoughts of the remembrance of Christ and the fellowship with the members of His body are the focuses of the celebration of the Lord's Supper.

45. Cullmann, "The Meaning of the Lord's Supper in Primitive Christianity" in *Essays on the Lord's Supper* by Oscar Cullmann and F. J. Leenhardt, p. 21.

A remembrance of Christ. The remembrance of Christ in the
biblical sense is very different from our modern notion of "remembering" as a mental transportation of thought back to the
moment of the occurrence of an event. It is rather the dynamic
recalling of the past so that it again becomes a present reality
which is operative and in which one may share. "To recall, in
biblical thought," says Martin, "means to transport an action
which is buried in the past in such a way that its original po-
tency and vitality are not lost, but are carried over into the present."[46] This dynamic sense is seen in the tracing of the death of
her son by the widow of Zarephath to Elijah's calling her sin to
remembrance (1 Ki 17:18). So in the Jewish Passover the head of
the household, with the bread in his hand, recites a formula based
upon the explanation of Deuteronomy 16:3: "This is the bread
of affliction which our fathers ate when they came out of Egypt."
Although it is not the same bread, a real link is conceived which
allows the participant to relive the experience of history, making
it his very own.

The remembrance of the Passover not only looked to the past,
making it present, but was also anticipatory of a future redemption. Similarly, the remembrance of Christ in the Lord's Supper
has the threefold significance of Christ's past redemptive sacrifice,
His saving presence, and His future coming.

1. A remembrance of Christ's death. The very elements of the
rite and the words of institution emphasize the communion as a
remembrance of the death of Christ. This is not to overlook the
fact that it is a "remembrance of me," that is, of Christ Himself
as the person of the Saviour who gave Himself, but rather points
out the fact that the climax of His ministry and foundation of
salvation was the giving of His life as a ransom for many (Mk
10:45). The separate bread and wine, signifying His body and
blood, speak of sacrificial death, for in ancient Hebrew the "body
and blood" already referred to "the two component parts of the
body, especially of a sacrificial victim, which are separated when
it is killed"[47] (cf. Heb 13:11). His death is thus a sacrifice which
Jesus explained as the basis of the new covenant (Mk 14:24).
In so doing He proclaimed His death as the event which brought

46. Ralph P. Martin, *Worship in the Early Church,* p. 126.
47. Jeremias, *The Eucharistic . . . ,* pp. 143-44.

the promised forgiveness of sins and final reconciliation of God and man to fulfillment.

Thus, in instituting this remembrance of Himself, Christ desired that the church proclaim His death as the final salvation act of God, even as He did to the disciples at the Last Supper. For this reason, Paul gives the meaning of the command "this do in remembrance of me" as the proclamation of the Lord's death until He comes (1 Co 11:25-26). This is not in the sense of an evangelistic sermon to outsiders, but the church's own continual recollection of the basis of its salvation in the redemptive death of Christ.[48]

In this remembrance of the death of Christ there is no thought of a reenactment of His death as in the sacrifice of the Roman mass and also among some Protestants.[49] The sacrificial death in the Lord's Supper, as in the Jewish Passover, is presupposed, and the ritual and the explanatory words serve as a remembrance and a proclamation of what God has already done. Commenting on the phraseology of "offering Christ" or "offering Christ's sacrifice" which is often used in connection with the Lord's Supper, Aulen states,

> The formula does not occur in either the New Testament or in the documents of the primitive church. . . . In reality it is contrary to the fundamental conception of the sacrifice of Christ which we find in the New Testament. The sacrifice of Christ is entirely and solely His sacrifice—and God's. This is the essential point: God was in Christ reconciling the world to Himself. Through this sacrifice, perfected once for all, He abolished all man-made sacrifices. A formula such as this that we "offer Christ" turns the biblical kerygma upside down. It is not strange therefore that all kinds of erroneous associations have become attached to it.[50]

48. Gray states that "the recitation of the story of the death of the Lord, in other words of the acts of redemption in which the Christian Church originates and on which it depends, corresponds exactly to the Haggadah at the Jewish Pascal meal, the recitation of the act of redemption from Egypt on which the Jewish nation depended" (George Buchanan Gray, *Sacrifice in the Old Testament, Its Theory and Practice*, p. 395).

49. For a discussion of a new emphasis on the Lord's Supper as a sacrifice among some Protestants, see A. M. Stibbs, *Sacrament, Sacrifice and Eucharist*. Typical of the sacrificial interpretation of "remembrance" is that of Clark, who says that Christ is made present "for the 're-calling' of his sacrifice before God, thus making it here and now operative" (Neville Clark, *An Approach to the Theology of the Sacraments*, p. 62).

50. Gustaf Aulen, *Eucharist and Sacrifice*, pp. 198 f., cited by Stibbs, p. 31.

Rather than any sacrifice to God, the rite is totally concerned with the movement of grace from God to man which flows from the prior Godward sacrifice. This direction is indicated in the Lord's words over the bread and cup, "This is My body, which is for you," and "This is My blood of the covenant, which is to be shed on behalf of many" (1 Co 11:24; Mk 14:24, NASB). The elements signify something that is done toward man. For this reason, the actions of breaking the bread and pouring the wine do not represent the dying of Christ, but are only involved in the giving of the fruit of His death to the disciples. "It is not the action of breaking, but the food received out of Jesus' hands that is spoken about 'in the form of prophetic allegory.' "[51]

The fulfillment of the Lord's command for His remembrance, according to Paul, is in the receiving and appropriating this food. "For as often as you eat this bread and drink the cup, you proclaim the Lord's death until He comes" (1 Co 11:25, NASB). In the Lord's Supper, therefore, the church in remembering Christ, makes present the risen Lord who is also the crucified one who invites all to continually appropriate the saving efficacy of His sacrifice which was made once for all at Calvary.

2. A present fellowship with Christ. The remembrance of Christ is not the recalling of a figure of history who has long since passed away, but the proclamation of the death of the risen Lord who is present in the church. He who invited the disciples to share the Last Supper continues to be the real Host at each communion service. The church gathers at the "Lord's table" (1 Co 10:21) to eat the "Lord's supper" (11:20), and an invitation to share a meal, especially to the Oriental, is an invitation to fellowship. "Every table fellowship is a fellowship of life."[52] So in the communion the believer shares intimate fellowship with Christ. This communion is centered in the partaking of the bread

---

51. Herman Ridderbos, *The Coming of the Kingdom*, p. 429. It is significant to note that the better Greek manuscripts do not have the word "broken" in the Lord's statement concerning His body in 1 Co 11:24. The emphasis is upon the fact that His body was given "for you." Jeremias, likewise, excludes the action of breaking the bread and pouring the wine from the Lord's command, "Do this." "Jesus was not interpreting the actions . . . but was clearly explaining the bread and the wine themselves" (*The Eucharistic . . .* , p. 143).
52. Jeremias, *The Eucharistic . . .* , p. 136. Jeremias notes that Jesus' admission of sinners to fellowship meals with Himself meant "an offer of salvation . . . and the assurance of forgiveness."

and the cup which the apostle explains as the communion or partaking of the body and blood of Christ (1 Co 10:16-17). But the supper is more than the fellowship of sharing a meal with Christ, for He gives Himself as the very substance of that meal.

How the nature of Christ's presence in the Lord's Supper is to be understood has been the cause of much controversy and division throughout the history of the church. Four major views with slight modifications are presently held among churches.

a. Roman Catholic. Commonly known as transubstantiation, the Roman Church teaches that the literal body and blood of Christ are present in the elements of bread and wine. When the priest utters the formula of consecration over the bread and wine they are transformed, so that while the characteristics of the bread and wine remain the same (e.g., color, taste, smell, etc.), their substance is truly changed into the body and blood of Christ. This view was formally stated in 1551 in the canons and decrees of the Council of Trent which state,

> But since Christ our Redeemer declared that to be truly His own body which He offered under the form of bread, it has, therefore, always been a firm belief in the Church of God, and this holy council now declares it anew, that by the consecration of the bread and wine a change is brought about of the whole substance of the bread into the substance of the body of Christ our Lord, and of the whole substance of the wine into the substance of His blood. This change the holy Catholic Church properly and appropriately calls transubstantiation.[53]

As indicated in the statement of Trent, the Roman position is based primarily upon a literal interpretation of Christ's words concerning the bread and the cup, "this is my body," and "this is my blood." Several facts however, preclude this literal understanding. (1) As Christ spoke, He was present in body so that the disciples could hardly have thought that they were literally eating His body and drinking His blood. (2) The copula "is" or some form of it is frequently used in Scripture in a metaphor, and does not always call for a literal understanding (e.g., "I am the door," Jn 10:9; "that Rock was Christ," 1 Co 10:4). In the very words of institution the metaphorical use is obvious with respect to the cup, "this cup is the new covenant" (Lk 22:20, NASB).

53. H. J. Schroeder, *Canons and Decrees of the Council of Trent*, p. 75.

So it must be similarly understood with respect to the bread in the previous verse. (3) The concept of drinking literal blood would have been abhorrent to the Jewish disciples and against the law (Lev 3:17; 7:26-27; especially 17:10-14). (4) The elements in the celebration of the Passover to which the Lord's Supper is analogous were interpreted symbolically and never identified with the realities represented.[54]

In addition to these reasons which make the literal interpretation of Christ's words untenable, the doctrine of transubstantiation materializes the presence of Christ in the elements so that they become objects of worship. Not only is there an absence of biblical support for the practice of such worship, but the presence of Christ thus tends to be rendered impersonal in the physical elements.

b. Lutheran. The Lutheran position also holds to the real presence of the body and blood of Christ, but without any transformation of the elements as in transubstantiation. Rather, the body and blood are said to be "in, with, and under" the bread and wine which remain as such. A statement of this position, popularly termed consubstantiation, although not with any idea of mixing the two substances, is given by Mueller:

> In the Holy Supper a peculiar union (the sacramental union) occurs by virtue of Christ's institution between the bread and the wine, on the one hand, and the body and blood of Christ, on the other, and because of this union all communicants (*manducatio generalis*) receive in, with and under the bread and the wine in a supernatural, incomprehensible manner Christ's true body and blood (*manducatio oralis*) as a pledge of the gracious remission of their sins.
>
> .   .   .   .
>
> The words of institution, it is true, demand also a spiritual eating and drinking, or *faith in the words* "Given and shed for you for the remission of sins." This is proved directly by Christ's command: "This do in remembrance of Me." But what the words of institution declare in particular is that, "in, with, and under the bread and wine Christ presents His true body and blood to be truly and substantially eaten and drunk by us." In other words, the words of institution say: "That which I offer you, which you are to receive and eat, is not only bread, but also My

54. Jeremias, *The Eucharistic* . . . , p. 145.

body. That which I offer you, which you are to receive and drink, is not only wine, but also My blood."[55]

Although the theory of consubstantiation does not demand a contradiction of the senses as in transubstantiation, where the elements are supposed to be something other than they appear, the same arguments against a literal understanding of Christ's words used against the Roman position are applicable against this view.

c. Zwinglian or memorial. The name of Zwingli is usually associated with the interpretation of the Lord's Supper, primarily as an act commemorating the Lord's death. Zwingli absolutely rejected any idea of the real bodily presence of Christ. However, he did believe that Christ was spiritually present to those of faith. According to this view, the words of institution are to be interpreted simply in a figurative sense, making the bread and the cup symbolic of the spiritual truth of Christ's death and its blessings. Zwingli himself made statements suggesting that, in addition to a simple memorial emphasizing the believer's witness to faith in the redemptive power of Christ's death, he also recognized a work of God in the supper.[56] Nevertheless, his emphasis upon the commemoration and witness aspects is what characterizes the memorial view today. According to this understanding, then, Christ is present spiritually, and eating and drinking of Him signifies faith in Him and reliance on His death. Although rightly rejecting the bodily presence, it is questionable whether this position adequately emphasizes the concept of communion with Christ through partaking of the elements of the supper as indicated by the apostle Paul (1 Co 10:16).

d. Reformed. This position, which is usually called the Calvinistic, unites with the memorial position in rejecting the physical bodily presence. But it does believe that Christ is present through the Spirit in such a way that His entire person—body and blood—is enjoyed in the supper. The presence of the body and blood is a dynamic presence in which the efficacy of Christ's sacrificial death is made effective in the believer through partaking of the elements in faith. According to Berkouwer, Calvin held to a true

55. John Theodore Mueller, *Christian Dogmatics* (St. Louis: Concordia, 1934), pp. 509-12; cf. *The Augsburg Confession*, Art. X.
56. For a discussion of Zwingli's position, especially in relation to that of Calvin, see Charles Hodge, *Systematic Theology*, 3:626-50.

communion with the body and blood, but these "are to be understood in terms of Christ's act of reconciliation, not in themselves."[57] The body and blood of the crucified Christ are thus present by the redemptive presence of the glorified risen Christ.

> Christ's surrender of His body and blood is not an event detached from His person, but it is his act, and in the reality and power of that act Christ Himself is in the full sense present in the Lord's Supper. In the Lord's Supper, the believer has communion with the glorified Christ because he has communion with his body and blood. This communion is not a communion with Christ's glorified "body" and "blood" as a substantial, isolated reality, but a communion with him in his offering and in his true body and blood.[58]

In the Reformed view, then, the elements of the Lord's Supper are more than mere symbols of His death, but in the partaking of them by faith there is a real partaking of Christ in His redemptive presence.

In turning to the Scriptures, the apostle speaks of a real presence of Christ in the Lord's Supper of which the participant partakes. There is a real communion with His body and blood, but this is not with the idea that Christ's presence is in the elements. Rather, the elements are symbols of the saving efficacy of His personal presence. Partaking of His presence is therefore not a physical eating and drinking, but an inner communion with His person which uses the outward action as an expression of inward spiritual faith.

The real presence of Christ in the supper is thus no different than His presence in the Word.[59] In the one He encounters His people in visible elements and in the other in words. In both He is really, but spiritually, present as the glorified Lord by the ministry of the Spirit, and in both He is likewise received spiritually in faith. The only difference is that in the supper He gives the church visible symbols of the significance of His presence and invites them to partake in actions which visibly symbolize spiritual participation in the salvation of His sacrificial death.

57. Berkouwer, p. 229.
58. Ibid., p. 235.
59. Eduard Schweizer, *The Lord's Supper According to the New Testment*, pp. 37-38.

3. An anticipation of Christ's return. In the remembrance of Christ in the Lord's Supper, there is not only a looking back at the sacrifice of Calvary and a fellowship with His risen person, but there is also a forward look in anticipation of His return. This hope is expressed by Jesus when in the institution of the supper He said, "Verily I say unto you, I will drink no more of the fruit of the vine, until that day that I drink it new in the kingdom of God" (Mk 14:25; cf. Mt 26:29; Lk 22:16, 18). The same eschatological motif is carried by Paul when he explains the Lord's Supper as a proclamation of the Lord's death "til he come" (1 Co 11:26). The present spiritual fellowship of the Lord's table with the ascended Lord is not the final fellowship. It is only anticipatory of the direct fellowship of the kingdom which is often pictured in the Scriptures as sitting down to enjoy a meal (Lk 14:24; Mt 22:2 ff.; Rev 19:9; cf. Is 25:6; Zep 1:7).

The supper given to the church during the absence of direct fellowship with the Lord is not simply prefigurative of the great eschatological banquet, but also provisional. At the same time that Christ spoke of eating the fulfilled Passover and drinking the wine "new" (*kainos*) [60] in the future order of the kingdom of God (Lk 22:16; Mk 14:25), He instituted His table for the church. At this table the church already feasts provisionally in the final salvation through participation in Christ. While it is true that all of the experience of the life of Christ through the presence of the Holy Spirit is in reality a foretaste or an "earnest" of the full inheritance of salvation, nowhere is this more clearly signified than in the eating of the provisions of salvation at the Lord's table.

Along with the recollection of His death, this eschatological outlook was always present in the celebration of the supper. For this reason the New Testament observances were not characterized by the solemnity of a funeral, but were full of exultation in anticipation of Christ's coming as well as the present enjoyment of His person through the Spirit.

A fellowship of believers. Fellowship with Christ in the supper also implies fellowship with other believers. To be united to

---

60. "*Kainos* is the epitome of the wholly different and miraculous thing which is brought by the time of salvation" (Behm, "*kainos*" in *TDNT*, 3:449).

Christ through sharing in His redemptive death means at the same time a uniting with His people who are also in Him. This horizontal fellowship in the celebration of the Lord's Supper is a central feature, according to Paul's instructions to the Corinthians, and one which they were guilty of neglecting. In the eating of the meal, which in the Corinthian practice was included in the Lord's Supper along with the bread and cup, there was no recognition of the unity of the church. Some, apparently the rich, began to eat their food before the arrival of their poorer brethren, who were detained longer, probably because of their occupation. Moreover, some ate to excess while others went hungry (1 Co 11:21). Such actions can in no way be called the eating of the Lord's Supper, according to the apostle (11:20). The Lord is one and therefore those sharing in Him are one, and this oneness is made visible especially in the partaking of the bread where all partake of the same bread: "For we being many are one bread, and one body: for we are all partakers of that one bread" (10:17). By an easy transition in the meaning of the bread, Paul teaches that as the many believers partake of the bread which signifies union with Christ (v. 16) they become one with the bread which is now viewed as the body of Christ, the church (v. 17). Thus, there can be no genuine experience of fellowship with the Lord at His table until all divisions, whether social or otherwise, are healed and fellow believers are received as equal participants in Christ.

Horizontal fellowship around the Lord's table, however, without the vertical communion of the participants in Christ, is likewise impossible. Genuine unity of believers in the observance of the table is possible only if they share a similar understanding of the meaning of that table. For this reason, attempting to unite different church bodies, as is sometimes done today, through the rite of communion without first uniting in the meaning of the death of Christ which it proclaims is impossible. Berkouwer, while acknowledging the contradiction between the plurality of the Lord's Supper in the churches and the one body of Christ of which it speaks, yet rightly concludes,

> One will not be able to solve the problem by superficializing the confession of the Church, unless one wants to abandon the

Lord's Supper to absolute irrationality. One may think that he has thus preserved the Church, or at least its prospects for unity, but at the same time he has lost the Lord's Supper, which has been given to us through the sacred institution and which therefore asks for faith and can be received in the communion of the Church only if that faith is present.[61]

THE EFFICACY OF THE LORD'S SUPPER

The fact of blessing. Having been instituted by Christ for the regular practice of His disciples in the church, it goes without saying that the Lord's Supper was designed to be a blessing to the church. The concept of communicating divine gifts by eating and drinking was very familiar to the Oriental mind, even as is seen in the Scripture with its references to bread (Jn 6:35, 50), the water (Jn 4:13-14; Rev 21:6; 22:1, 17), and the fruit of the tree of life (Rev 22:2, 14, 19), all of which are symbolic of the communication of divine life and healing. So also is the common use of the idea of "the feast of salvation which imparts the gift of redemption" (e.g., Mt 5:6; 8:11; 22:1 ff.; 25:10; Lk 22:30; Rev. 19:7-9).[62] The "Lord's Table" is thus set before the church that believers might partake and thereby be nourished and strengthened in the life of God.

As we have seen in the meaning of the Lord's Supper, Christ, under the symbols of the bread and the cup, signified the giving of the fruit of His sacrificial death to the disciples. His command to repeat the same partaking of the bread and cup indicates that this same meaning is intended each time it is done. The efficacy of the rite is thus summed up in the fact that in it Christ again and again makes Himself present with the church, offering the saving efficacy of His death. So effective is His encounter with His people that failure to acknowledge the significance of this rite brings judgment upon those involved (1 Co 11:27, 29).

But the presence of Christ in communion is not of a different kind than it is to faith apart from the rite. Where two or three are gathered in His name He promised His presence without any mention of the Lord's Supper (Mt 18:20). And Paul's prayer for

61. For a good discussion of this question, see Berkouwer's entire chapter entitled, "The Lord's Supper: A Common Table?" p. 279 ff.
62. Jeremias, *The Eucharistic* . . . , pp. 154-56.

the Ephesian believers is "that Christ may dwell in your hearts by faith" (Eph 3:17). Moreover, He is present in His Word as the Spirit of God illumines the Scriptures, confronting the hearers with the living Christ who is revealed in them. In all of these instances Christ is present in His saving efficacy, even as in the supper.

It cannot, therefore, be said with the Roman Catholic Church that the practice of the Lord's Supper is necessary, implying a special communion with Christ which is unattainable through faith. Rather, through the means of signs, Christ dynamically and vividly presents Himself to His people as the crucified one, even as He does through the vehicle of words. The efficacy of the Lord's Supper is thus concerned not with a special presence of Christ but with the further enjoyment of His continual presence in the believer's life.

Nature of the blessing. The benefits conveyed by Christ in the Lord's Supper and represented by the bread and the cup are those which flow from the death of Christ. In relating His blood to the new covenant, Jesus identified these blessings with the fulfillment of this promised covenant. That which is received in bread and cup, as Ridderbos explains, is "the sacrificial food and drink of the new covenant, the fruits of the New Testament sacrificial blood."[63]

The two basic provisions of the new covenant were the forgiveness of sins and the gift of the Holy Spirit (cf. Jer 31:31-34; Eze 36:25-27). Although these were received initially in salvation and symbolized in baptism, the Christian's walk is not static but dynamic. He has been saved but he is also being saved. Involved in this continuous walk is the fresh need of forgiveness of sins and the power of the Spirit. In the Lord's Supper these are offered anew in order that the one partaking in faith might have fresh assurance of sin forgiven and a new appropriation of the life which is in Christ by the Spirit. Jesus said, "Whoso eateth my flesh, and drinketh my blood, hath eternal life." (Jn 6:54). Partaking at the Lord's table in faith means nothing less than increasing in that life through a fresh appropriation of the Saviour.

Manner of the blessing. The blessings of the Lord's Supper

63. Ridderbos, p. 427.

are communicated through the reception in faith of the elements which Christ made symbolic of the fruit of His death. Believers in the church, even as the disciples at the Last Supper, are commanded to "take," "eat," and "drink," and it is in this "taking" and "eating" that they partake of Christ's body and blood in the Lord's Supper. This does not mean that the bread and cup are magically infused with spiritual power, but by virtue of Christ's promise there is a real connection between the reception of these signs and the spiritual realities which they represent. The same parallel, which has been previously mentioned, between the Word and the elements exists here. "The nature of the elements need not even be mentioned—the visible manner in which they are the bearers of salvation does not lie upon a different plane from the audible way in which this salvation is communicated by the divine Word—the essential and exclusive thing is the 'nature of *Christ's promises.*' "[64]

This communication of Christ's saving presence both by means of words and the visible symbols of the Lord's Supper does not occur on the physical level merely by hearing or partaking. Rather, He comes on the level of personality, demanding the corresponding personal reception. So, as with the reception of the Word, the real saving presence of Christ is communicated in the reception of the elements only when it is "mixed with faith" in those who partake (cf. Heb 4:2).

PARTICIPANTS OF THE LORD'S SUPPER

Believers. As the Lord's Supper was given to the disciples and the church, only believers who are a part of the body of Christ are entitled to partake of it. In the early church those who practiced the "breaking of bread" were those who "gladly received his word" (Peter's proclamation of Christ) and "continued steadfastly in the apostles' doctrine and fellowship . . . and in prayers" (Ac 2:41-42). Similarly, the disciples are mentioned as breaking bread together with Paul at Troas (Ac 20:7). By its very nature as the communion of the body and blood of Christ (1 Co 10:16) the Lord's table is set only for those who have a share in Him and His salvation.

Examined believers. Believers must, furthermore, be in proper

64. Ibid., p. 438.

relationship with God and their fellow members of the body of Christ. For this reason the apostle gives instruction that "a man examine himself, and so let him eat of that bread, and drink of that cup" (1 Co 11:28). To come in an improper spiritual condition is to participate "in an unworthy manner" (v. 27, NASB), resulting in the chastening judgment of God which can take the form of sickness and even physical death (1 Co 11:30-32). The criterion of a worthy participation is the proper recognition of the significance of the rite. Paul writes, "For he who eats and drinks, eats and drinks judgment to himself, if he does not judge the body rightly" (v. 29, NASB). Some have interpreted this in the light of the apostle's rebuke of the Corinthians for failing to consider the other members of the church and so understand "the body" as a reference to the church. Unworthy participation is "failure to recognize the church for what it is, the body of Christ, in which the living Lord is present."[65]

However, the close proximity of the use of "body" in verse 27, apparently in the same thought context, argues for a similar meaning here. There Paul states that "whoever eats the bread or drinks the cup of the Lord in an unworthy manner, shall be guilty of the body and blood of the Lord" (NASB). The failure to judge the body is thus a failure to recognize it for what it is, the communion with the body and blood of Christ, and to distinguish it from a common meal. The proper judgment, of course, would include the recognition of all other believers as fellow partakers, and therefore as equal members of the one body which is formed through communion with the one Christ.

The concept of partaking in a worthy manner is not speaking of a condition of sinlessness, even through confession, which may be thought to make one worthy to receive God's grace. Instead, it concerns the believer's basic attitude toward his Lord and his fellow believers. As Barclay so aptly says, the prohibition of unworthy participation "does not shut out the man who is a sinner and knows it to be so. . . . If the table of Christ were only for perfect people none might ever approach it. The approach is never closed to the penitent sinner. To the man who loves God

65. Higgins, pp. 72-73.

and loves his fellow man the way is ever open, and his sins, though they be as scarlet, shall be white as snow."[66]

Assembled believers. The supper, which expresses the communion of believers in the body of Christ, is for the church as it is met together. The "disciples came together to break bread" with Paul at Troas (Ac 20:7). Moreover, it was to the church that the apostle gave his instructions concerning the supper in 1 Corinthians. Seven times in chapters 11-14 the word translated "came together" is used, indicating that the supper was observed when the church was assembled for worship. While its normal celebration is for the established church, this does not seem to preclude its observance under other conditions. Christ instituted it for the disciples before the church was inaugurated, and surely the promise of His presence in the midst of two or three (Mt 18:20) may be appropriated in the case of the supper when necessary. The experience of unity of the body, however, is best served in the larger gathering of the church.

THE MODE

The procedure. According to the gospel accounts, the institution of the Lord's Supper took place in conjunction with the eating of the Passover meal. It seems probable to assume with Jeremias that the Lord used two of the customary parts of that celebration to give the bread and the cup new significance. Although there is still some debate over the exact proceedings at the Passover celebration, it is probable that the blessing of the bread occurred after the preliminary course but before the main meal, while the blessing of the cup followed the meal just prior to the singing of the second part of the *Hallel.*[67] This sequence appears to be borne out when Mark states that it was "while they were eating, He took some bread, and after a blessing He broke it" (14:22, NASB), while Luke specifically mentions that it was "after they had eaten" that Jesus distributed the cup (22:20, NASB). In Luke there is mention of a second cup prior to the distribution of the bread over which Jesus pronounced the eschatological words concerning not sharing again the fruit of the vine until the time of the kingdom. However, the commands

66. William Barclay, *The Letters to the Corinthians*, p. 117.
67. Jeremias, *The Eucharistic* . . . , pp. 58-60.

instituting the continual remembrance are not attached to this first cup, and it is therefore not considered a part of the observance (cf. Lk 22:18-20; 1 Co 11:24-25).

The supper in the early church also seems to have been always connected to a common meal (1 Co 11:17-22; Ac 20:7, 11; 2:46). Later known as the love feast (*agapē*, cf. Jude 12), this practice continued until the time of Ignatius. While the table fellowship served as a meaningful introduction to the communion, providing opportunity for the tangible expression of love and unity in the body, it was not considered as part of the observance which was instituted by the Lord. The apostle clearly distinguishes the partaking of the bread and the cup from the meal, indicating that the reception of these two symbolic elements was that which was commanded to be repeated in remembrance of Christ (1 Co 11:23-26). The later popular suspicion that these meals, which were eaten in the evening, were scenes of licentious revelry and even crime, together with the rise of the sacerdotal spirit which turned the memorial supper into a mysterious priestly sacrifice, combined to bring about the cessation of the love feast in connection with the Lord's Supper.

From the instruction of the apostle to the Corinthians it is evident that the early church followed closely the procedure of Christ in instituting the supper. The mentioning of the cup "after supper" (11:25, NASB) suggests that the bread was taken during the meal and the cup later, following the pattern of the Last Supper.[68] They were later brought together when the meal was discontinued. The essential elements of the supper, as instituted by Christ and practiced by the church, include:

1. Prayer over the elements, setting them apart as symbols of the body and blood of Christ's sacrificial death. These prayers consisted of thanksgiving and praise for Christ's sacrifice and the fruits of salvation which flow from it.[69]

2. The distribution of the bread and cup to all. The breaking of the bread and pouring of the wine, as we have noted, do not

---

68. Archibald Robertson and Alfred Plummer, *A Critical and Exegetical Commentary on the First Epistle of St. Paul to the Corinthians*, p. 246.
69. Praise is especially suggested in the pronouncement of blessing (Mk 14:22; Mt 26:26). Cf. Hermann W. Beyer, "eulogeō" in *TDNT*, 2:760-61.

have a special symbolism but are only involved in their distribution.

3. The recalling of the words of Jesus explaining the bread and cup as representative of His body and blood in sacrifice for His people and inviting them to "take" and "eat." The difference in wording of the biblical accounts seems to indicate that the exact wording was not considered essential.

4. Eating and drinking the elements, signifying reception of Christ and His sacrificial death for the spiritual nourishment of His people. In order to truly celebrate the supper the entire person must be involved in the performance of these acts. Unless the spirit is involved in appropriating in faith the realities symbolized in the elements and actions it is not only a meaningless ritual but brings down judgment upon those who participate in a superficial manner.

The elements. In the institution of the Lord's Supper Jesus used two elements, the bread and wine, which were close at hand as parts of the Passover meal. In using them, however, Jesus imparted to them the new meaning of His own sacrificial death. The emphasis in Scripture is not on the nature of the bread and wine, but rather upon their symbolic significance. This is evident in the frequent use of "cup" for the "fruit of the vine." The actual term "wine" (*oinos*) is not used in either the accounts of the synoptics or in Paul's writing.

In biblical life, bread and wine were commonly used for nourishment and early came to be used as symbols of the spiritual nourishment and blessing of God (cf. Gen 14:18; 27:28, 37; Amos 9:13; Jn 6:35, 48). Both eating bread and drinking the fruit of the vine are anticipated in the blessings of the coming kingdom (Lk 14:15; 22:18, 30). In the supper the bread and wine, symbolic of the sacrifice of Christ, also speak of the nourishment and blessing which are received as the sacrificial food from Christ's offering.

According to the accounts of institution, both elements were received by all the people. There is no biblical justification for the practice of withholding the cup from the laity, allowing only the priests to partake of it while the laity receives only the bread. This practice has been common in the Roman Catholic Church since the Council of Constance in 1415. Christ instituted both elements as symbols of His death and invited the partaking of both as representative of receiving the fullness of that death.

Administration of the Lord's Supper. The person who should administer the Lord's Supper is not specified. The command to continue the observance was given to the disciples, as representatives of the future church, even as were the commands of the Great Commission. It is, of course, logical to assume that the leader of the Lord's Supper was one of the recognized leaders of the church. But the absence of specific biblical instruction implies that the position of presiding over this rite was not reserved for a distinct class of clergy. This reservation is seen only later in the second century.

Frequency of observance. The New Testament gives no specific directions on how often the Lord's Supper is to be celebrated. However, the words of the apostle, "as often" imply that it is to be done frequently.[70] The statement of Acts 20:7 suggests that at Troas, at least, it was observed regularly when the believers met together on the first day of the week. Perhaps a more frequent observance is indicated in the early church at Jerusalem in the report that they were "continuing daily with one accord in the temple, and breaking bread from house to house" (Ac 2:46). There is nothing to suggest, however, that this was to be the normative pattern or that it became so as other churches were established. After examining the evidence and admitting that none of it securely establishes an invariable practice, Moule concludes, "We must be content to say that it is likely enough to have been a weekly practice."[71] Shortly after New Testament times a weekly observance is clearly seen in the injunction of the *Didache* (14:1) to come together every "Lord's Day" to break bread, as well as the similar testimony in Barnabas (15:9) and Justin (*Apol. I.,* 67.3).[72] Without doubt the Lord's Supper was observed with considerable frequency in the early church, demonstrating the significance that the remembrance of Christ by this means had in the life of the community.

---

70. Robertson and Plummer, p. 249.
71. Moule, p. 29.
72. Ibid., pp. 28-29.

Bibliography

THE BIBLIOGRAPHY is divided into four sections: (1) works concerning the church in general, including the meaning of the term, the nature of the church and its historical beginning; (2) works concerning the organization, government and ministry of the church; (3) works concerning the worship of the church, including the ordinances or sacraments; and (4) general theologies, commentaries and other sources used. Particularly significant or helpful works in each area have been noted with an asterisk. Although published too late for use in the writing of this study, the significant works, *A New Face for the Church* by Lawrence O. Richards and *One People* by John R. W. Stott, have been included.

GENERAL WORKS ON THE MEANING AND NATURE OF THE CHURCH

Bannerman, D. Douglas. *The Scripture Doctrine of the Church*. Grand Rapids: Eerdmans, 1955.

Brunner, Emil. *The Misunderstanding of the Church*. Philadelphia: Westminster, 1953.

*Campbell, J. Y. *Three New Testament Studies*. Leiden: Brill, 1965.

Cerfaux, Lucien. *The Church in the Theology of St. Paul*. New York: Herder & Herder, 1959.

*Clarke, Arthur G. *New Testament Church Principles*. New York: Loizeaux, 1962.

*Cole, Alan. *The Body of Christ*. London: Hodder & Stoughton, 1964.

Dargan, Edwin Charles. *Ecclesiology, A Study of the Churches*. 2d rev. ed. Louisville: Dearing, 1905.

Flew, Robert Newton, *Jesus and His Church; A Study of the Idea of the Ecclesia in the New Testament*. London: Epworth, 1960.

*Hort, F. J. A. *The Christian Ecclesia*. London: Macmillan, 1897.

*Johnston, George. *The Doctrine of the Church in the New Testament*. Cambridge: U. Press, 1943.

Kik, Jacob Marcellus. *Ecumenism and the Evangelical*. Philadelphia: Presbyterian & Reformed, 1958.

Knox, W. L. *St. Paul and the Church of the Gentiles.* Cambridge: U. Press, 1961.

Kuiper, R. B. *The Glorious Body of Christ.* Grand Rapids: Eerdmans, n.d.

*Küng, Hans. *The Church.* New York: Sheed & Ward, 1967.

Lang, G. H. *The Churches of God.* London: Paternoster, 1959.

McKelvey, R. J. *The New Temple: The Church in the New Testament.* London: Oxford U., 1969.

Metzger, Bruce M. "The New Testament View of the Church." *Theology Today* 19 (Oct. 1962):369-80.

*Miller, Donald G. *The Nature and Mission of the Church.* Richmond: John Knox, 1957.

———. *The People of God.* London: SCM, 1959.

Minear, Paul S. "Church, Idea of." In *The Interpreter's Dictionary of the Bible*, ed. G. A. Buttrick, 1:607-17. New York: Abingdon, 1962.

*Minear, Paul S. *Images of the Church in the New Testament.* Philadelphia: Westminster, 1960.

Nygren, Anders, ed. *This Is The Church.* Philadelphia: Muhlenberg, 1952.

*Radmacher, Earl D. "The Nature of the Church." Doctor's dissertation, Dallas Theological Seminary, Dallas, 1962.

Robinson, J. A. T. *The Body.* Studies in Biblical Theology. London: SCM, 1957.

Robinson, William. *The Biblical Doctrine of the Church.* St. Louis: Bethany, 1948.

Schlatter, Adolf. *The Church in the New Testament Period.* London: SPCK, 1961.

*Schmidt, Karl Ludwig. "ekklesia." In *TDNT*, 3:501-36.

Schnackenburg, Rudolf. *The Church in the New Testament.* Trans. W. J. O'Hara. New York: Herder & Herder, 1965.

Scott, Ernest Findlay. *The Nature of the Early Church.* New York: Scribner, 1941.

*Stibbs, Alan. *God's Church.* Chicago: Inter-Varsity, 1959.

*Thornton, Lionel Spencer. *The Common Life in the Body of Christ.* 4th ed. London: Dacre, 1963.

*Watson, J. B., ed. *The Church; A Symposium.* London: Pickering & Inglis, 1949.

THE ORGANIZATION AND MINISTRY OF THE CHURCH

Beyer, Hermann W. "diakonēo, diakonia, diakonos." In *TDNT*, 2:81-93.

———. "episkopos." In *TDNT*, 2:608-22.

Davies, W. D. *A Normative Pattern of Church Life in the New Testament: Fact or Fancy?* London: Clark, n.d.

Farrer, A. M. *The Apostolic Ministry.* Ed. Kenneth E. Kirk. New York: Morehouse-Barlow, 1946.

Forrester, E. J. "Church Government." In *The International Standard Bible Encyclopaedia*, 1:653-55. Grand Rapids: Eerdmans, 1955.

*Green, E. M. B. *Called to Serve: Ministry and Ministers in the Church.* Philadelphia: Westminster, 1956.

*Hay, Alexander Rattray. *The New Testament Order for Church and Missionary.* St. Louis: New Testament Missionary Union, 1947.

*Hodge, Charles. *The Church and Its Polity.* London: Nelson, 1879.

Käsemann, Ernst. "Ministry and Community in the New Testament." In *Essays on New Testament Themes*, pp. 63-94. Naperville, Ill.: Allenson, 1964.

Lampe, G. W. H. "Church Discipline and the Interpretation of the Epistles to the Corinthians." In *Christian History and Interpretation: Studies Presented to John Knox*, ed. W. R. Farmer, C. F. D. Moule and R. R. Niebuhr, pp. 349-51. Cambridge: U. Press, 1967.

*Lightfoot, J. B. "The Christian Ministry." In *Saint Paul's Epistle to the Philippians*, pp. 181-269. Grand Rapids: Zondervan, 1953.

Lindsay, T. M. *The Church and the Ministry in the Early Centuries.* London: Hodder & Stoughton, 1903.

Manson, Thomas Walter. *The Church's Ministry.* London: Hodder & Stoughton, 1948.

*Morris, Leon. *Ministers of God.* London: Inter-Varsity, 1964.

Reid, John Kelman Sutherland. *The Biblical Doctrine of the Ministry.* Edinburgh: Oliver & Boyd, 1955.

Reingstorf, Karl Heinrich. "apostolos." In *TDNT*, 1:407-45.

*Richards, Lawrence O. *A New Face for the Church.* Grand Rapids: Zondervan, 1970.

Salmon, George. *The Infallibility of the Church.* London: Murray, 1914.

*Schweizer, Eduard. *Church Order in the New Testament.* London: SCM, 1961.

Shepherd, M. H., Jr. "Deaconess; KJV Servant." In *The Interpreter's Dictionary of the Bible*, 1:786-87. New York: Abingdon, 1962.

*Stott, John R. W. *One People.* Downers Grove, Ill.: Inter-Varsity, 1968.

Swete, Henry Barclay, ed. *Essays on the Early History of the Church and the Ministry.* London: Macmillan, 1918.

Telfer, W. *The Office of a Bishop.* London: Darton, Longman & Todd, 1962.

Vine, A. R. *The Congregational Ministry in the Modern World.* Ed. H. Cunliffe-Jones. London: Independent, 1955.

WORSHIP OF THE CHURCH, INCLUDING THE ORDINANCES

Adeney, W. F. "Worship (in NT)." In *A Dictionary of the Bible,* ed. James Hastings, 4:941-44. New York: Scribner, 1909.

°Aland, Kurt. *Did the Early Church Baptize Infants?* Philadelphia: Westminster, 1963.

°Aulen, Gustaf. *Eucharist and Sacrifice.* Edinburgh: Oliver & Boyd, 1958.

°Beasley-Murray, G. R. *Baptism in the New Testament.* London: Macmillan, 1962.

°———. *Baptism Today and Tomorrow.* New York: St. Martin's, 1966.

°Berkouwer, G. C. *The Sacraments.* Grand Rapids: Eerdmans, 1969.

Best, Ernest. "Spiritual Sacrifice." *Interpretation* 14 (July 1960): 273-99.

Bromiley, G. W. *The Baptism of Infants.* London: Church Book Room, 1955.

Carson, Alexander. *Baptism in Its Mode and Subjects.* 5th Amer. ed. Philadelphia: Amer. Baptist Pubn. Soc., 1853.

Clark, Neville. *An Approach to the Theology of the Sacraments.* Naperville, Ill.: Allenson, 1956.

°Cranfield, C. E. B. "Divine and Human Action." *Interpretation* 12 (Oct. 1958):387-98.

Cullmann, Oscar. *Baptism in the New Testament.* London: SCM, 1951.

°———. *Early Christian Worship.* Naperville, Ill.: Allenson, 1953.

———. "The Meaning of the Lord's Supper in Primitive Christianity." In *Essays on the Lord's Supper* by Oscar Cullmann and F. J. Leenhardt, pp. 21-23. Richmond: John Knox, 1958.

Gibbs, A. P. *Worship.* Denver: Wilson Foundation, n.d.

Higgins, A. J. B. *The Lord's Supper in the New Testament.* Chicago: Regnery, 1952.

°Jeremias, Joachim. *Infant Baptism in the First Four Centuries.* Philadelphia: Westminster, 1962.

———. *The Eucharistic Words of Jesus.* New York: Macmillan, 1955.

Jewett, Paul K. "Baptism (Baptist View)." In *The Encyclopedia of Christianity*, 1:517-26. Wilmington, Del.: Natl. Foundation for Chrn. Ed., 1964.

Lietzmann, Hans. *Mass and Lord's Supper: A Study in the History of the Liturgy.* Trans. Dorothea H. G. Reeve, pp. 204-8. Leiden: Brill, 1953.

Marcel, Pierre. *The Biblical Doctrine of Infant Baptism*. London: Clarke, 1953.

*Martin, Ralph P. *Worship in the Early Church*. Westwood: Revell, 1964.

*Moule, C. F. D. *Worship in the New Testament*. London: Lutterworth, 1961.

Mounce, R. H. *The Essential Nature of New Testament Preaching*. Grand Rapids: Eerdmans, 1960.

*Murray, John. *Christian Baptism*. Philadelphia: Presbyterian & Reformed, 1962.

Oepke, Albrecht. "baptō, baptizō." In *TDNT*, 1:529-46.

Reicke, Bo. "A Synopsis of Early Christian Preaching." In *The Root of the Vine* by Anton Johnson Fridricksen et al., pp. 128-60. Westminster: Dacre, 1953.

Schweizer, Eduard. *The Lord's Supper According to the New Testament*. Philadelphia: Fortress, 1967.

———. "Worship in the New Testament." In *The Reformed and Presbyterian World* 24 (Mar. 1957):196-205.

Small, Dwight H. *The Biblical Basis for Infant Baptism*. Westwood, N.J.: Revell, 1959.

Strathmann, H. "latreuō, latreia." In *TDNT*, 4:58-65.

———. "leitourgeō, leitourgos." In *TDNT*, 4:215-31.

*Stibbs, A. M. *Sacrament, Sacrifice and Eucharist*. London: Tyndale, 1961.

"The Case for Infant Baptism." *Christian Today* 9 (Oct. 9, 1964): 7-11.

von Allmen, J. J. *Worship, Its Theology and Practice*. New York: Oxford U., 1965.

Warns, Johannes. *Baptism*. Grand Rapids: Kregel, 1958.

*White, R. E. O. *The Biblical Doctrine of Initiation*. Grand Rapids: Eerdmans, 1960.

COMMENTARIES AND OTHER WORKS

Abbott, Walter M., ed. *The Documents of Vatican II*, New York: America Press, 1966.

Alexander, J. A. *Commentary on the Acts of the Apostles*. Grand Rapids: Zondervan, 1956 reprint.

Allis, Oswald. *Prophecy and the Church*. Philadelphia: Presbyterian & Reformed, 1945.

Anderson, Sir Robert. *The Gospel and Its Ministry*. London: Pickering & Inglis, n.d.

Arndt, W. F. and F. W. Gingrich. *A Greek-English Lexicon of the New Testament and Other Early Christian Literature.* Chicago: U. Chicago, 1957.

Barclay, William. *The Letters to the Corinthians.* Philadelphia: Westminster, 1954.

———. *Letters to the Galatians and Ephesians.* Philadelphia: Westminster, 1959.

———. *The Letters to Timothy, Titus and Philemon.* Philadelphia: Westminster, 1956.

Barr, James. *The Semantics of Biblical Language.* Oxford: Oxford U., 1961.

Barrett, C. K. *The Gospel According to St. John.* London: SPCK, 1960.

Barth, Karl. *Church Dogmatics.* Edinburgh: T. & T. Clark, 1957.

Berkhof, Louis. *The Kingdom of God.* Grand Rapids: Eerdmans, 1951.

———. *Systematic Theology.* Grand Rapids: Eerdmans, 1941.

Berkouwer, G. C. *The Conflict With Rome.* Philadelphia: Presbyterian & Reformed, 1958.

Bigg, Charles. *A Critical and Exegetical Commentary on the Epistles of St. Peter and St. Jude.* The International Critical Commentary. Edinburgh: T. & T. Clark, 1902.

Bright, John. *The Kingdom of God.* New York: Abingdon-Cokesbury, 1953.

Broadus, John A. *Commentary on the Gospel of Matthew.* An American Commentary on the New Testament. Ed. Alvah Hovey. Philadelpha: Amer. Baptist Pubn. Soc., 1886.

Brown, Francis; Driver, S. R. and Briggs, Charles A., *A Hebrew and English Lexicon of the Old Testament.* Oxford: Clarendon, 1959.

Bruce, F. F. *Commentary on the Epistle to the Colossians.* The New International Commentary on the New Testament. Grand Rapids: Eerdmans, 1957.

———. *The Book of the Acts.* The New International Commentary on the New Testament. Grand Rapids: Eerdmans, 1954.

———. *The Letters of Paul: An Expanded Paraphrase.* Grand Rapids: Eerdmans, 1965.

Brumback, Carl. *"What Meaneth This?"* Springfield: Gospel Pub., 1947.

Brunner, Emil. *The Christian Doctrine of the Church, Faith and the Consummation, Dogmatics.* Vol. 3. Philadelphia: Westminster, 1962.

Bullinger, Ethelbert. *The Mystery.* London: Eyrie & Spottiswoode, n.d.

Burton, Ernest DeWitt. *A Critical and Exegetical Commentary on the Epistle to the Galatians*. The International Critical Commentary. Edinburgh: T. & T. Clark, 1952.

Buttrick, George A., ed. *The Interpreter's Bible*. 12 vols. New York: Abingdon, 1953.

Calvin, John. *The Institutes of the Christian Religion*. 2 vols. Philadelphia: Westminster, 1960.

Chafer, Lewis Sperry. *Systematic Theology*. 8 vols. Dallas: Dallas Seminary, 1948.

Charles, R. H. *A Critical and Exegetical Commentary on the Revelation of St. John*. The International Critical Commentary. Edinburgh: T. & T. Clark, 1920.

Cranfield, C. E. B. *A Commentary on Romans 12-13, Scottish Journal of Theology Occasional Papers No. 12*. Edinburgh: Oliver & Boyd, 1964.

Cremer, Hermann. *Biblico-Theological Lexicon of New Testament Greek*. Edinburgh: T. & T. Clark, 1954 (1895).

Cullmann, Oscar. *Peter, Disciple, Apostle, Martyr*. Philadelphia: Westminster, 1962.

———. "The Tradition." In *The Early Church*. Ed. A. J. B. Higgins, pp. 55-99. London: SCM, 1956.

Delitzsch, Franz. *Biblical Commentary on the Psalms*. 3 vols. Grand Rapids: Eerdmans, 1959.

Denney, James, *The Death of Christ*. New York: Armstrong, 1902.

Eadie, John. *Commentary on the Epistle of Paul to the Colossians*. Grand Rapids: Zondervan, 1957.

———. *Commentary on the Epistle of Paul to the Galatians*. Grand Rapids: Zondervan, n.d.

———. *Commentary on the Epistle to the Ephesians*. Grand Rapids: Zondervan, n.d. Reprint from 1883 ed.

Edersheim, Alfred. *The Life and Times of Jesus the Messiah*. Grand Rapids: Eerdmans, 1956.

Ellicott, Charles J. *St. Paul's Epistle to the Galatians*. London: Longman, Roberts, & Green, 1863.

Ellis, E. "II Corinthians v. 1-10 in Pauline Eschatology." In *New Testament Studies*, 6 (Apr. 1960):211-24.

Ellison, H. L. *The Mystery of Israel*. Exeter, England: Paternoster, 1966.

Fairbairn, Patrick. *Commentary on the Pastoral Epistles*. Grand Rapids: Zondervan, 1956.

Findlay, G. G. "St. Paul's First Epistle to the Corinthians." In *The Expositor's Greek Testament.* Grand Rapids: Eerdmans, 1951, 2:729-953.

Fisher, George P. *The Beginnings of Christianity.* New York: Scribner, Armstrong, 1877.

Gee, Donald. *The Pentecostal Movement: Including the Story of the War Years (1940-47).* Rev. ed. London: Elim, 1949. p. 10.

Godet, F. *Commentary on the Epistle to the Romans.* Grand Rapids: Zondervan, 1956.

———. *Commentary on the Gospel of John.* Grand Rapids: Zondervan, n.d. Reprint from 1893 ed.

Gray, George Buchanan. *Sacrifice in the Old Testament, Its Theory and Practice.* Oxford: Clarendon, 1925.

Guthrie, Donald. *The Pastoral Epistles, Tyndale New Testament Commentaries.* London: Tyndale, 1957.

Hatch, Edwin. *The Organization of the Early Christian Churches.* Oxford and Cambridge: Rivingtons, 1881.

Hendricksen, William. *A Commentary on the Gospel of John.* Two vols. complete and unabridged in one. London: Banner of Truth, 1954.

———. *I-II Timothy and Titus, New Testament Commentary.* Grand Rapids: Baker, 1957.

———. *Colossians and Philemon, New Testament Commentary.* Grand Rapids: Baker, 1964.

Hendry, C. S. *The Holy Spirit in Christian Theology.* Philadelphia: Westminster, 1956.

Hodge, Charles. *Systematic Theology.* Grand Rapids: Eerdmans, n.d.

Hoekema, Anthony A. *What About Tongue Speaking?* Grand Rapids: Eerdmans, 1966.

Hoekendijk, J. C. *The Church Inside Out.* Ed. L. A. Hoedemaker and Peter Tijmes. Trans. Issac C. Rottenberg. Philadelphia: Westminster, 1966.

Hoskyns, Edwyn. *The Fourth Gospel.* London: Faber & Faber, 1947.

Hughes, Philip E. *Commentary on the Second Epistle to the Corinthians.* The New International Commentary on the New Testament. Grand Rapids: Eerdmans, 1962.

Jeremias, Joachim. *The Parables of Jesus.* Rev. ed. New York: Scribner, 1963.

Kent, Homer A., Jr. *The Pastoral Epistles.* Chicago: Moody, 1958.

Kittel, Gerhard and Friedrich, Gerhard, eds. *Theological Dictionary of the New Testament.* 6 vols. published. Trans. and ed. Geoffrey W. Bromiley. Grand Rapids: Eerdmans, 1964-68.

Lenski, R. C. H. *The Interpretation of St. Paul's Epistles to the Galatians, to the Ephesians and to the Philippians.* Columbus, O.: Wartburg, 1946.

———. *The Interpretation of St. Paul's First and Second Epistle to the Corinthians.* Columbus: Wartburg, 1946.

Liddell, H. G. and Scott, Robert, eds. *A Greek-English Lexicon.* London: Oxford U., 1959.

Lightfoot, J. B. *Saint Paul's Epistles to the Colossians and to Philemon.* Grand Rapids: Zondervan, n.d. (1879).

———. *The Epistle of St. Paul to the Galatians.* Grand Rapids: Zondervan, 1957.

Meyer, H. A. W. *Critical and Exegetical Handbook to the Acts of the Apostles.* New York: Funk & Wagnalls, 1889.

Morris, Leon. *The Apostolic Preaching of the Cross.* Grand Rapids: Eerdmans, 1955.

———. *The First and Second Epistles to the Thessalonians.* The New International Commentary on the New Testament. Grand Rapids: Eerdmans, 1959.

Moule, C. F. D. *Christ's Messengers, Part I, World Christian Books No. 19.* London: Lutterworth, 1957.

———. *The Epistle of Paul the Apostle to the Colossians and to Philemon.* Cambridge Greek Testament Commentary. Cambridge: U. Press, 1962.

Moulton, W. F. and Geden, A. S. *A Concordance to the Greek Testament.* Edinburgh: T. & T. Clark, 1950.

Moulton, James H. and Milligan, George. *The Vocabulary of the Greek Testament.* Grand Rapids: Eerdmans, 1959.

Murray, John. *The Epistle to the Romans.* The New International Commentary on the New Testament. Grand Rapids: Eerdmans, 1965.

McClain, Alva J. *The Greatness of the Kingdom.* Grand Rapids: Zondervan, 1959.

Newell, William R. *The Book of the Revelation.* Chicago: Moody, 1947.

Oehler, Gustave. *Theology of the Old Testament.* Grand Rapids: Zondervan, n.d.

O'Hair, J. C. *A Dispensational Study of the Bible.* Chicago: O'Hair, n.d.

Paterson, W. P. "Marriage." In *A Dictionary of the Bible.* Ed. James Hastings. New York: Scribner, 1908, 3:262-77.

Pentecost, J. Dwight. *Things to Come.* Findlay: Dunham, 1958.

Persson, Per Erik. *Roman and Evangelical.* Philadelphia: Fortress, 1964.

Peters, George N. H. *The Theocratic Kingdom.* Grand Rapids: Kregel, 1957.

Plummer, Alfred. *A Commentary on St. Paul's First Epistle to the Thessalonians.* London: Scott, 1918.

———. *An Exegetical Commentary on the Gospel According to St Matthew.* Grand Rapids: Eerdmans, 1956.

Prenter, Regin. *Creation and Redemption.* Philadelphia: Fortress, 1955.

Richardson, A. *An Introduction to the Theology of the New Testament.* London: SCM, 1958.

Ridderbos, Herman. *The Coming of the Kingdom.* Philadelphia: Presbyterian & Reformed, 1962.

Robertson, Archibald and Plummer, Alfred. *A Critical and Exegetical Commentary on the First Epistle of St. Paul to the Corinthians.* The International Critical Commentary. Edinburgh: T. & T. Clark, 1955 (1911).

Robertson, A. T. *A Grammar of the Greek New Testament in the Light of Historical Research.* Nashville: Broadman, 1934.

Robinson, D. W. B. "The Salvation of Israel in Romans 9-11." *The Reformed Theological Review* 26 (Sept.-Dec. 1967): 81-96.

Robinson, J. Armitage. *St. Paul's Epistle to the Ephesians.* London: Clark, n.d.

Sauer, Eric. *From Eternity to Eternity.* Grand Rapids: Eerdmans, 1955.

Schroeder, H. J. *Canons and Decrees of the Council of Trent.* St. Louis: Herder, 1941.

Selwyn, Edward G. *The First Epistle of St. Peter.* London: Macmillan, 1961.

Stewart, James S. *The Life and Teaching of Jesus Christ.* Edinburgh: Church of Scotland, 1954.

Stott, John R. W. *The Epistles of John.* The Tyndale New Testament Commentaries. London: Tyndale, 1964.

———. *Our Guilty Silence.* Grand Rapids: Eerdmans, 1967.

Strong, A. H. *Systematic Theology.* Three vols. in one. Westwood: Revell, 1907.

Terry, Milton S. *Biblical Hermeneutics.* New York: Hunt & Eaton, 1893.

Thayer, Joseph H. *A Greek-English Lexicon of the New Testament.* Edinburgh: T. & T. Clark, 1901.

Trench, Richard C. *Synonyms of the New Testament.* Grand Rapids: Eerdmans, 1958.

Vincent, Marvin R. *Word Studies in the New Testament.* 4 vols. Grand Rapids: Eerdmans, 1946.

Vine, W. E. *An Expository Dictionary of New Testament Words.* 4 vols. Westwood, N.J.: Revell, 1940.

Walvoord, John F. *The Millennial Kingdom.* Findlay: Dunham, 1959.

———. *The Revelation of Jesus Christ.* Chicago: Moody, 1966.

Warfield, B. B. *Miracles: Yesterday and Today, True and False.* Grand Rapids: Eerdmans, 1954.

Westcott, B. F. *The Epistle to the Hebrews.* Grand Rapids: Eerdmans, n.d.

———. *St. Paul's Epistle to the Ephesians.* London: Macmillan, 1906.

Zahn, Theodor. *Introduction to the New Testament.* 3 vols. Grand Rapids: Kregel, 1953.

Subject Index

Abrahamic covenant, 74-82, 84, 89
Apostles
  in early church, 67, 98, 101, 107-11, 113, 115, 120, 132, 135-38, 155, 178
  foundation of church, 34, 36, 61-64, 134, 137-38
Apostolic succession, 106-12

Baptism (water)
  efficacy of, 196-98
  general practice of, 59, 61, 65, 87, 91, 104, 109, 116, 129, 170, 172, 190-91, 228
  institution of, 192-93
  meaning of, 193-96
  mode of, 208-12
  subjects of, 198-208
Believers
  branches, 53-56, 59
  called Christians, 23
  called of God, 19-20, 23, 97
  parts of Christ's body, 24-32, 59-60, 64-65, 75, 88, 102, 119, 124, 128-29, 136, 177
  priests, 38-44
  rulers, 91
  set apart, 19-20, 40-41
  stones (living), 35-37, 63
Bishop, 52, 99, 106-15, 140-53

Christ
  Bridegroom, 44-49, 59
  cornerstone, 34-35, 61
  foundation, 33-34, 61
  Head, 24-32, 46, 62, 96, 116-17, 119, 126, 136, 195
  High Priest, 39-40, 44, 127, 171-73
  Judge, 180
  King, 39, 58, 74, 83, 88, 90-91
  Lord, 87-88, 100, 166, 173, 177, 180, 187, 194
  Mediator, 127, 171-73
  Messenger, 80

  Messiah, 58, 60, 80, 89, 142, 207
  rock, 63
  Saviour, 46, 180
  Servant, 80-81, 130
  Shepherd, 49-53, 59, 129, 144
  source of church's life, 29-30
  Sovereign, 28-29
  sustenance of church, 30-32
  union with, 20, 29, 45, 47, 53-56, 59, 65, 103-4, 172, 193-95, 103, 226
Church
  assembly, 12-19, 21, 25, 90
  body, 24-32, 59-60, 64-65, 75, 88, 102, 119, 124, 128-29, 136, 177
  bride of Christ, 44-49, 88
  building, 33-38, 65, 119, 126-28
  defined, 11-18
  distinct from Israel, 70-74
  flock, 49-53, 59, 128
  gives glory to God, 97
  God's primary tool today, 7
  government of
    congregational, 114-18
    episcopal, 106-12
    presbyterian, 112-14
  habitation of God, 37-38, 165
  local, 16, 18, 25
  meaning of Greek words for, 11-15
  mystery, 59-60
  new creation, 60
  officers. See Deacons, Elders
  organization of, 98-120
    fact of, 98-99
    laws of, 100-102
    practices of, 100
  priesthood, 38-44
  seed of Abraham, 74-77
  servant, 94
  unity of, 17-18, 26, 34, 67, 102, 190, 226-27, 231-32
  universal, 16-18, 25
Church age, 76, 80-81, 89-91

246

Scripture Index

249